Engineering Productivity through CAD/CAM

Engineering Productivity through CAD/CAM

Dimitris N. Chorafas, M.E., E.E., M.S.E., Dr Sci (Math), P. E.

Butterworths

London Boston Durban Singapore Sydney Toronto Wellington

First published 1987

© Dimitris N. Chorafas, 1987

British Library Cataloguing in Publication Data

Chorafas, Dimitris N.
  Engineering productivity through CAD/CAM.
  1. Engineering design–Data processing
  I. Title
  620'.00425'0285   TA174

  ISBN 0-408-01588-8

Library of Congress Cataloging in Publication Data

Chorafas, Dimitris N.
  Engineering productivity through CAD/CAM.

  Includes index.
  1. CAD/CAM systems.   2. Production engineering.
I. Title.
TS155.6.C495   1986   670'.28'.5   86-23307
ISBN 0-408-01588-8

Photoset by Butterworths Litho Preparation Department
Printed and bound in Great Britain by Robert Hartnoll (1985) Ltd., Bodmin, Cornwall

Preface

The new engineering workstations are networked supermicros fitting within a system designed to improve product design productivity. Advances in software and hardware help engineers computerize not just drafting, but also analysis, verification and simulation previously done by hand or with a variety of standalone computer devices.

The object of this book is to promote a new perspective in computer-aided design solutions, to open new horizons. It is therefore intended for technical management – not just for engineering professionals studying the introduction of CAD/CAM or the revamping of the system they now have.

The need for improved productivity in engineering design can be summed up as follows. There is a shortage of electrical engineers, along with a likelihood of continuing slow growth in their numbers because of the high cost and difficulty of educating them. At the same time, industry is experiencing a need for increasingly complex and innovative products to maintain competitive positions. These more sophisticated products have shorter life cycles, as companies constantly seek to maintain or increase their market positions. Management has also become cost-conscious: only low-cost producers can survive, and computer-based media are instrumental in promoting low product cost.

Computer-aided engineering is a major innovation. While it can be looked at as an evolutionary step from computer-based drafting, it is significantly different. Original CAD approaches allowed computer-based entry, manipulation and storage of symbols. They were primarily useful for graphic or topological representation.

The new computer-aided design (CAD) technology captures and keeps track of the substantive information the symbols represent. It makes possible significant analysis of engineering designs which was not previously possible, and it creates an engineering database. In other words, the technology of the 1970s helped draw diagrams; that of the 1980s designs and analyses systems.

Furthermore, productivity improvement resulting from the new CAD could lead to a huge market. Intelligent engineering workstations give such a boost to the designer's productivity that every engineer who works full time on design (about half a million people in the world) should eventually have one. This is a significant change from the old approach of sharing a few CAD workstations among many engineers and designers.

Productivity improvements come not only from the computer-assisted design features but also, or even primarily, from the creation and use of the engineering database (EDB). This, too, is an evolutionary step and for this reason I do not believe in a distinction sometimes made in the literature, where CAD is used mainly in the sense of drafting while computer-aided engineering (CAE) is considered to be a totally different approach – which it is not.

What is new is the integration concept, which is now starting to dominate. Until about 1980, the main CAD area industry addressed was layout, and that was done mainly by the CAD/CAM companies. Everything else in creative design – simulation for instance – was accomplished on a mainframe or by specialized equipment.

The integration concept will see to it that formerly disparate approaches now converge under one system – and this convergence goes well beyond classical design references. It includes bills of materials, quality control aspects, integration with manufacturing (particularly robotics) and the ability to follow up product reliability and maintainability at the end-user site.

This is the range of background notions on which the present book focuses. Such notions constitute the theme of Chapter 1 and are framed in terms of advice in Chapter 2. Chapter 3 addresses itself to ways and means of successfully implementing CAD, the theme of Chapter 4 is CAD/CAM and the end user, and Chapter 5 advances a new design philosophy. Earlier CAD solutions allowed engineers to manipulate drawings easily and to store often-drawn details, thus improving productivity. Yet several factors made such approaches less than optimal for complex design applications. For example, as we add elements to an electronic design we do more than change the physical layout. We change its logical characteristics – and we need a new design philosophy to do that job successfully.

Before discussing software and hardware components of a CAD system, I have chosen to give precise examples of its successful usage, in Chapters 6 and 7. Chapter 8 stresses the goals any CAD installation should reach, and engineering performance is further elaborated in Chapter 9.

Ironically, very little of the substantial investment made in CAD/CAM has been directed to the data itself. Thus, even though the cost of new systems continues to grow rapidly, data quality often remains unsatisfactorily low.

Timely access to technical information requires knowledge of what kinds of text, data and drawings exist; how they are related; where they are stored and retrieved – whether in filing cabinets, in conventional computerized files, or in databases. It is important to know how information elements are used and by whom; how they are updated and by what procedures. This subject requires a serious systems study, an issue treated in Chapter 10. Chapter 11 elaborates on how to organize data in a rational manner, using proper classification and identification methods.

Chapters 12 and 13 deal with Fourth Generation Programming Languages (4GL) and Expert Systems, while Chapter 14 focuses on graphics languages. All aim to facilitate and promote *end-user computing*.

In the coming years, user-driven computing will become one of the major fields of automation. It is expected that user-driven computing will reach over 65 per cent of the total MIPs available, with user-oriented databases becoming an integral part of the working environment.

For integrity, security and cost reasons, the appropriate tools have to be carefully customized to the user's requirements. They must also be embedded into a total information management concept and supported by the intelligent, interactive workstations to be built in to every engineering desk (Chapter 15).

The range of subjects we have covered brings forward a fundamental requirement: strategic planning for CAD/CAM. Chapter 16 addresses itself to this issue: CAD/CAM has become a strategic product.

The greater the competitive pressure to design new products rapidly, and the quicker the old ones become obsolete, the greater the need for computer-based approaches. This leads to more rapid adoption of CAD in consumer electronics, architectural design and service-oriented companies than in older businesses less subject to product and process evolution. Yet these, too, can be revitalized through newer, more competitive CAD-assisted products.

Let me close by expressing my thanks to everybody who contributed to the making of this book. From my colleagues, for their advice; to the organizations I visited in my research, for their insight; to Professor Mike Pratt of the Cranfield Institute of Technology, for his collaboration in shaping the contents of this text; and to Eva-Maria Binder for the drawings, the typing of the manuscript, and the index.

D.N.C.

Contents

Chapter 1

New directions in engineering

The story of man, his sciences, his tools, and the methodologies he uses – from the design and manufacture to the marketing of man-made products – is well known. In the course of an evolution spanning nearly eight thousand years, the concepts, images and means of implementation have changed, but the drive for better performance is steady and ongoing in spite of obstacles – or maybe because of them.

We are now applying the high technology of computer modeling to the ancient craft of metal forming. The objective is to change the process of producing dies from a half-understood art to a scientifically based, predictable process. This is a story of basic change in the way we look at engineering.

New design and production ideas aim to stamp out sheet metal parts on a computer early in the tooling process to see if we can actually manufacture the part as designed. This gives new flexibility to designers, because they are able to specify new shapes and materials without the fear that they might turn into manufacturing nightmares.

Formability is a constant battle between two disasters, buckling and tearing. If we try to form too much, the material breaks. If we don't do it enough, it wrinkles. It is a fine balance and the process is difficult to analyse as a whole. Mathematical models are built on the *finite elements* of stress analysis.

This is not only valid in mechanical and civil engineering, but also in electrical and electronics. Any field of engineering design is open to computer-based experimentation – and this is just as true of manufacturing processes.

A single-line diagram of a typical power system consisting of 100 buses, 90 lines, 60 loads, 40 transformers, 20 generators, and 20 shunts would involve the plotting of 200 alphanumeric and nearly 1000 numeric values. The single-line diagram itself would consist of 500 graphical symbols. A study which manually takes weeks to execute can be completed in less than two hours by using the computer.

But, within the engineering profession, computer-based approaches should not be limited to the design task. The whole management perspective must be examined, with emphasis on performance improvements that can bring down costs, improve quality, and shorten time-scales.

1

Technology in the offing makes feasible the implementation of global computer message systems: from electronic mail to computer conferencing; the merging of voice, text, data, graphics; efficient planning and scheduling tools; the ability to store/retrieve a large number of drawings; and expert systems – not only for decision support but also to help in engineering analysis.

A strategic approach

Technology is now at our disposal to provide assistance in engineering work and answer the ever-increasing challenges. This is the basic message to convey when we talk of processes assisted by computers and in which communications play a vital role.

Whether in the office or in the factory, solutions based on computers and communications require that the system be *object-based*; the *nodes* with memory and processing power be well defined; *protocols* exist for tasks running on one node to access the other; and *programs* be system-wide, rather than for this or that machine.

Above all, there must be a *strategy*:

- Where do we wish to go?
- What do we want to accomplish?
- At what cost?
- Within what time-scale?

Having satisfactorily answered these questions, we must look at the mechanics: How can we simulate the complete system that we project? What investment is to be made at each workstation (WS)? What level of facilities is to be supported at each node?

While many answers are specific to the situation, basic principles are general enough to help as a guideline: With computer-aided design (CAD) the most widespread demand is *not* for CPU cycles but for access to disk. Thus, it is advantageous for the *database* to be distributed to a *number* of nodes that can store information elements.

Such nodes can be workstations or dedicated rear-end engines – what is important to the user is that there exists *one logical source* of data: the *engineering database* (EDB). At the same time, the *system architecture* with which we work must be flexible, easy to implement and to maintain.

The chosen *protocols* must provide reasonable assurance of error correction and a guaranteed engineering file delivery. The supported *communications band* must be wide enough to cover the projected application(s).

The featured *services* must answer the applications requirements in a cost-effective manner. The *strategy* should be to develop an architecture that can promote lots of parallelism – and be open to future developments.

The design must make sure that we built an engineering design system that is flexible and expandable. It is almost certain that, as applications experience accumulates, we will need to

- increase the number of attached nodes;
- accommodate diverse types such as storage nodes and multifunction workstations:

- blur the distinction between one processor and the other; and
- pay particular attention to end-user considerations.

The WS is the real man–information interface, and therefore the point of our major concern. In all text/data manipulation cases involving user workstations, productivity gains are realized through:

(1) Immediate and consistent response time that primarily depends on what the user himself is doing.
(2) Avoidance of key entry for any type of text/data already stored and updated in databases.
(3) Isolation from a communications failure of any type that cuts the WS from the database source.
(4) Enhanced interactivity attainable on a workstation, involving all users on a network.
(5) A comprehensive, properly structured design process as outlined in Figure 1.1.
(6) Easy migration to the personal computer (PC) environment assured through sessions providing access to all existing functions.

THe workstation today is characterized by the *3 megas:* one million instructions per second (MIPS); one megabyte of central memory; one megapixel of softcopy (video presentation); and also a hard disc. By early 1988, this workstation will cost about $5000.

At such a price, for the facilities which it provides and the productivity enhancements it makes feasible, the workstation will be a bargain. Endowed with communications disciplines to work through both local area networks and long haul, such a workstation should be under every engineering and managerial desk. *All the work must be interactive.*

As we will see in the following section, this was not the original concept of computer-aided design. If we look back and critically examine the values prevailing during the last 20 years we find that the very first approaches were batch – to be replaced by interactive of a centralized kind, which then gave way to the fully distributed environments we are starting to enjoy today, which will dominate the years to come.

The institution of a forward-looking solution in computer-aided design is a strategic consideration. On it will depend the productivity and profitability of the engineering department during the next decade. We will be returning to this argument.

There are significant benefits to the end user – that is, the professional engineer – from a personal computer oriented solution. Among them, we distinguish a significant acceleration of development time; shorter implementation time-scales; the ability of the end user to develop his own applications without waiting in long service queues for development and maintenance; and modernization of engineering workstations at state-of-the-art level.

Other benefits include better availability to the design engineer of experimentation capabilities; the dissociation of application(s) from database design, permitting application changes without upsetting applications programming and work done on the database; integration into the WS of different equipment today spread over the user's desk

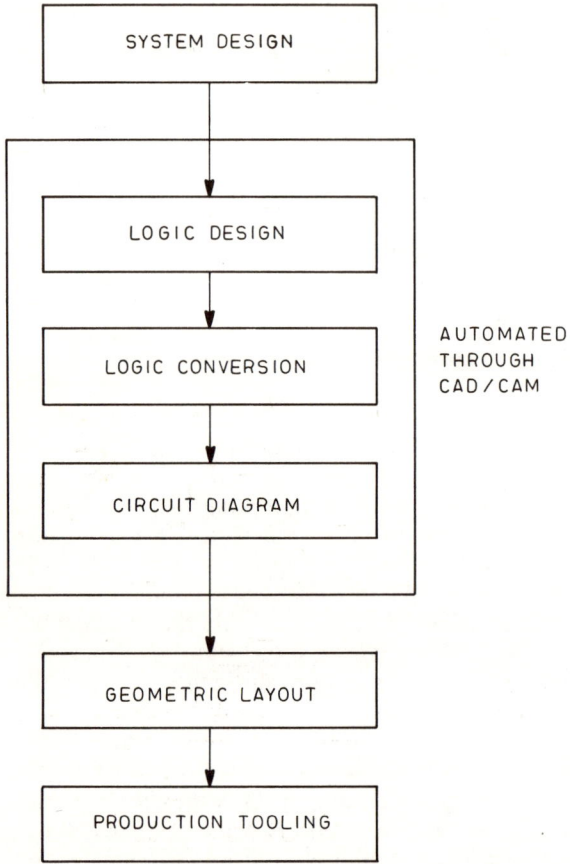

PCB DESIGN PROCESS

Figure 1.1 There is an increasing level of automation in design due to the facilities provided by CAD/CAM. Are you using all available facilities?

(calculators, non-intelligent terminals, et al.); and, most importantly, greater end-user productivity and easier conversion to further implementations.

The personal computer to which reference is being made for computer-aided design applications will typically have: a 32-bit microprocessor; half megabyte to one megabyte central memory; a high resolution screen of one megapixel (10^6 pixels – picture elements); a 10 to 20 megabyte disc; graphics tablet; and, optionally, printer or plotter.

A few years ago such a unit would have cost over $50,000. Today it costs half that. As mentioned previously, its cost will soon drop to $5000 – but by that time technology will see to it that the engineering workstation will need to support much more in terms of facilities to be worth its salt. Expert systems will be one of the focal points.

Just as clearly, there are benefits to the computer center from a personal computer solution for CAD. Among these is the dissociation (from an applications viewpoint) of the end user from the central system software; less, even nil, impact from applications changes effected by the end user; and sharp reduction of user interference with mainframe project developments.

Other benefits include the end of delays due to changes; diminution of project complexity due to application separation; specialization of mainframe projects to database and datacomm; an acceleration of project development; and faster and easier user changeover to new systems.

There are also prerequisites to be fulfilled. First, the requirements for engineering workstations must be clearly spelled out. They include:

(1) *Strategic* consideration to establish goals, timetables, budgets – in brief, the information systems plan.
(2) *Multipurpose* operations to serve data processing and word processing needs.
(3) The ability to *evolve* in time, without modifying applications.
(4) *Modularity* in terms of physical expansion.
(5) *Adaptability* to the user's requirements, making his job easier and more productive.
(6) *Standardization* of various logical and physical modules, providing homogeneity, compatibility, and portability.
(7) *Online access* to a properly designed engineering database (EDB).
(8) Communications *transparency* so that the user is unaffected by the technique of routing used to accomplish a link (local or long haul).
(9) *Economic* considerations to assure that sound engineering principles are observed.
(10) *User-friendly* interfaces, including prompting, help and forgiveness.
(11) *On-call* assistance, not only for training but also for time out and other cases.
(12) *Steady review* and re-evaluation to ensure actuality and to chop the dead wood.

The most important and most difficult of the changes to be carried out is to designers' concept of what CAD is. A look at the history of evolution of computer-based design approaches proves that, whether we talk of CAD facilities or product design *per se*, old images are totally unsuited to this new perspective.

The first thirty years

Originally, computers were used as number crunchers. The concept came from man's acquaintance with calculators, handling a small amount of data and producing larger quantities of numerical information.

The ability to handle engineering-type applications in calculator fashion was considered an important milestone in the use of the early computers, back in the 1950s. We no longer think in these terms. Furthermore, three decades ago few organizations could afford more than one computer. This gave rise to centralized data processing practices.

Another 1950s concept, now totally outdated, influenced input methods for many years. Input approaches were crude: punched cards and paper tape read sequentially into mechanical devices. Output fared just as poorly. Almost everything was printed and presented in a non-selective form to the user. As a result of these slow, paper-based practices, job turn-around was measured in days. The engineer got very little real assistance – and practically nothing to make his job more effective or more challenging.

While some results were obtained with the early use of computers in engineering departments in situations characterized by heavy computing loads, from the viewpoint of the individual user the work that needed to be done did not change. In fact, there were cases where the actual time to complete a design job lengthened.

No wonder, then, that to overcome these problems and handle applications for which batch computing was impractical, terminals were introduced to speed man's interaction with the machine. With them, processing, storage and retrieval facilities could be taken right into the engineer's workplace.

The early 1960s saw imaginative approaches in what was then called 'design augmented by computers'. This was based upon two key ideas:

- First, that the user could enter data into the system as and when it originated, and at a time and place more convenient to him.
- Second, rather than depending for input on holes punched in paper and for output on hard copy, input could be done and output obtained through the same unit: a video device (screen, soft copy)

This gave rise to the use of interactive terminals attached online to mainframes, either directly cabled or through phone lines with appropriate interfacing (teleprocessing). Once the terminals were installed they could be used for further activities such as online enquiries, time-sharing of central resources and so on.

New opportunities opened up for engineering designers. Relative to batch processing, response time significantly improved. Input/output delays were eliminated, and for the first time the engineer was able to use the computer for design activities. This was the state of the art in the late 1960s.

Online terminals and the time-sharing of central processors provided an opportunity for a close match between the computer power and the needs of the user. They offered the engineer the possibility of getting more involved in the design and development of the product or process he was working on – but they also introduced constraints of their own.

One of the constraints has been software. The engineering designer is not necessarily a programmer; neither, it is said, would he like to become one. It has therefore been necessary to match hardware capabilities with appropriate software support, prior to seeing the diffusion of what was by then called *computer-aided design* (CAD). In the early 1970s this gave rise to turnkey systems and brought to the foreground a number of specialized CAD companies.

While large engineering firms in the aeronautical, motor vehicle and computer fields led by developing their own computer-aided design software, commercially available systems started on an interactive turnkey basis around 1970. Their advent created a new and flourishing industry.

One of the challenges was conceptual. With the advent of the *engineering database* (EDB) for design purposes came the view that there must be a necessary extension of computer-based engineering design into the domain of *computer-aided manufacturing* (CAM). To make it happen, we need to automate vital linkages characterizing the transition from design to production.

Another conceptual challenge was the change of emphasis from drafting to design. Though we often spoke of computer-aided design, we came to realize that the real pay-off of higher productivity through interactive computers was *and is* with the more imaginative activities of the designer. There is where the primary emphasis is due.

As the practice of time-sharing gathered momentum, hidden constraints showed up. While turnaround was vastly better than with equivalent batch systems, heavy loads on the central computer resources had a negative effect on the productivity of professional engineers. The same is true of response times, which become increasingly longer and, therefore, unacceptable.

Several factors can contribute to a long response time: a machine not really designed for interactive work, overloading at the host; too many accesses to the database; busy communications network; and so on. This matter is discussed further in later chapters.

Solutions came by way of partial decentralization, but they were not lasting. The 1970s saw the development of the minicomputer at a cost which made it feasible to install in user departments. Databases were also distributed where possible, seeing to it that users were better able to exercise some control over their use of information technology.

But by the late 1970s/early 1980s, as the level of user involvement and motivation increased, minicomputers and midicomputers no longer had sufficient power to handle the greater demands posed upon them. This focused interest on multifunction workstations, which are now available for CAD/CAM at an affordable cost.

Increasingly, these machines work as an integral part of a complex information system for design purposes, linked through *local area networks* (LAN) and long-haul connections. The applications themselves are changing. Engineering design blends with *office automation* (OA) into an aggregate of services to characterize the mid to late 1980s.

This new generation of engineering systems will benefit from technological advances in the dual sense of intelligent features and lower costs. Today's engineering workstation with its *megapixel* of video resolution will most likely sell for about $5000 in 1987/88.

The $25,000 unit will be a symbolic machine with 6 megabytes (MB) central memory; 200 MB hard disk; voice input/output (I/O); and user-generated computing. It will allow fast development of algorithms and heuristics.

By 1990, the engineering professional will be able to tell his workstation the results he wants, and the relational database will ask the questions and do the job. This means an *expert system* orientation, which currently is at the research and early applications stage.

Computer-aided design

Since the beginning of modern engineering there has existed a growing need for methods of processing information which is related to the shape of components. This need accelerated with the use of computers in manufacturing processes.

Conventional engineering drawings and blueprints are, however, largely unsuitable for direct entry to computers. They depend upon human interpretation to recognize solid shapes from combinations of two-dimensional projections of different designs – and they are not directly transferable to machine processing in a *robotics* factory. New approaches

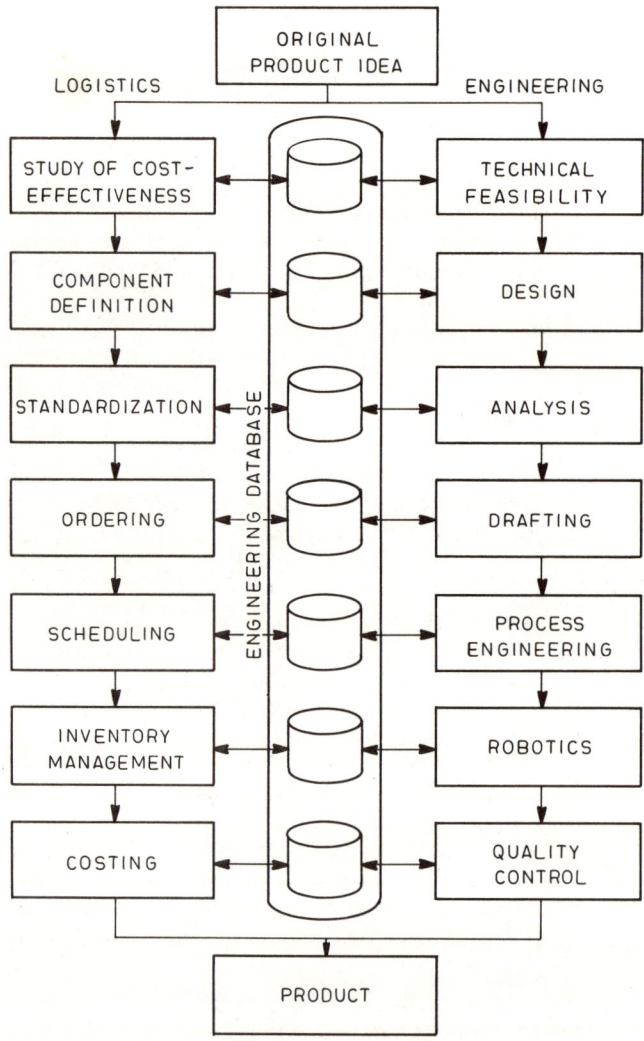

Figure 1.2 Any technical study involves engineering and logistics support. Both should be served by computers, and the engineering database is a vital reference to both

are necessary and they should take full account of intelligent machine capabilities microprocessors can offer. We can better appreciate the great change induced by microprocessors in engineering design if we look into the history of their development and the product impact they have had.

The late 1940s saw the birth of the transistor; the mid-1950s its commercialization. At the factory floor this meant the first generation of *numerical control* (NC) machine tools, beyond what vacuum tubes could offer.

In the late 1950s we experienced the early *integrated circuitry* (IC), and in the early 1960s a start to experimentation with industrial robots. The mid-1960s saw IC in production, a new generation of numerical control machines with integrated circuitry, and full automatic transistor production.

Microprocessors were an early 1970s development. The mid-1970s saw the one-chip microprocessor, a newer generation of NC blended with factory information systems, microcomputer-based continuous casting and microcomputer-controlled sewing machines.

The landmark of the late 1970s in microelectronics was very large-scale integration (VLSI), while there already existed a range of products, including consumer items, distinguished by the incorporation of semiconductor-based devices. Examples are electronic cameras (mid-1960s); electronic automatic transmission (late 1960s); anti-skid equipment (early 1970s); electronic ignition and LSI-controlled fully automatic washing machines (mid-1970s); microprocessor-controlled air-conditioning and other environmental equipment (late 1970s).

The design and process engineering for increasingly high density semiconductors and related circuits is made feasible through computer-aided design. The same is true of studies centering on intelligent machines in every one of the examples we have been considering. Computer-based processes start at the planning stage – from the original idea to the study of feasibility. Design, analysis, and drafting are steps well known to have been automated. What is less appreciated, however, is a parallel process, which addresses logistics.

Figure 1.2 outlines seven processes interacting with the product database. But the computer-based tactical issues, though necessary, are not enough for successful computer-aided design. The prerequisites are strategic and include:

(1) Statement of direction.
(2) Definition of the processes to be undertaken (describing is not defining).
(3) The proper organization for professional productivity.
(4) Design steps for obtaining a fault-tolerant product (reliability is built in at the design stage).
(5) The use of robotics.
(6) Great care in becoming and staying a low-cost producer.
(7) Built-in quality and maintainability.

The observance of these seven steps is instrumental in turning computer-aided design from a vague concept to a profitable reality. It is not enough that the use of computers in place of conventional drawing techniques offers greater accuracy, fast repetition of details, rapid amendment, and high-speed output to any scale.

Properties contained in drawings, such as dimensions and areas, can be exploited to the full by the computer. The database provides centralized storage of designs readily accesses through workstations. Computer software assures a full range of geometrical constructions, variety of line styles and character sets, selection of drawing content, and reasonable security of design data. But unless there is a clear statement of direction with spelled-out objectives, the results will be a small fraction of what management expects or hopes for.

Today, CAD systems should be implemented through intelligent workstations and local network solutions, with shared engineering databases and peer stations. Hierarchical centralized approaches are obsolete, expensive, and unjustifiable under current technology. Another basic requirement is logical integration. Distinct, standalone services are weak approaches with short life cycles.

Basic concepts should include the service and impact of modeling systems and the fact that CAD enables complete three-dimensional part descriptions to be created and manipulated. Engineering parts with planar and curved surfaces can be modeled; profiles can be created, swept, rotated to make prismatic and other objects.

CAD-generated boolean operations allow objects to be built up from combinations of basic shapes. The computer should be used as a logical engine rather than just being extremely effective in speeding up the production of engineering drawings and plans. For a CAD utility, it is necessary to adopt a form of shape description which is neither biased toward particular applications nor dependent upon human assistance for interpretation.

A method is required that describes solid shapes completely and unambiguously. However, shape information forms only part of the complete description of a component or assembly. Material type, surface finish, part numbers, and other vital references must be incorporated for a complete product description to be built up in the computer.

This is the approach taken by the leaders in CAD/CAM such as Boeing, General Motors, and General Electric. The results they have obtained are in proportion to management's stand on what is necessary in terms of preconditions.

Computer-aided solutions should hit at the concept level of *structuring, formalizing,* and *recording.* CAD provides support along four axes of reference:

(1) analysis, in terms of design (pre-processing);
(2) calculation to be assured by the computer;
(3) integration through a properly structured database, accessed by all authorized users;
(4) standardization of output as part of post-processing.

Boeing and GE created formatting standards and led to an organization which promoted the use of pre- and post-processors. The advent of competitive modeling is credited to a GM development – designing a Cadillac after analysis of appealing (Mercedes) characteristics. As a result, back in 1976, the design of the 'Seville' took 28 months to complete against the classical 48 months Detroit time.

CAD applied from the original design stage means both greater quality and higher productivity. If polyvalent contributions and procedural changes are made in the design, then productivity can improve significantly. But, as always with computer-based systems, the equipment itself is a small part of the total. Much more important is the applications perspective.

Office automation

Like computer-aided design, office automation (OA) amplifies a wide range of communication and control capabilities. This is the reason why it influences many activities of managers and professionals.

Improvements in overall effectiveness arise primarily from improvements in executive capabilities. These trace their roots to the implementation of off-the-shelf advances in office technology. However, the purchase and use of OA equipment without prior system study can be counter-productive.

Even if an hour or more is saved by executive and/or clerk, only a thorough detailed study can suggest how to use this hour. Otherwise, work expands to fill the time available for its completion.

Work also expands to fill the amount of equipment available. This is true of personal computer (PC) capacity, of processing power expressed in millions of instructions per second (MIPS), and of disk storage. There is no such thing as a 'large enough' storage space.

In a CAD/OA environment, a single universal product description should be accumulated as a design proceeds from initial conception to manufacture. A consistent source of information for everyone working on a product should be provided – whether he or she works with engineering, manufacturing, purchasing, or sales.

The flow of common data should provide the thread that links interdependent processes which culminate in manufacturing and marketing. Since the product is maintained in the engineering database, it can be associated with other stored information. Thus component lists, catalogues and so on – which normally use part numbers or references to drawings – can have explicit references to the component itself.

The blending of computer-aided design and office automation allows a more unified approach to costing, marketing, and quantity estimation. All aspects of the component can be brought together in the database.

A significant benefit is the reduction in the errors so commonly made when data is passed manually between departments, generated from separate, possibly inconsistent documentation, and using (in most cases) outdated information.

Computer-aided design and office automation solutions have many things in common – starting with the workstation (WS) characteristics. In regard to software and hardware, a CAD system will involve the:

(1) computer;
(2) video screen and eventual hard copy device (printer and/or plotter);

(3) local database (microfile);
(4) access to central and regional databases (public or private);
(5) interactive datacomm capability;
(6) applications programming (AP) library;
(7) end user facilities.

The references are as valid for a management workstation as for computer-based facilities provided to any other professional. The software will be different, but there will always be available an applications library. The same is basically true regarding the resolution of the screen, as well as the nature and number of attached devices.

The evolution toward intelligent, communicating workstations may have been slow, but the pace is accelerating. Sometimes the emphasis is near-sighted: in telex, the trend has been toward higher capacity lines, yet it is the broader development, towards electronic mail, which makes the difference in service.

Whether we talk of engineering or managerial workstations, micro-computer-based distributed resources:

- make available local power at an affordable cost;
- help manage interactivity;
- ensure better response times; and
- avoid overloading the central facilities.

Particularly helpful as a major part of CAD/CAM is the interaction between users, as real development activity starts with the prototype. Whether we talk of engineering or managerial applications, computer modeling:

- cuts time lags;
- assists in reducing costs;
- improves quality; and
- promotes reliability.

In engineering, the overall philosophy is to try to eliminate the redesign phases by computer modeling. In management, we are particularly interested in decision support.

Both engineering and managerial workstations have been evolving over the years. For both engineering and management, the design operations to be done are *not* so complex. The most important part is preparation – the break with the tradition of keeping everything in one's own head and going about our work in a non-structured manner.

We know that structured approaches mean;

(1) the ability to state the reasons *why* we make the choices we do;
(2) the power to define *how* we are going to go about them;
(3) the wisdom to select as a first application a process complex enough to demonstrate the results of the system and yet not so complex as to discourage the needed mental conversion.

Within a broader applications horizon, it becomes evident that the potential of a CAD/CAM system goes much beyond the visual interactivity. What we see on video is the tip of the iceberg in terms of the results we can obtain.

But to obtain the wanted results we must establish our goals, prepare, and work with timetables and milestones. This is just as valid if we are interested in:

- Choice of axonometric, isometric, oblique or orthographic projections, or selecting among alternative plans of action.
- Drawing pictures as wire frame or full solid color views, or presenting risk evaluation on money loans.
- Adjusting the angle and intensity of directional lighting, or evaluating alternative investments.
- Moving, rotating, copying, deleting or making invisible any object in the picture, or answering 'what if' questions in budgetary allocation.
- Planning the line of sight across the scene, or evaluating the aftermath of a control action.
- Setting or resetting the angle of vision, or setting or resetting goals for divisional operations.

To start in the right way it is important to keep in mind that, in *any* automation project, the most sophisticated element, the one that is the most fragile, the most complicated and most likely to malfunction, is *the user*. From this we can derive two basic axioms.

The first is that the user must *not* write software in the old, classical way. He should either use packages or employ Fourth Generation Languages (4GL). The second principle is that, rather than spending precious time in reinventing the software wheel, brainpower should be applied to:

- rethink and reorganize the procedures;
- classify/identify all entities (logical, physical).

Information elements, the building blocks of the database, are logical items. Machines and spares are physical.

Whether we talk of engineering or managerial workstations, feasibility studies should be made with two criteria in mind:

(1) cost/benefit;
(2) the upgrading in quality of the organization and its people.

The first is heavily influenced by the mental and physical productivity we are going to obtain, the second by the degree and depth of the preparatory work preceding the introduction of office automation and/or computer-aided design.

Chapter 2

Key functions of a Technical Division

Efficiency in the technical operation of an industrial organization should be the concern of everybody in the top management team, not only of the technical personnel.

Under the impact of present-day industrial developments, the task of technical management takes on new importance. We must establish the Technical Division as a unique function able to handle seemingly unrelated activities, which however have both a background coherence and a great impact on the life of the firm.

The efficient implementation of a system that performs well – from product planning, through design and reliability to manufacturing and after-sales service – is key to the well-being of a firm. Performance can determine the success or failure of an enterprise and, with it, the careers of individuals.

Engineering designers must go well beyond the functions their task involved in the past. They must be able to create order out of poorly structured environments. The generation of engineering drawings is only a minor part of the new technical mission. Because of a steady integration, in probably no other field of management is the job to be done more confusing and, at the same time, more challenging.

While design engineering is usually thought as the principal objective of the Technical Division, other functions occupy an equally important role. The latter can be classified into two main groups:

(1) *Office management* – from ordinary administration and personnel to financial control, costing, standardization, purchasing and the management of inventories.
(2) *Manufacturing engineering* – including process studies, proprietary equipment design (necessary in certain industries), robotics systems, production planning, production control, and the very important area of steady improvements in efficiency.

Good product design is intimately linked to the bill of materials. The same is true of process design. Any project management worth its salt will pay great attention to:

- *Component standardization*, and therefore classification/identification of parts, sub-assemblies, assemblies.

- *Procurement optimization*, placing particular emphasis not only on specifications and costs but also quality and delivery dates – including the tracing of supplier dependability.
- The *automation of inventory management*, including raw materials, semi-manufactured goods, ready products, associated tools, machine parts, and machine aggregates.
- *Field feedbacks* as a result of maintenance action. This data is a valuable contribution to the engineering database, greatly affecting future design considerations.

These technical objectives go a long way beyond the old approaches to computer-aided design which dominated the 1970s. If understood and appreciated, they can help management look at the technical process in a more elegant, effective, all-encompassing manner.

The transition from R and D to manufacturing

An effective approach to the relationship between research and development (R and D) and manufacturing is not always the case in industrial operations. This gives rise to much confusion. Many companies, surprisingly, allow their production people to play around with product specifications or, conversely, permit their R and D people to pass a product file to manufacturing for actual production, before the product has had a chance to settle down.

Light-hearted approaches to 'debugging' have been found to be the origin of many product failures. This is a good example not only of what should not be done but also of a new vital role CAD/CAM can play in terms of file transmission and coordination.

Computer-based assistance can be incorporated in all phases of the development cycle. Once a product passes into the development stage, it is reasonably easy for the management to:

- analyze its potential salesworthiness;
- evaluate the degree of competition it may face;
- determine the general objectives and specificiations, including costs;
- project approximate target dates;
- coordinate time schedules;
- assign engineering skill.

The evaluation of development, as distinguished from that of research, mut be in terms of progress toward definite goals. Many companies establish schedules of development work as a method for defining what each person is expected to do and when he is expected to do it. The management needs to obtain information about the progress and prospects of technical projects for two reasons: first, as a basis for deciding whether a project should be continued, expanded, contracted, changed, or stopped; second, as a basis for appraising the performance of the development work as such.

Scheduling the work to be done at the development stage involves:

(1) breaking down the job into component parts or operations;
(2) estimating when each operation should be started, how long it should take and what resources are required;
(3) arranging the separate operations in proper order in relation to other operations and to other planned uses of the resources.

While R and D people often argue that scheduling cannot be used in development 'because nobody knows exactly how long each project will take', it is wise to remember that schedules are used for many operations for which a precise estimate of the time required cannot be made. This is said on the premise that even a rough approximation is better than no plan at all.

Questions of scheduling in development work are part and parcel of the responsibilities of the Technical Division. They are related to the time at which a certain product is brought to the market. Often this becomes a matter of evaluation in terms of time and cost versus operability.

In a competitive market, timing is an extremely important factor, and it works both ways: too early may be as bad as too late. Time is as much a resource as manpower, advanced technology, equipment and capital.

Because of the importance of new products for tomorrow's markets, and the cost of badly planned new products, better managed companies have devised plans and controls entrusted to the Technical Division. Their objective is to make sure that

- products are planned to the least detail;
- design and manufacturing processes are computer-based;
- materials are optimized;
- the bill of materials is kept dynamic;
- the engineering database is constantly enriched and consulted;
- interactivity is assured between all departments and projects working on the same or related products;
- coordination between research, development, manufacturing, maintenance is guaranteed through online information systems.

These are roles early CAD/CAM approaches did not tackle. Yet they should be the backbone of a computer-based system able to help engineering perform a better job for the company – significantly aiding its profitability and survival.

Apart from the question of optimum timing, the transition from research to production involves a substantial number of technological problems. Many of them are specific to the situation and to the product, but a problem common to almost all cases is that of the sharp decline in dependability of the product as soon as it passes from development to mass production.

New tests and adjustments are then necessary. In many cases there is a recovery, and the product gains once more the percentage dependability it had achieved when it was in the pilot stages. In other cases the recovery is followed by a new decline when the engineering product gets into operation. Ironically, this decline is sharper, and needs longer time for recovery.

Figure 2.1 is a view of this transitory stage. With paper-based processing, the crucial aspects of the transition call for great skill on the part of the person in charge. The engineer involved in the stages from development to production, or in their evaluation, should understand the role of each component of the system. Only then he will be able to predict vulnerability to change due to the new environment. In order to do so in an able manner, he should expect the unexpected, and should possess the skill of making dependable predictions based on the obtained results.

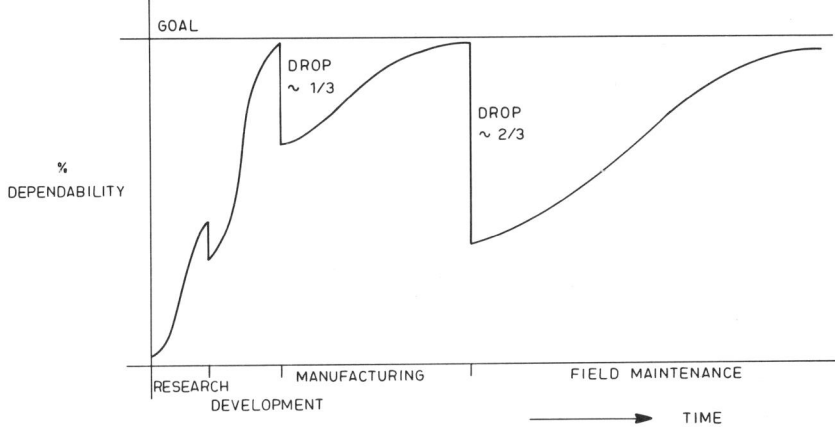

Figure 2.1 In the passage from research to development, manufacturing and field maintenance, there is a drop in dependability. CAD should help correct this classic situation

This and similar needs require the engineer engaged in development work to acquaint himself with how:

- the production system operates;
- commodities are produced;
- alternative ways for manufacturing can be devised;
- selection must be done among these alternatives;
- the various constraints which are present in material or other subjects can be distinguished.

Only then he can appreciate what goes into the production effort, and be able to communicate with the production people in the factory.

In a process automated through CAD/CAM the engineering expertise should be the same or greater, but the mechanics of the file transmission process are immensely simplified. What is confusing, slow, messy and prone to errors is paper-based mechanics.

Online CAD to CAM (supposing the factories are equipped with CAD/CAM units) helps:

(1) minimize the drop in dependability;
(2) accelerate the transmission procedures;
(3) present the right images (drawings, etc.) to the appropriate departments;
(4) handle efficiently the bill of materials;
(5) standardize procedures and processes;

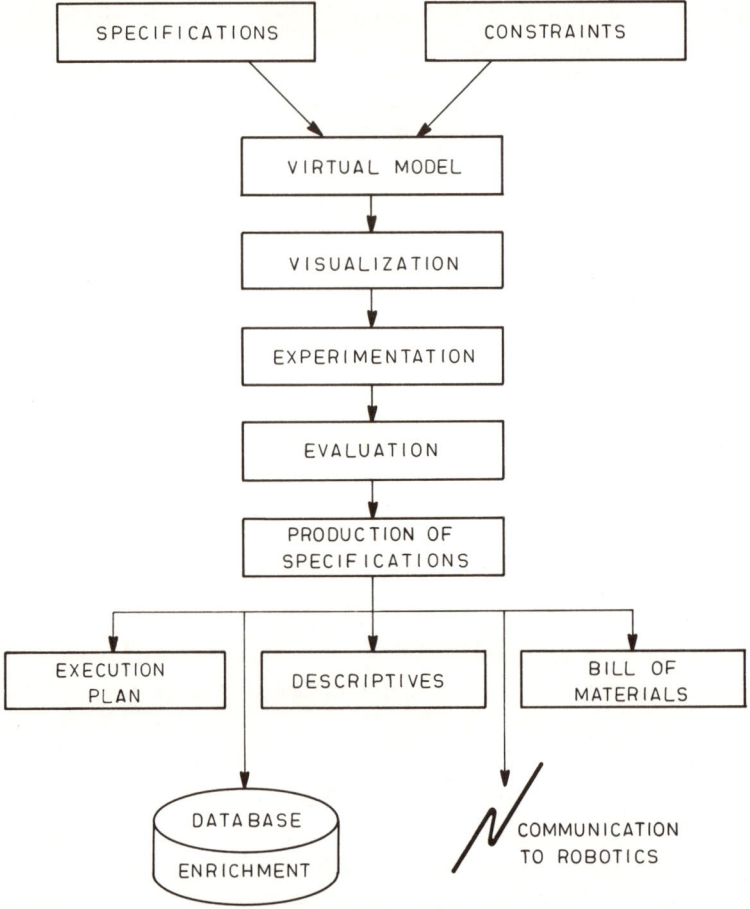

Figure 2.2 A whole new approach is necessary to improve the cost-effectiveness and the reliability of man-made products. The key is ingenuity, not just CAD

(6) lead to robotics without major changes in the way of handling engineering documents;

(7) assure a more effective handling of field maintenance problems.

With technological products today field service problems are much more critical and further from solution than comparable reliability in research, development and manufacturing.

To help answer these challenges satisfactorily, a whole new approach has been developed in engineering design. It constitutes an organized effort to raise value, lower cost, and provide for better coordination.

By changing materials and components, we aim to get the same performance without affecting quality. Being a low-cost producer should constitute a basic discipline of the development and design engineering.

This is one of the fundamental reasons why working with CAD should be not only a company policy but also a requirement starting at the very beginning of the design cycle. The degree of factory efficiency, tooling ingenuity and purchasing resourcefulness determines how closely the factory approaches minimum cost requirements. But even the most efficient factory methods, ingenious tooling and resourceful purchasing cannot reduce the cost of the product below the minimum established by the design engineer.

But the introduction of CAD/CAM at the early stages of the engineering cycle also poses challenges. Among them:

(1) *What to do with old drawings?* The answer is to sort them out; select those still actual; and do something about those selected. For instance, store them on optical disk for easy retrieval through a personal computer.

(2) *What to do with the new drawings coming from subcontractors?* Here the answer is to ask for and obtain CAD output and appropriate standard at the source. But also to establish rules regarding File Exchange Standards (IGES, GKS, PHIGS, VDI, PLPS).

(3) *What to do with new drawings from one's own R and D?* The solution in this respect must be much more structured than in any previous case. Such solution is related to the final selection of software and hardware; training of all engineers; the company-wide standards and associated test runs.

CAD/CAM will be that much more effective and profitable if Technical Management takes care to train *all* engineers and draftsmen. There should be a policy that slide rules, calculators, batch number-crunching, etc. are forbidden. Everybody working in the Technical Division should know how to work with CAD/CAM.

Not only must every engineer work through computer-aided design, but the company should use the results from 1, 2, and 3 above to create the Engineering Database (EDB) of the organization. Every person in the Technical Division – engineer, physicist, mathematician, draftsman – should work online to the EDB.

It is equally advisable for management to establish *productivity standards* – just as every self-respecting company has standards of quality and reliability.

Furthermore, without any doubt management must bring in CAD/CAM at the production site – in each and every factory. Here again, it is advisable to use uniform standards.

Just as wise is to establish a policy of enriching the EDB with field feedbacks from maintenance engineers. This will not only help improve quality but also, through the use of CAD/CAM, assist in steadily cutting costs.

Moving beyond the design process

We have been talking of a range of activities that go well beyond the original limited view of what computer-aided design is or could do. The goal should be to provide a vital service for the building and interrogation of product databases. The design engineer needs a powerful, general purpose set of commands for building, interrogating and manipulating component definitions. He should also be able to add information to them.

From a macroscopic viewpoint, provision must be made for interfacing to a variety of data management systems, drawing from Romulus's range of picture-generating facilities and providing output to any type of graphical device. Beyond doubt, this requires a system solution and should be so approached.

Unlike the 1960s and early 1970s, drafting is not longer the focal point of CAD. Computer-aided design has the same relation to drafting that office automation has to word processing (WP): drafting and WP are components of larger systems, playing junior partner roles in their respective automation frameworks.

As such, drafting and word processing should occupy less than 10 per cent of both the system analysis effort and the allocation of available facilities. In both cases (CAD and OA) databasing and data communications count for much more than the junior partners just mentioned.

Both CAD and OA must be interfaced to a network. Communications will be a key feature in all future systems – even more important than processing. All managers and professionals working in the same department and/or on the same project must be able to communicate with one another, both on a local area network basis and long haul.

The CAD system must work online not only with the other engineering departments of the firm but also – and most importantly – with:

- the company's own manufacturing plants;
- the suppliers and their CAD/CAM systems;
- the engineering organizations of the clients.

Within the company's own operations, the CAD users must be able to exchange messages, switch files, pass on graphics output, receive annotations and comments. They must also be able to make direct calls to private and public databases and to receive whichever program they need downloaded from subroutine libraries.

For processing purposes, the organization will typically maintain a rich set of routines for building, interrogating and manipulating models – as well as commands tailored to particular needs and direct programming interfaces.

Programs are necessary to unite objects, subtract objects from others, and find common intersections; to check for interference and extract arbitrary profiles or profile sections from a model; to construct two- and three-dimensional geometric points; to work on curves and surfaces; and to proceed with profile generation.

Other programs are needed for linear and rotational sweeping; for the identification of useful features of an object; for translations, rotation, removal and copying of features; to move models in any direction, rotate models about any axis, and mirror objects about any plane.

The designer needs programs to add linear, point-to-point dimensions; to provide textual annotations; to enquire about the geometry of a model; to list topological entities of a model; to save a model in a textual neutral file; to retrieve stored models; and to execute previously generated command files.

Through software, he will copy bodies, rename entities, build bodies by adding edges, delete bodies, provide local or full hidden line removal, obtain stereo views, assure the labelling of topological entities, rotate views, and zoom in or out.

A significant number of the programs needed for processing purposes can be found as packages – but choosing packages is itself an art. Among the critical issues in the choice of a package are:

(1) *Availability*. How long has the package been in general use? How many installations? Can we talk to users?

(2) *Flexibility*. Will the package run on different equipment or machine configurations? Can its functions grow? Is it modular?

(3) *Hardware*. What is the minimum configuration the software will run on? The input/output specifications? The communications requirements?

(4) *Software*. Is the package written in a modern and efficient language? What operating system does the package run under?

(5) *File design*. Is it feasible to evaluate the package's master files? Their organization? Special input/output options? Communications capabilities?

(6) *Documentation*. Does documentation include system and run-level narrative descriptions? Operating instructions? Input/output and file descriptions? Prompts and self-help? Communications protocols?

We should always try to get the best documentation we can. A package stands or falls on its documentation.

(7) *Applications references*. Are current users satisfied with the package? Is the system thorough and efficient? Does the application run smoothly? Does the system's performance meet the user's expectations?

(8) *Support*. How much support will the vendor supply during installation? Will the vendor train operating personnel, systems professionals, programmers, designers, managers?

(9) *Maintenance*. Is maintenance regularly provided? Does the vendor charge extra for maintenance after installation? What about steady enhancements? How will we be notified about new features and improvements of the package?

(10) *Cost*. Is the package available for purchase or lease? Are there extra-cost options and special features? How much will the vendor charge for training, installation, conversion, maintenance and any modifications that might be necessary?

On all these issues it is important to obtain applications references. Contacting other users of any package is a vital precautionary measure. The same is true of benchmarking.

Even if other engineering users say that the package is 'tops', it has to be tested to the organization's own needs. The tests should definitely include *response time* and the assurance that *user exits* are provided to add value as experience accumulates.

The emphasis on the use of packages has as its core the wisdom of avoiding the re-invention of the wheel. Instead of spending valuable brainpower on tasks which have already been solved, we should be investing it in the more challenging and rewarding effort of organizational studies and the fulfillment of prerequisites for a successful CAD implementation.

The advice can therefore be phrased in simple terms: 'If we find a package which suits our CAD applications, we should buy it. We should not write the program.' But we should also be careful to assure consistency in our choices. Both program portability and design portability are foremost.

Talking of choices, compatibility and rationality suggest that we should first choose the software and only then the hardware of CAD/CAM; in precise terms, the hardware that supports the software we have chosen.

Furthermore, for the value-added items for which we may need to write applications we should use Fourth Generation Languages (4GL) for prototyping – and for subsequent programming except run-time optimization. A major part of the time thus saved should be used to update steadily our information plant. This involves:

- steady database enrichment;
- classification/identification;
- inventory/purchasing coordination;
- CAD/CAM policies and equipment.

This is absolutely necessary to remain competitive. It is as important as steadily updating the skills of *all* our engineers, production and maintenance people to the new technology the company acquires.

Perspectives on file portability

While the processing aspects of a CAD system are known and, therefore, reasonably appreciated, less well known but just as vital is the need for file exchange between diverse computer-aided design equipment.

As a matter of policy, only one standard should exist within the same organization. The need for interfaces comes from the need to communicate and exchange CAD files with clients and suppliers. There exist today different graphics exchange standards and choices must be made in this regard.

(1) Nearer to the equipment level is the Virtual Device Interface (VDI) and the somewhat older Virtual Device Metafile (VDM).

In June 1984, ISO WG2 (Graphics) set a format title for VDM: 'Information Processing – Computer Graphics – Metafile for Transfer and Storage of Picture Description Information'; in short: 'Computer Graphics Metafile', or CGM.

There is a second-generation (post-VDM) draft of the Virtual Device Interface (VDI) studied by ANSI X3H3. ISO WG2 also established a new title for VDI: 'Information Processing – Computer Graphics – Interface Techniques for Dialogs with Graphical Devices'; in short: 'Computer Graphics Interface', or CGI.

However, at present the graphics standard of the personal computer world is the bit map of the IBM PC. There is talk that before too long we will see hardware from IBM as a *de facto* standard at the VDI level. At the same time, Unix may be moving toward an object-code-level interface. And we should not forget the Quickdraw set of primitives carried into at least some Macintosh clones and other machines.

In this sense, VDI, bit map, and Quickdraw are competing technologies near the device level. Besides this plurality there is a need to verify that various implementations of a graphic standard meet formal requirements of CAD/CAM in the broadest sense – from management to engineering and manufacturing.

(2) Interfacing to the VDI level is the representation of graphic sets. Here the Videotex agreements signed in Geneva, In February 1983, are the best frame of reference.

Eight graphic sets are defined by the North American Presentation Level Protocol (NA PLPS), valid for the United States and Canada. Seven graphic sets (of which only part is compatible with NA PLPS) have been established by the European CEPT standard.

Images are described as either alphageometric or alphaphotographic representations by means of Picture Description Instructions (PDI). This permits the growth of large information bases through terminal independence. There is no problem in accommodating new developments and improvements as new technologies become available.

This is a significant benefit, as the growth of character-oriented systems is restricted not so much by their display methods but by their image description techniques. Besides the virtual independence from terminal configurations there is independence from communication networks and database construction. Larger input buffers can store several pages of a document transmitted as a single burst of information.

(3) The Programmer's Hierarchical Graphic Standard (PHIGS) will most likely evolve as a separate product in the course of time. It is intended to serve users who display and manipulate a large amount of graphics in a highly interative environment.

Four aspects are especially important. First, the implementation of a hierarchical display list to allow display-list subroutines and to permit the description of relationships between portions of the graphics data. Second, provision for the flexible modification of the display list so that application programs can manipulate the graphics data as appropriate. Third, the use of modeling transformations for describing the position and motion of objects in the graphics data space. Fourth, the use of GKS concepts and functions wherever possible, differing from GKS only when required to meet the needs of the intended audience.

PHIGS issues have been reviewed by X3H3, which is addressing some of the items of its design. PHIGS has also been presented to an ISO meeting, in June 1984.

(4) The Graphical Kernel System (GKS) was originally developed as a two-dimensional standard. (Mostly editorial in nature, it was originally

known as DIS 7942). More recently there has been a GKS 3-D extension. ISO is interested in it, and ANSI is participating in the drafting effort.

Basically a German development adopted by American standardization bodies, GKS benefits from the establishment of validation and certification center for GKS in a German state institution. Testing is performed at three levels:

- the operating interface;
- the interface to the corresponding GKS tables;
- the comparison of a candidate implementation with the reference implementation.

In America, the federal government is trying to procure the validation techniques being developed in Europe, to validate GKS implementations that vendors want to sell to the federal government.

Because of the ongoing work, the Graphical Kernal System will most likely be the first to define the interface between graphics applications and the underlying graphics support system.

Bindings of GKS to FORTRAN and BASIC have been completed. The FORTRAN binding is to be part of dpANS X3.124 in the US. Bindings to Ada, Pascal, C, and PL/1 are under way in ANSI X3H34.

(5) The Initial Graphics Exchange Specification (IGES). Its goal has been to establish information structures to be used for the digital representation and communication of product definition data. It permits the compatible exchange of product definition data used by various CAD/CAM systems.

IGES has been developed and built in the United States, one of the key initial sponsors being the Department of Defense. The National Bureau of Standards and companies in the aerospace and motor industries, as well as CAD/CAM system manufacturers, all participated in the effort.

Several technical committees work on IGES. The most important are E&R (Extension and Repair) and TE&S (Test, Evaluation and Support). Technical subcommittees address themselves to issues such as advanced geometry, piping, finite element analysis, electrical engineering, test library, problem areas, recommended practices.

In a calendar of progress, the following dates can be mentioned: The effort started in September 1979 and January 1980 saw the publication of the first specifications (Version 1.0). In June 1981 was developed the Draft Standard, and in April 1982 the ANSIs Standard.

Though ANSI seems to have accepted IGES since May 1980, it has also worked on its own standard: the Core System since 1979 and on GKS since 1982. As a result, there are two distinct methodologies within the ANSI Standard: IGES and ANSI's own.

Since overlaps are unavoidable, it is important to realize what IGES is and what it is not. In principle, the whole effort is descended from CAD/CAM ideas and technology. It is not an attempt to tackle commercial databases. As a result, IGES has been often criticized for ignoring fundamental issues in database design.

A good deal of the original effort was funded by the US Air Force in the ICAM (Integrated Computers and Manufacturing) program. The US Army, Navy and NASA also sponsored the program under contract to NBS.

The original goal was no different from that of the other file exchange standards: developing a computer-independent interface for transferring information from one CAD system to another. This left its mark on strategy and structure: IGES is a *Communications File* solution – designed, targeted on and intended for exchange of data between turnkey graphics systems. It is not a database, nor does it have a database management system (DBMS).

To help position IGES within the engineering design effort, we should look at interfacing requirements between the database kept for pre-processing, that for post-processing, and other information elements of the engineering database kept on mainframes, minis, workstations, file servers of local area networks, as well as text and data warehouses.

Beyond doubt, five standards which are partially overlapping are too many. The more so as the role of graphics standards is to define a set of common procedures for developing graphics applications.

Graphics devices are not transaction-type processors oriented to structured activities, usually at operation control. Structured activities are characterized by:

- clear definition of what constitutes a problem;
- known, documented alternatives;
- already optimized solutions.

Engineering design is a creative task, and therefore an unstructured activity. It involves complex or dynamic choices, exploratory problems, planning premises.

This is the critical role of online graphics – whether for engineering design or management control. The demand for versatile systems is so overwhelming that the lack of trained analysts, programers and users can be a constraint. The same is true of the ability to transfer files between machines.

Standards must be developed to relieve this bottleneck. To such standards must be interfaced all software and hardware, and the Technical Division will be well advised to give such standards due priority in the selection of physical and logical machines.

Placing emphasis on response time

The lion's share of automation resources should be allocated to those activities of the Technical Division which count more and can give the highest return on investment. With CAD, this is the role of the chief design engineer and of his immediate assistants. In OA, the main emphasis should be placed on management productivity functions.

In both cases, time is at a premium. It cannot and should not be spoiled by slow responses and messy files. Furthermore, both with CAD/CAM and with OA it is important that every manager, every engineer, designer or other professional has his own intelligent workstation (WS) and interacts directly with the database.

This direct, online interaction with the engineering database is in the background of the statement made in the preceding section that one of the key missions of a Technical Division should be the streamlining of handling product files. From research and development to manufacturing and field maintenance, files should be homogeneous, compatible and portable.

Another major challenge facing a Technical Division confronted with the automation of its design and production resources through CAD/CAM is the improvement of response time. We implement computers and communications to improve response and obtain higher productivity from the managers and professionals we employ.

Response time requirements should be answered both through procedural and software/hardware means. The use of intelligent engineering workstations connected to the central CAD unit will ease its load, improve response time, and make feasible a broader array of personal design capabilities. To realize this requires both the appropriate physical connection and logical constructs.

Several experiments have been made to evaluate the connection of microprocessor-based engineering workstations to a central resource. Typically, such applications have been page-independent, with the possibility of changing presentation without altering the application. Different database organizations were used for tests: direct index-sequential, and sequential transaction files.

Two types of application were employed in one of these experiments: (1) retrieve from master file; (2) update master file and append transaction file. The test took place under simultaneous-access conditions by all workstations, thus testing worst conditions in terms of response time. It was felt that, because of high visibility of the workstations by the end user, 'worst condition' evaluation provided better guarantees.

In this experiment, with one non-intelligent engineering WS accessing the central CAD unit, the response time was nearly 2 seconds. This became '3 plus' seconds in the case of a two-WS access; grew to 5 seconds with three; then 12 to 15 seconds for five workstations; and hit 20 to 26 seconds for six WS. Typically, response time depends on:

(1) access time on disk;
(2) number of accesses of the disk;
(3) CPU time;
(4) transaction time between terminal and central processor;
(5) implementation inefficiencies (operating system, DBMS, special software interfaces, drivers);
(6) the DBMS enveloping requirement of 200 kilobytes (KB) per terminal, leading to roll-in, roll-out;
(7) system interlocks.

A further test identified the necessity of studying response time very carefully, including: overhead at every level; file organization (to which response time seems to be very sensitive); the effect of programming tools;

and other factors entering into the response time equation, such as the type of application.

The best results were obtained (a steady 2 second response time) when the central CAD unit was relieved of all processing functions, acting mainly as File Server. The processing needs were located at intelligent engineering workstations. Further improvements were made in database organization and in the function of the applications environment.

This is an example on how characteristic studies of the Technical Division have changed with OA and with CAD solutions. Stress analysis or powerloads will no longer be done by engineers working with slide rule and calculator. Computers and software will perform not only the basic computations but also the optimization.

Support by computers and communications should help preserve the most valuable resource we have in an organization: human capital. That is why the time of the professional working on the system should be the subject of careful, factual, documented studies.

As Figure 2.3 outlines, the *elapsed time* is composed of three component parts: *user, system and idle times*. Each one of them should be analyzed so that fast, reliable interactivity is assured. I see this as a prerequisite to the proper implementation of CAD/CAM, which we will be discussing in the following chapter.

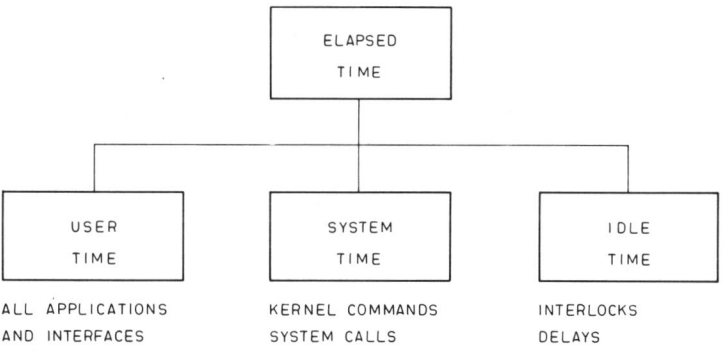

Figure 2.3 Elapsed time and response time are not always considered in technical studies. Yet they are critical in a man-machine dialog

The examples we have been considering provide sufficient evidence that working with computer-based support in a communications-intensive environment poses challenges which can only be answered through fundamental studies. To these, the Technical Division must now focus its attention. As we will see in the following chapter, change to the new environment involves both concepts and means. It also requires new directives.

Chapter 3

Implementing computer-aided design

We have spoken of new directions in engineering and the evolving functions of the Technical Division. In the background of this discussion has been the process of computer-aided design – but we also said that major conceptual changes are necessary.

When we move out of paper and into the world of electronics, the means we have at our disposal and their power, improve by more than an order of magnitude. Our approach must also evolve, otherwise the benefits will be minimal.

Training *all engineers* to the new concepts and tools must be a steady process. As technology moves forward, our know-how should evolve. Rubinstein, the famous pianist, once said: 'If I don't exercise for a month, the public will notice it. If I don't exercise for a week, my friends will notice it. If for a day, I would notice it.' Training must be steady.

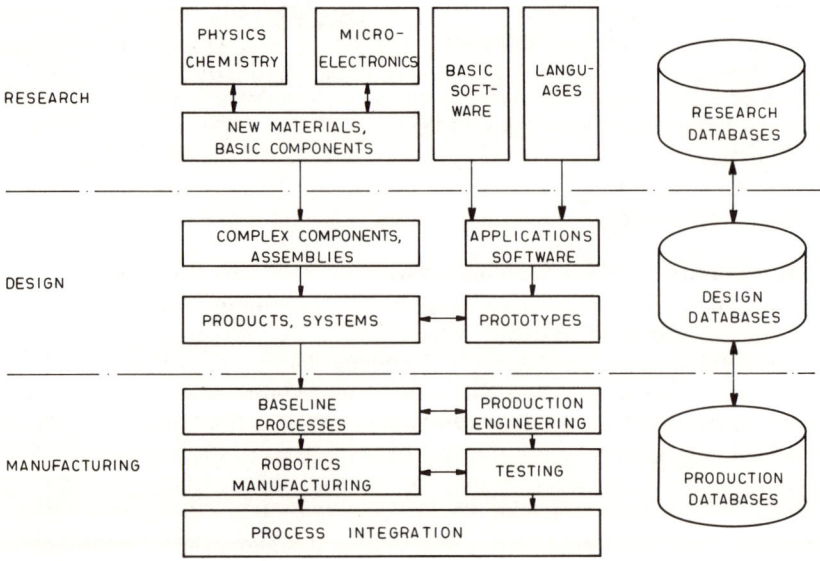

Figure 3.1 A whole new concept is necessary in order to integrate research, design and manufacturing, and to interconnect the corresponding databases

Training must see to it that every engineering professional understands the CAD system as an aggregate of *software* (SW), *hardware* (HW) packages, *algorithms* and *data* needed to create an interactive facility with user-friendly, fast, dependable access to and manipulation of information elements (IE). This definition of CAD is valid whether we talk of research, design or manufacturing (Figure 3.1).

R and D/manufacturing coordination, file exchange standards, response time requirements, and the all-important classification/identification perspectives, are component parts of the same effort: improving engineering productivity, bettering product quality and cutting costs. The able use of CAD/CAM, it is said, can improve the productivity of engineers by 400 to 3000 per cent. But such improvements will not come of their own will.

Implementing CAD/CAM is an activity vastly greater and more complex than purchasing equipment or software. Throwing money at the problem is an insignificant part of the effort. The key problem is the change that must take place within the organization. Such change is often tied to:

- Management concepts;
- Engineering skills;
- Product demand;
- Labor unions and social factors.

Management must appreciate that in a highly competitive environment the quality of engineering services will deteriorate without the proper computers and communications support. Costs will be going up in all operations that remain labor-intensive.

Most importantly, as products and processes become increasingly complex and are themselves computer-based, designers cannot work in isolation. The product description they generate has to be used by many other knowledge workers.

Since in engineering the greatest asset of a company is its data, organizing a smooth flow of data is crucial to efficiency. This underlines the role of the engineering database, which we touched on in the first chapter and which we will further expand in this.

Improvements on present procedures will not come through a miracle or a revelation. They require insight, foresight, know-how, hard work, and a well-directed, steady, consistent effort. This is the sense of properly implementing CAD/CAM.

From drafting to designing

We said that we have to automate for product quality as well as for cost savings. Parts and assembly automation tips the scales beyond labor cost advantages. It alters the way of interconnecting the design office to the production floor.

Because of extensive use of CAD/CAM, Chrysler's new H-car family has more than two-thirds of its components designed and engineered on computer screens. Some experts are hailing it as America's most advanced computer-aided design and manufacturing system.

When the engineer designs a project on a video screen, the computer helps fill in point and figure calculations. It stores the design, or, if it is finished, sends it to a computer-driven production machine, such as an automated drill press, where the prototype is produced.

Meanwhile, the design data is in the database, so the computer can create bills of materials, purchase orders, inventory reports, and any other information necessary to keep management up to date.

Because the integration of CAD/CAM reduces work in progress it also results in significant cost savings. Intermediate production stocks can be reduced by specifying *which* parts are needed to make or assemble a product, as well as *when* the parts are needed.

Computer-based links of engineering and manufacturing help to create efficient parts schedules: bills of materials can be entered into the system and tied to the appropriate items on the schedule; inventory records can be entered and tied to bills of materials.

Then the system produces adjusted schedules, ordering requirements, and warnings about problems that cannot be solved without unusual intervention by various departments. The computer-based system can forecast needs and arrange deliveries.

Information distilled by the system will be reported to management, translated into production reports and financial records: balance sheet items reflecting inventory, present and projected receivables, and present and projected payables covering parts.

As materials requirements are reviewed by the system, delivery dates for materials on open purchase orders can be checked. If a date changes, the system will note this for purchasers and other directly affected parties. The system simulates daily operations, using actual data entered into the computer each day. By simulating material requirements planning, it alerts the purchasing department to possible shortages months in advance.

These are convincing examples that two decades of experience in computer-aided design have moved our point of emphasis away from drafting and into broader, more rewarding areas of endeavour. Whether we call the new concept computer-aided engineering (CAE) or keep on using the CAD title is unimportant. Important is the need to alter our preconceptions.

Drafting is essentially a two-dimensional task: the production of an engineering drawing. It contains many repetitive jobs, and is amenable to improvement using computer aids.

The engineering designer faces the more demanding job of creating a three-dimensional part, assembly, or aggregate, which must perform a specified task. The product will have to meet geometric and functional constraints, and may need to be styled attractively. In other words, the designer works essentially in three dimensions. Although he is forced to record his design on an electronic drawing board in 2-D, he will often be seen producing scale models, and also resorting to expensive mock-ups.

If he is going to work through the computer in 3-D, the engineering designer has two requirements, which are crucial.

(1) He needs to be given an effective means of interacting with the model, stored and maintained by the computer.

(2) He must be assured that a complete and accurate model of his work will be produced – involving a full product description, including geometry, surface finish, dimensions and other attributes.

This implies that every face and edge of the model will be accurately represented and that the proper characteristics can be attached to the data structure. The designer will also expect to be able to obtain the mass properties of the product, check for interference between components, and produce high quality pictures for sales and technical literature.

Structure and functionality should dominate his effort – together with the ability to design for low-cost production. As Figure 3.2 shows, the concepts entering this approach are design goals, physical attributes, symbolic elements (hence, icons), and specifications for geometric elements.

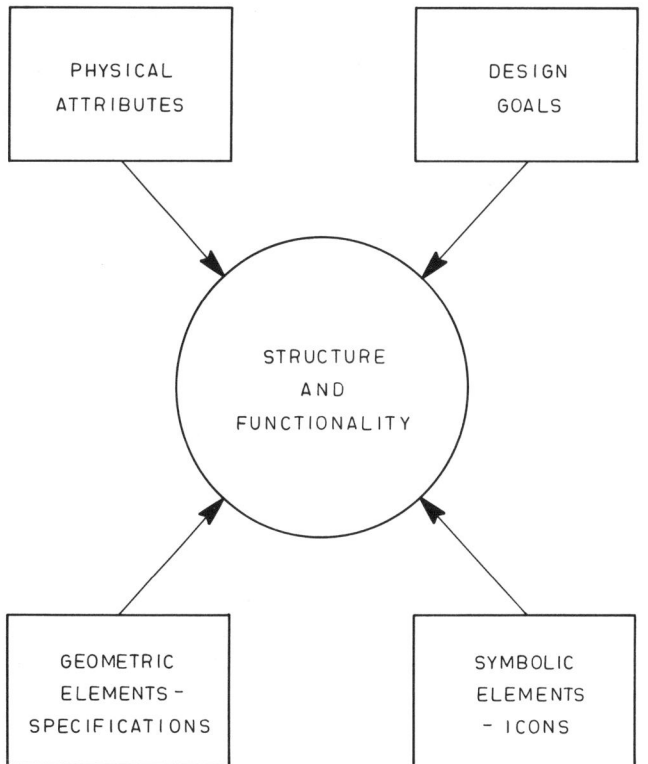

Figure 3.2 Structure and functionality should dominate engineering design. This requires thinking in parallel on four different axes of reference

Working online to the engineering database, the designer has at his disposition a wealth of information elements, which he does not need to re-invent every time he has a new project. He can also follow an orderly procedure, iterate different steps, experiment and optimize.

For instance, designing electronic circuitry requires several steps. The design of a complex system starts by laying out a block diagram equivalent to an architectural plan. This specifies in broad terms: the *functions* the design is to perform; and how they *integrate*.

Then the design is broken down into functional blocks, containing greater detail as to what logic will be included. Detailed drawings specify the contents of the functional blocks as interconnected logical components.

While all digital electronic systems can be projected as interconnected logic gates, the gates themselves are meaningless as production data. They must be presented as interconnected integrated circuits (IC) and discrete semiconductors for printed circuit board (PCB) design. Transistor interconnections must be shown for gate array design, and the same is true of the actual multi-layered components.

To arrive at production data for the first two design functions (PCB and gate arrays) generally requires only two-dimensional representation. But ICs call for a complex three-dimensional one. This is fundamental in the emerging use of computers for gate array design.

Throughout this process, both the evolving system and its components are checked, simulated and verified to avoid logical inconsistencies; to prevent the propagation of errors and/or delays; and to assure that parts of a design, worked on by separate work groups, fit well into an aggregate.

Product simplification and reliability

Product simplification is one of the key benefits to be obtained through computer-aided design. Designers did that manually in their time – but only great designers.

In 1937, for instance, Messerschmitt (the well-known aircraft producer) asked the manufacturers of the Argus 8C 300 CV motor to reduce the number of pieces in the helix from 377 to 12. The engine manufacturers balked. For them, this was not possible. Messerschmitt himself went to work and reached his goal in three months.

There are not many top designers around who can beat the computer by using their brains. In general, 'the computer knows best'.

Chip and computer manufacturers offer a good example of how the adoption of a new technology helps reduce costs, keeping the company competitive. Apple reduced the component count in its IIE model from 110 to 31 by replacing many chips wired into printed circuit boards (PCB) with two LSI custom chips.

The cost of the custom chips themselves might be equal to or higher than the cost of the standard chips they replace when their fixed engineering cost is included, but they make possible significant savings in:

- assembling circuit boards;
- simplifying many aspects of the system's design and/or construction;
- increasing system reliability.

Reliability is, of course, a prime consideration. If for no other reason, the use of facilities closely associated with computer-based processes like CAD/CAM should be given the proper attention. In the longer run they may become not just an important co-product but a mainline product of computer-aided design.

Experts in the relatively new discipline of risk analysis caution that assessing the collective risk of the world's potential calamities is not an easy matter. Experimenting on the individual probabilities provides at least a first approximation, and computer-based aggregate studies can be relatively accurate as well.

Norman C. Rasmussen, Professor of Nuclear Engineering at the Massachusetts Institute of Technology, put his thoughts in the following manner: 'The probability of a dam failure is about 1 in 10,000 a year. There are now about 10,000 dams. And they fail about one a year.' The numbers change as plants age – and that, too, must be taken into consideration.

Then came Chernobyl. In 1974, it was predicted that a core-damaging nuclear accident should only happen once in, say, 20,000 years of operation. Now it has happened twice in seven calendar years. Some 300 functioning reactors exist in the world. Even if we assume that one fourth of them are closed for repair, we manage 225 years of operation in one calender year. What's the frequency with which we should expect the next accident?

Some experts said in 1982 that accidents were 30 times more likely than was calculated at earlier times. This might give us a likely accident every 3 years. Which is what we have had lately. Soon some 200 more nuclear reactors will come into operation. So an educated guess might be made that nuclear reactor accidents will happen every second year, or so. In 1986, Chernobyl gave evidence of this.

The reason such estimates cannot be considered as awfully pessimistic is that there is at present a great inconsistency in the assessments of differing risks. Risk assessment in today's interdependent world involves balancing very small risks against very large consequences, and the art of doing so is not under control. But high technology at management's side can be of help – as, of course, can steady vigilance.

Equipment becomes worn and safety procedures inevitably relax. Both should become the subject of experimentation. Without a long, hard look at life cycles, in today's highly technological world a disaster such as the one at Bhopal is quite probable.

The real problem is that technological man undertakes too many hazardous things. What particularly worries designers is that the time between calamities may be getting too short.

The US alone has some 6000 chemical plants; the world-wide total is at least twice that. Add in nuclear power plants and related facilities, equipment for handling liquefied natural gas and other explosive fuels, laboratories for studying potent new biological organisms, and – perhaps most critical of all – the many instances when these and similar substances are transported (including aging tankers and highway transport) and we are dealing with potential calamities number in the tens of thousands.

Even if there is *only* 1 chance in 100,000 of a major accident at any one place in a given year, some calamity is bound to occur somewhere in the world perhaps every 10 years – or less. Worse yet, risk analysts agree that their calculations can easily be off by a factor of 10 or even 100. The true value of an estimate of one in a million might really be one in a trillion – or just 1 in 10,000. Moreover, a plant that starts life with one chance in a million of have a major accident in any given year may pose a much greater risk 10 years later.

Thus, the best answer lies in database experimentation in the early phases of design:

- tightening standards where necessary;
- improving warning systems and emergency response plans;
- choosing costlier but less hazardous processes, when possible;
- doing things on a smaller scale;
- isolating the danger whenever feasible;
- realizing that industrial catastrophes are no longer distant improbabilities.

Though it may not be a self-evident truth at first sight, product simplification and the ability to experiment on life cycle behavior can tremendously boost engineering productivity. In strict technical terms, productivity refers to measures of output primarily based on physical units: production in relation to an input factor such as labor hours.

We all know that, to be meaningful, measures of productivity must be tailored to the problem and production system in hand. We also appreciate that there exist different viewpoints regarding productivity measurements:

- Economists stress the ability of a production system to deliver goods and services for consumption.
- Business managers usually compare the input/output relationships of similar departments or businesses.
- In manufacturing, we compare output to worker-hour input.

With this we attempt to gauge how changes in production methods affect output. The trouble is that there exists no universally valid measure of input when we talk of thought processes and of creative activities.

For the last 100 years, labor has been a useful thing to measure because it was such a large part of the cost of most products. With automation this is no longer true. If productivity is tied closely to labor, it is necessary to look at the worker within a broad context. We should not consider technical factors alone; many other forces are also at work.

Work backlog is an example where design automation can be the solution. Such a backlog of work is symptomatic of our society's radical shift toward an information economy with increasingly greater demands posed at the design phase.

The problem is especially accute in firms that lack a cogent information policy. An increase in complexity causes productivity problems, which cannot be solved unless the development team has become proficient with new design tools. Add to this reliability and maintainability requirements and you get the composite picture necessary to make valid decisions.

In other terms, an organization's productivity cannot always be measured simply in terms of labor per hour. We must also account for factors ranging from managerial effectiveness to run-time safety and customer satisfaction. Productivity objectives for systems development include:

(1) reduced costs;
(2) faster implementation;
(3) less manpower;
(4) system quality;
(5) dependability in performance;
(6) user control;
(7) overall flexibility.

But it is also true that increasing the designer's productivity is not merely a matter of providing him with better software or faster computer. We also have to be be willing to improve other aspects of the job – particularly his mental images.

We have to realize that today (and even more so for the years to come) we are dealing with big systems. Big systems are not small systems that have outgrown their original size. They are totally different in perspectives, fundamental studies, and engineering demands.

Computer-aided design should be seen as the way to augment the range and depth covered by our brain. As processes and products get immensely complex we cannot handle all the details and integration requirements in our mind. The intellectual capabilities of the human brain reach their limits – and we are only in the 20th century.

The instrumental role of the database

An engineering database is a dynamic model of a system. It is utilized for design and management purposes, being accessible online by a large number of authorized workstations.

Such a database is the storehouse of information elements (IE) which can be data, text, graphs or images, and eventually voice. The IE is the building block of the engineering database. It can be a bit, byte, field, record, file, or a subset of the EDB.

When we think of engineering databases, we have to consider not only the past but also their future evolution. Practical statistics on text and data usage are not yet available, but an MIT study has established that ratios of 3 or 4 to 1 between text and data will be typical in business. There is no evidence to suggest that engineering databases will be characterized by a different ratio.

A pivotal point in a good design is the ability to integrate data and text, keeping the options open for the integration of graphics on a corporate-wide level – from engineering to manufacturing and field maintenance. This is the next frontier of CAD/CAM.

For a wide-ranging engineering database structure, we also need to provide new languages. Technology and science cover a tremendous spectrum. (CAD people express interest in relational DBs, while they have little interest in the hierarchical kind.)

The value of a database largely depends on how rich its content is and how high the volume of usage. The implementation of computer-aided design will face an inherent drawback if we cannot load those of the older, hand-kept drawings that are still active.

Many companies shy away from this responsibility – yet they can well use the old drawings' transcription as a means of training their professional people. It is also possible to automate this process under acceptable financial terms, if the necessary preparatory work is done in sorting out what is still valid.

Another issue that increases the value of an engineering database is the availability of first-class supports. A *data dictionary* (DD) and a *database management system* (DBMS) are necessary for its administration. Text and data can be managed through the same DBMS if properly structured in terms of encapsulation. We talk of encapsulation when access to an IE is at group level and is achieved through the linguistic (programming) interfaces at our disposal.

Elementary IE can be structured, then grouped, into larger information elements with *virtual storage* (VS) characteristics: pages, multipages, scrolls. Structuring is necessary for automatic retrieval capabilities, leading to recognition memories and associative solutions.

For storage and retrieval purposes, preparatory work is at a premium. Able database design has prerequisites. The topmost are:

(1) the overall concept;
(2) organization;
(3) integration;
(4) partition.

Only when such prerequisites are properly satisfied can we talk of:

(5) distribution;
(6) implementation;
(7) maintenance.

Any EDB represents an organized, orderly collection of IE, designed in an applications-independent manner. It can be distributed, shared by authorized persons (therefore, engineering and managerial workstations) and serve design purposes.

The database must be organized with the objectives of providing online facilities and interactive capabilities – through local area and long-haul networks. It must also assure file exchange, and we have spoken of evolving file transfer standards in the last chapter.

The choice of data structures is important in any application. In solid modeling it has proved to be crucial to the success of the product. The data must represent every item of interest to the designer: assemblies, components, faces, edges and vertices. It must enable the designer to select these items using a graphical input device, and allow the system to generate suitable pictures quickly. It must also allow the user a wide variety of modeling operations.

Not only traditional drafting techniques are needed for producing profiles, but also methods for generating simple solid shapes, together with means of combining such devices through logical (boolean) operations.

The designer must be able to work through levels of abstraction and to effect transformation concepts on data structures needed for the system on which he is working (Figure 3.3). One major appeal of the distributed approach is that each user can pick the CAD system that best suits a particular need. Problems arise, however, when a company tries to transfer CAD data between departments.

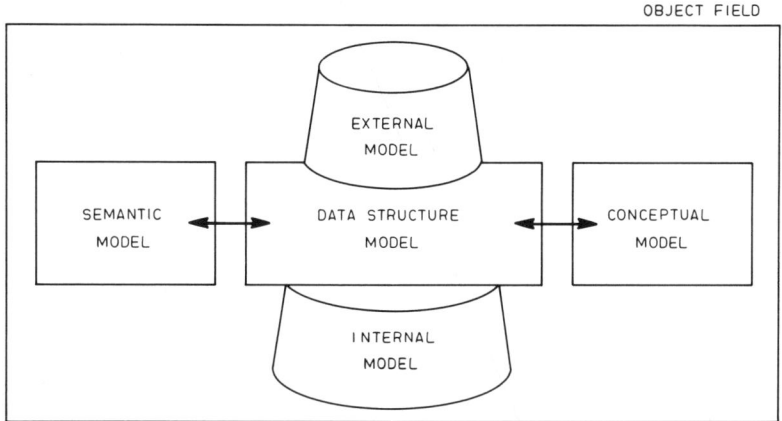

Figure 3.3 The engineering database will typically run under a database management system. Data structures interface between internal and external models

As stated earlier, because of the lack of standardization the CAD equipment from one vendor may not be able to communicate with a system from another vendor. Hence design data may have to move through interfaces or be manually re-entered, with delays, costs and mistakes being unavoidable. After two decades of letting its divisions go their own way in CAD, General Motors is spending monumental sums on forging communications links between CAD installations. This need is particularly underlined with the move toward computer-aided manufacturing (CAM).

Computer-aided manufacturing leads to computer-integrated manufacturing (CIM), which poses a system problem: who is to integrate the computers which run the factories and their machines? An inventory taken at General Motors indicated that there are in the whole company some 65 000 types of programmable controlling machines from large computers to small drives – and they are not necessarily compatible.

This is not the exception, but the rule. From the factory floor to communications networks, large industrial organizations spend a significant amount of their capital investment in providing interfaces among incompatible computer equipment, controllers, and protocols. This led General Motors to establish uniform standards for vendors who want to do business with the corporation. Hence the Manufacturing Automation Protocol (MAP). Boeing did the same by establishing the Technical and Operations Protocol (TOP).

Unless the environment is properly controlled, even small discrepancies can result in parts that do not mate properly on the assembly line – which the CAD/CAM system should reach to be worth its salt. Therefore, not only must mapping standards be chosen but also telecommunications requirements must be kept in perspective.

All information elements must be designed to serve – without conversion – both databasing and datacom. *A file is a message in the EDB, and each message must be designed as a file.*

The use of design systems linked to online databases allows the engineer to specify parts and instantly determine if those parts are currently used in production. If the specified parts and assemblies are not in inventory, an online link is possible to the production floor and/or the purchasing department. This helps minimize inventories. Also, engineers who are reluctant to change product designs just because one component has changed can review an entire design to see if one cost-saving revision can lead to others.

In conclusion, the CAD/CAM database is the key element in integrated design and manufacturing systems. Its proper usage can reduce product design time to a third of that normally required. In some instances, CAD/CAM has shrunk design time by a factor of 20.

More significantly, computer-aided design really pays off when engineering modifications are made. New drawings, machine tool instructions, and parts breakdowns can be developed, and revised contracts produced to keep them actual. In design and in manufacturing, faster reflexes mean bigger profits.

The importance of an online engineering database will be better appreciated if we recall that between 20 and 30 per cent of the designers' time in a company is spent duplicating items that already exist. CAD eliminates re-inventing things if something similar has been previously designed.

Administrative aspects in engineering

In terms of the automation of basic functions, the typical engineering company can be divided into two major work groups:

* administration, timetables, cost control – generally management group;
* design and engineering support group.

The administration group encompasses all elements of planning and control, from project cost and scheduling to staff management, finance, and accounting. The engineering group is basically scientific and production oriented.

Both groups need computer support. They must maintain a complete cost database available to all users through direct access via intelligent terminals. Such administrative database must be developed, pruned, kept actual. It must also integrate with the engineering database.

The discussion in these three chapters has provided evidence that automation at the engineering group end is a more complex problem than that of the administrative functions. In the past, automation in the engineering field meant standalone special-purpose equipment: 'scopes, analyzers, automatic testers, graphics machines. Next came high-speed terminals and the large, dedicated scientific computer with a library of scientific software programs. Today the terminals include intelligent workstations linked one to another, to graphics equipment and to the engineering database. This leads to the development of a system of distributed engineering workstations, each allowing its user to access information elements, compute, display, simulate, experiment, store, print or plot.

Distributed engineering workstations will typically feature *distributed databases*. With intelligent WS there is no reason why we should regularly access a central organizational database. We can nicely handle *local files* without a gigantic streamlining routine. This keeps everything small:

(1) The individual user can understand the system better.
(2) The *personal computing*, text/database and data communications specialist can more easily see how to manipulate a new function, and
(3) It becomes possible always to send information to the recipient in the way he wants to receive it.

At each local workstation level, text, data and graphics can be *linear, lean* and *simple*. But the distribution of intelligent workstations at every engineering desk also demands stringent, well-planned administrative procedures to ensure that the system will work as one entity.

Properly studied procedures are necessary to produce and handle the documentation of specifications and product descriptions in a uniform way; to develop engineering designs; to test end products, thus providing the possibility of life cycle simulation; to handle eventual modifications; and to generate performance statistics.

Administrative chores should look after the smooth passage from development engineering to manufacturing. Let us define production as the process through which men, machines, technology and capital operate upon raw materials under the direction of the management in order to create useful products.

An article to be manufactured must be capable of being produced at low cost; and to be capable of being produced at low cost, an article must be so designed. (The same can be said of maintenance. The notoriously low maintainability of man-made systems is largely because the designer rarely gives maintenance imperatives and after-sales requirements the attention they deserve.) *Design ingenuity,* then, should be an inherent attribute of computer-based engineering, which renders it capable of efficient production.

Design producibility is revealed in the physical characteristics of the product, its built-in reliability and the correctness of its tolerances. The designer's choice of materials, methods, processes, standard and commercial parts and furnishings must ensure efficient production.

It is the designer's responsibility to establish the specification of a product which can sell competitively. The product for which he develops the specifications must:

(1) meet established performance requirements;
(2) have a quality level compatible with the market in which it is to be sold;
(3) be capable of production at competitive cost.

The importance of these functions shows why the transitional stage from R and D to production encompasses more than purely technical functional considerations and extends into the phases of manufacturing. Knowledge of current problems and activities of purchasing, material control, tooling, manufacturing inspection, sales and service is essential to the development of efficient design.

Product planning collaboration with production can help develop highly competent analyses of the available alternatives, and reasonably good forecasts of the results.

This means that a major need in successful product planning/production integration is to open up and keep clear the channels of communication between these skilled and specialized areas of work. This can be accomplished through CAD/CAM. The same is true for providing means for coordinating all their contributions in the best interests of the company. The latter statement helps to underline the need for an analytic approach in production.

No matter what the particular line of a certain industry is, because of the rapid advances in technology every factory should establish a function beyond engineering design; a function which might be called 'manufacturing progress', or 'plant research'. This, too, should be carried on through CAD/CAM.

Furthermore, the able use of CAD/CAM facilities should be instrumental in reducing the levels of supervision prevailing in an organization. Multiple levels of supervision are 'managerial fat' and it should be cut out – to be replaced by direct access to databases.

The Japanese have understood the wisdom of this policy. At Toyota there are only five levels of supervision: from President to foreman. Ford was said to have 12 levels of supervision, and the company undertook a conscious policy of cutting two levels and aiming to cut more, in order to become competitive.

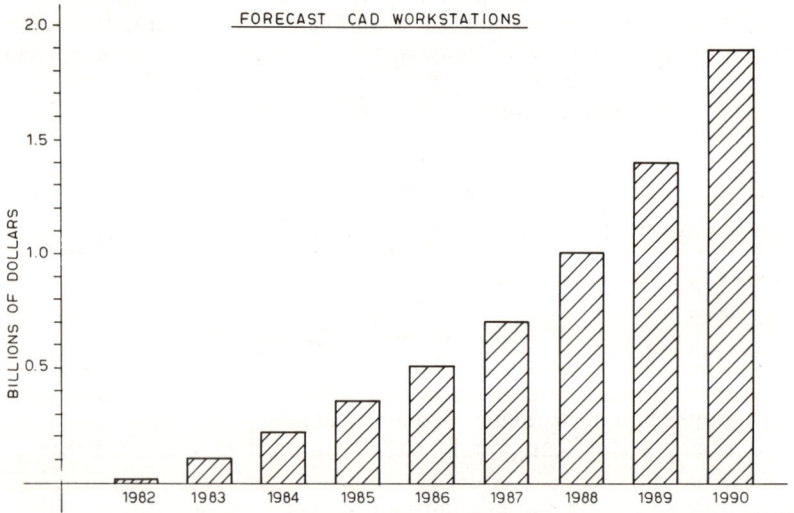

Figure 3.4 There is a fast-growing market for CAD workstations. The population increases much faster than the dollar value, as prices continue to drop

Precisely because the chances offered to improve the profitability of operations are great, the markets for computer-based design equipment, robots, and other automation devices are poised for an explosion. A CAD workstation forecast is given in Figure 3.4.

An increasing number of large manufacturing companies are putting computers and communications systems to work for development and factory managers through the use of concepts centering on resource planning. At the factory level, high technology production equipment, which descended from numerical control gear, can now control complex operations.

Robots are a good example. From an administrative viewpoint, management must however look beyond the initial costs of robots. Indirect costs – for installation, integration, insurance, maintenance, special tool fabrication, and equipment depreciation – can total two to three times that of the robots themselves.

Furthermore, one standalone robot is of no consequence. Deployed in groups, industrial robots become part of a large system with many integrated processes, Such configurations are commonly found in factories with large workflow lines, for example in automobile factories. Work goes from one robot station to another. The robot becomes a section of an assembly line. Groups of robots act like whole sub-assembly departments.

The key to success is breaking down jobs into functions that can be handled by groups of machines with the appropriate complement of arm motions and tooling payload capacities. Grouping robots is regarded as a more sophisticated approach to automation, and success generally requires some experience with simpler, less rewarding forms.

A similar reference can be made with CAD/CAM units. As the late George Marshall stated to a group of nuclear scientists who visited to convince him about the atom bomb: 'Even the most mighty weapon which exists in only one copy and can be used just once is of no consequence to the military. The military's value is in its continuous ability to deliver.' The same is true of engineering and science.

Chapter 4

CAD/CAM and the user

The aims computer-aided design wants to address have their roots in the very early utilization of computers for weapons systems engineering. As such, they are as old as the beginning of the computer era. How can we project better and faster than with the time-honored, relatively slow and heavily manual approaches?

Another vital point is how we can present the results to the end user so that the interaction is more effective. The final output of a CAD system must be a proper engineering document. The artwork should be acceptable – even superior to those drawings turned out manually. The system must be able to employ a variety of standard component specification files, addressing itself to the scientist, the engineer and the draftsman with little or no background in computers.

Reference was made to the beginning of the computer era. Thirty years ago, computer-based engineering applications were practically all batch. But by 1963, time-sharing had given the possibility of interactivity – and at about the same time the graphics work done at MIT opened up a new dimension. GM capitalized on these two developments by 1965, to create DAC-1.

Since the use of computers in engineering leaned toward experimentation, there should be no surprise in the interest in modeling. GM is credited with add-on modeling features related to the development in designing a Cadillac after analysis of competitive characteristics. As a result, back in 1976, the design of 'Seville' took 28 months to complete against the classical 48 months Detroit time.

While the large engineering firms in the aeronautical, motor vehicle and computer fields led by developing their own computer-aided design systems, commercially available CAD/CAM started, on an interative turnkey basis, around 1970. And the first significant applications have been in electronic printed circuit board (PCB) design.

The first turnkey CAD products were for integrated circuit (IC) projects, electrical schematics, and 2-D drafting. Most of the early offerings centered around the capability for 2-D drafting; as we shall see in the appropriate chapter, 3-D design came much later.

With experience, the engineering tasks handled through CAD became more complex; and this experience slowly spread toward computer-aided manufacturing (CAM). The industry moved into it in 1975, though the real impact in the factory will largely be felt from 1985 to 1990, in connection with robotics.

Computer-aided engineering (CAE) started as a phrase advanced by SDRC (Structural Dynamics Research Corp. of Cincinatti, Ohio), but it incorporated new aspects. For the CAE proponents, these are related to the fact that the original goal of CAD was drafting, and that this goal is now changing towards creative engineering.

Supports for computer-aided design

As always with computer-based systems, the equipment itself is but a small part of the total. More important is the needed software and the applications perspective. In terms of software and hardware, a CAD system will involve

(1) computer(s);
(2) engineering database;
(3) interactive datacomm capability;
(4) procedural prerequisites;
(5) applications programming (AP) library;
(6) end user facilities.

In terms of concepts, the three words forming CAD – *computer, aided* and *design* – can structure a three-dimensional frame of reference, including important support features, as Figure 4.1 demonstrates. This presentation accounts for the fact that any engineering design is the reflection of the

- know-how,
- imagination, and
- synthetic ability

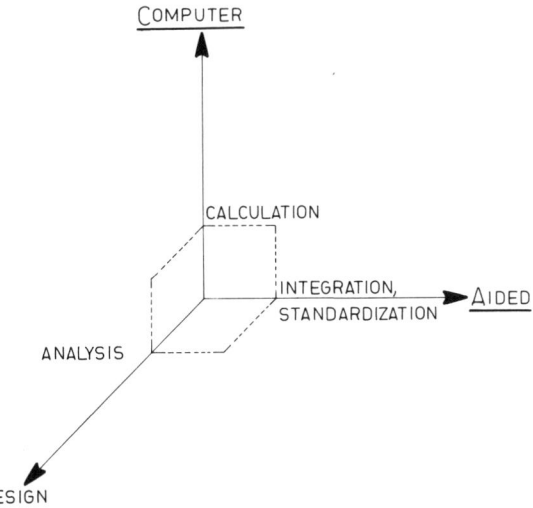

Figure 4.1 CAD means calculation, integration and analysis. International standardization is some time away, but a company should standardize its own operations

of the project engineer. The creative process sees to it that the engineer working on a project needs a concept – and this concept must be developed in some kind of rough design.

Computer-aided engineering aims to hit at the concept level of

- structuring,
- formalizing, and
- recording

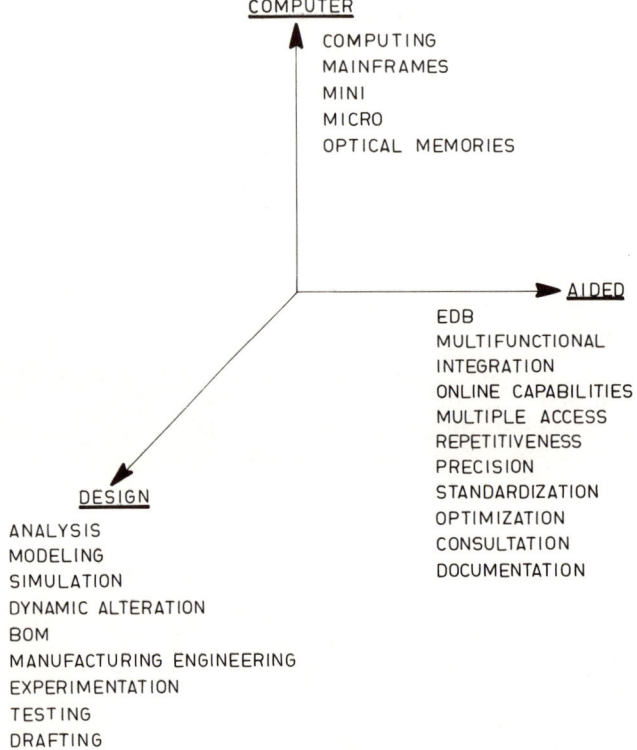

Figure 4.2 Multifunctionality characterizes each of the main reference lines in CAD. How well CAD is used is a function of how much the available characteristics are exploited

which together make up the process. Figure 4.2 brings this aspect into focus. The support CAD provides is in three key steps:

(1) analysis, in the design axis (pre-processing);
(2) calculation, to be provided by the computer;
(3) the end result of integration and standardization (post-processing).

Analysis and integration have been the steps primarily supported by the dedicated machines of the CAD technology while mainframes have been used to support calculation. This is now changing, with emphasis on a multi-dimensional approach to the design of CAD/CAM.

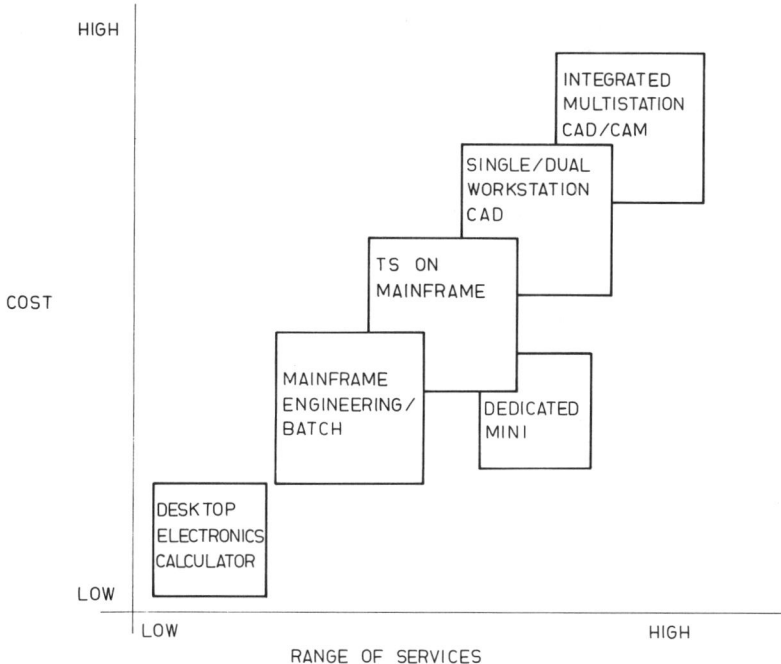

Figure 4.3 There is not just one, but a whole range of supports for computer-aided activities. Low-cost hardware/software often means very high cost in human intervention, and vice versa

The tendency is to have intelligent microprocessor-supported work-stations; maxicomputer-based computing capability; and online engineering databases. The evolution in range of services and corresponding costs is demonstrated in Figure 4.3. This:

- improves response time;
- helps manage interactivity;
- doesn't load the central resource.

Particularly helpful as a major part of the CAD/CAM is the interaction between user views. Real development activity starts with the prototype. Using computer modeling:

- cuts time lags;
- reduces costs;
- improves quality;
- promotes reliability.

The overall philosophy is to try to eliminate the redesign and prototype phases by computer modeling. The object of this approach is to:

(1) create geometry;
(2) prepare the geometry for analysis;
(3) proceed with the analytical steps;
(4) induce changes and study aftermaths;

(5) repeat through successive iterations steps 2, 3 and 4;
(6) test the outcome under all specified conditions;
(7) fully document the results.

One of the basic facilities in a multistation graphic exchange system is the sharing of text and data between different engineering workstations. In this sense, the production of a design is a relatively minor part of the overall system-supported features.

Such features are now further enhanced through color presentation, which replaces the former black and white, and 'pseudocolor' capabilities. (The latter give colors as different levels of gray, which is a matter of interpretation.) Behind the fact that we can see an object in color is the ability to project the geometry that exists behind the object, and our ability to bring it in perspective automatically.

Like any other tool, CAD has been evolving over years of practice. Figure 4.4 starts with the early experiences in the period 1958 to 1965 and projects into the late 1980s with the integrated robotics capability. The majority of commercially offered CAD/CAM systems is now in the 3-D area. The '2½' generation involves 32-bit processors for handling of surfaces and the resulting calculation facilities.

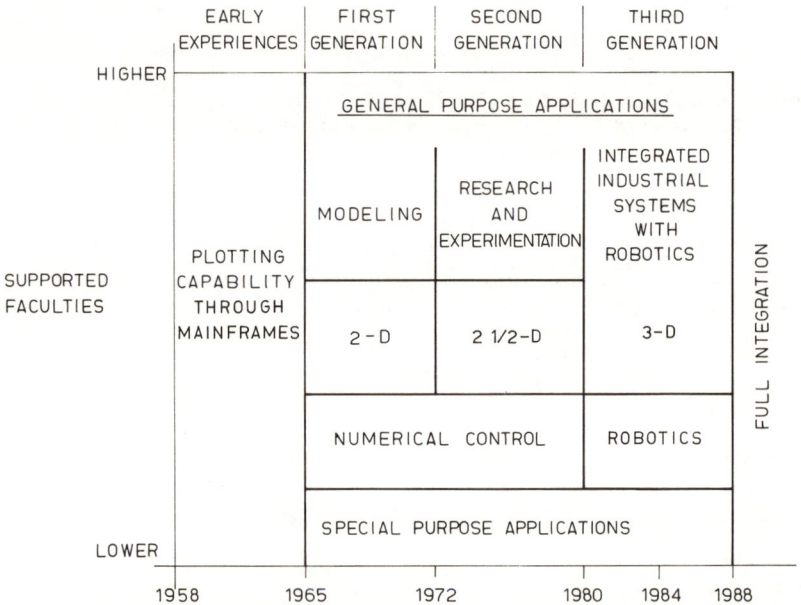

Figure 4.4 Thirty years of development have led to the CAD concept which dominates present-day practice. In a couple of years, nothing but full integration will be acceptable

Yet, even at this point, we have come a long way from the early experiences in CAD, which involved bits and pieces of the design domain and not the whole range. As we gain experience, we observe an accelerated expansion towards integrated industrial systems: from basic design to robotics capability.

Such an expansion presupposes standardization, formalization, and the existence of objectives. It is therefore necessary to remember that without the proper prerequisites results will leave much to be desired. In reality, the design operations to be done are *not* so complex. The most important part is the preparation – the break with the tradition of keeping everything in one's own head and going about our work in a non-structured manner.

Part of the problem is that even universities do not teach how to formalize the design process. The only structured approach taught is the language of mathematics. Yet we know that structured approaches mean:

- the ability to state the reasons *why* we make the choices we do;
- the power to define *how* we are going to go about them;
- the wisdom to select as a first application a process complex enough to demonstrate the results of the system and yet not so complex as to discourage the needed mental conversion.

An efficient answer to the question of *where* to start is with projects involving computing, analysis, design, and simulation. A valid answer to the question of *how* to start is with one's own equipment, packages, possible turnkey solutions – or in certain cases service bureaus.

The choice of the project is influenced by the decisions to be reached relative to the questions of where and how to start. The same is true about the construction of a logical database organization, which should properly:

- identify the current state;
- project on needed developments;
- integrate the information elements (IE) in the engineering database.

Next to the logical DB organization comes that of the physical storage: a decision should be reached whether it will be centralized on CAD or distributed by workpost.

Furthermore, when examining the physical and logical structure of the EDB we should remember that with any and every project we start not from a blank sheet of paper but from the existing engineering design references, which we modify and improve. Interactivity with the stored information elements is, in fact, a major benefit to be obtained from CAD/CAM solutions.

Database organization will be influenced by prospective usage, and the way chosen to describe the objects/entities. This may be an implicit procedural step, usually called 'constructive' evaluation, or a boundary analysis with experimental synthesis capabilities supported by CAD/CAM.

The proper preparation and database organization will necessarily include the ability to answer a range of applications perspectives:

(1) conceptual presentation;
(2) design;
(3) analysis;
(4) evaluation and redesign.

Steps 3 and 4 are computation bases and interact with one another. To move out of the loop we need

(5) modeling (the logical construction of prototypes).

Physical models for engineering studies are very expensive, involve the best people available in the organization, and take much time to create. Logical models can replace them in order to:

(6) formalize the engineering design;
(7) test this design;

and then move to:

(8) manufacturing.

Within this broader applications horizon it becomes evident that the potential of a CAD/CAM system goes far beyond visual interactivity. What we see on video is the tip of the iceberg in terms of the results we can obtain.

Also – and it cannot be repeated too often – one of the greatest advantages is the EDB and online access to it. Schematics, signs, rules help work in terms of expression. But once done, we can recall, repeat, revamp. (For non-repetitive work, we must establish whether we should start line by line from a white sheet or take elements from the existing EDB, improve and recompile.)

In every case, the fundamental background is the organizational work. This involves a substantial effort in procedural restructuring and standardization: the richer becomes the EDB, the more we capitalize on the power of CAD.

This is a dynamic proposition; if we look at the video in a static way, the result would be well below normal benefit. To gain the profit that CAD/CAM makes feasible we must work the system over its whole range of supported facilities.

A growing CAD population

The primary purpose of a CAD/CAM system is to improve and promote the productivity of the professional people employed in the engineering department. The next goal is better outgoing product quality and design processes, which would not have been feasible without CAD/CAM.

Lasting productivity effects do not come about by accident. A productive system is one that is fully supported through its life cycle. This calls for the appropriate methodology:

(1) productivity reviews;
(2) pre-installation evaluation;
(3) training tuned to enhance engineering productivity;
(4) post-installation controls;
(5) observations, tracking, recording;
(6) expert consultation and steady upkeep.

As with all new systems, a great deal of expert reaction is psychological. Here, considerable attention must be paid on how to overcome the fears that people have. A valid way is, six months prior to CAD/CAM introduction, to train the projected users intensively.

To ease the fears of a possible loss of jobs, it is advisable to lay stress on the statistics, which document that designers are not replaced by computers. By expanding the engineering horizon, CAD introduces more work than it replaces.

Many industries have found that through CAD/CAM they can do much more work than without. This is true of practically all fields: mechanical and electrical engineering, civil engineering, and cartography. Statistics show that there is no loss of jobs, but that there are considerable improvements in productivity and in product quality.

From the more successful current installations, the following lessons have been learned. The principal areas to be addressed during the preparatory period include:

(1) *Organization.* Should a multistation or single-station approach be taken? Which are the key choices that answer the prerequisites? Are there any *necessary* structural changes?

HOW TO GET STARTED :

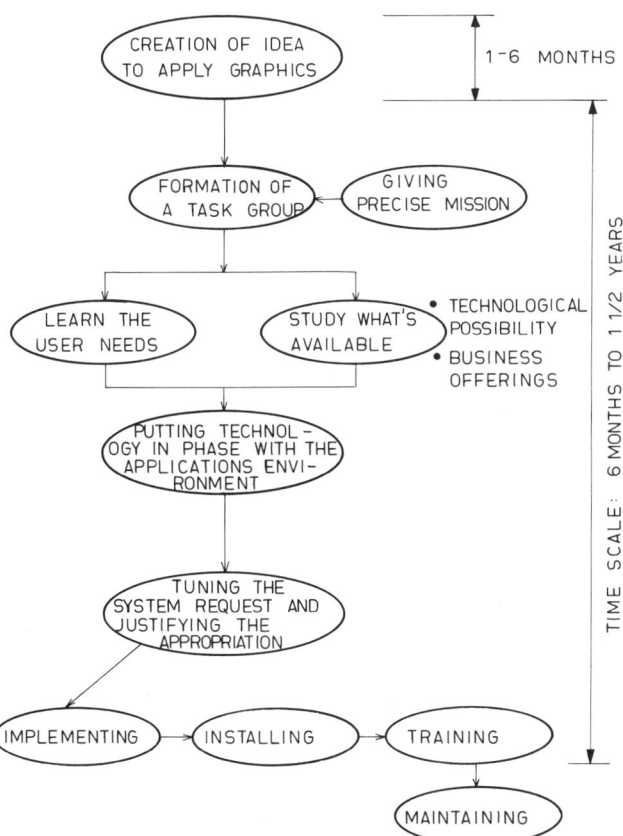

Figure 4.5 This block diagram suggests a timescale for introduction of fairly complex CAD systems. For simpler workstations, a quarter to half the time would do

At pre-installation time a productivity review should be done well ahead of installation and should include:

- a decision on the work to be done first;
- the selection of users;
- their training;
- the proper care in avoiding pitfalls;
- the installation layout and housing.

An orderly approach to getting started is shown in Figure 4.5. Figure 4.6 outlines the organizational steps to be followed over a 13-month period. (see also an accelerated timetable in Chapter 16.) While certain specific issues may vary from case to case, the baseline has the remarkable quality of remaining fairly steady.

(2) *System use.* The answer to this question involves choices on design, detail and digitizing mode of operations. The design mode is the most

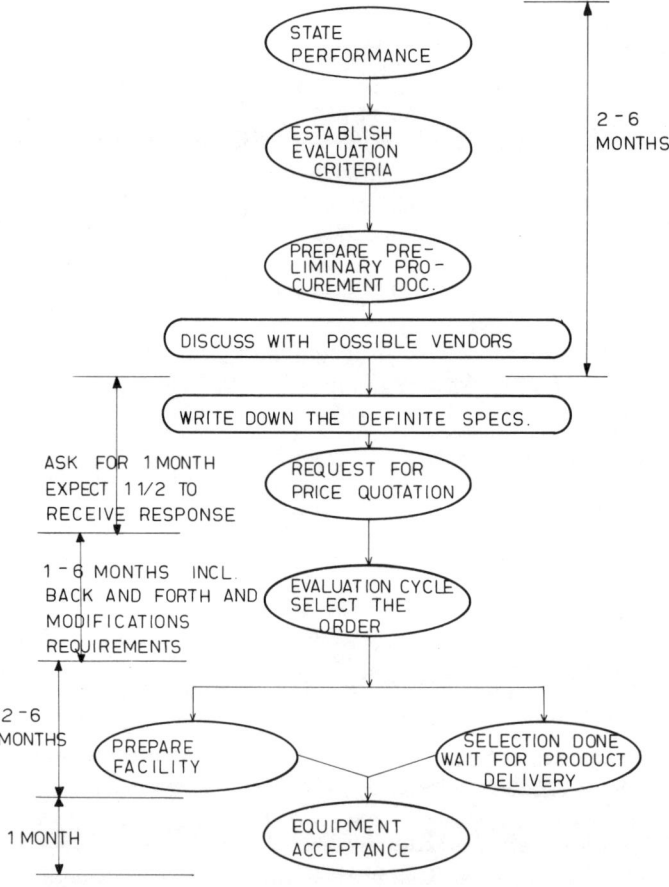

Figure 4.6 These organizational steps apply to a company with no CAD experience. If a firm already has CAD installation(s), such procedures should be part of smooth-running routine

complex, and it is often advisable for the organization to start off with something simple – to avoid building a wall of resistance.

Digitizing has characterized first-generation CAD. As an example, in the printed circuit board world, the engineer:

- gets manual data;
- does a manual layout;
- sends it to the drafting room where the different points are digitized.

With CAD, these three steps are done in one and the DB is created that way. Through interactive design approaches, the engineer inputs on the screen the schematics, eliminating the manual layout. Further advances such as the automatic logic development, will provide a topographical description of the schematic: a netlist will be assured, merged with the outline, layout, and drafting – eventually cutting out the schematic.

(3) *Training*. Should training be done on site or at the manufacturer's premises? Whom to send? What are the available training aids? The course outlines? Who will be the internal instructors? How best to train the instructors?

As with system use, the training plans must be elaborated step by step, improving the end user's capacity to work with the system. In this sense, simpler but just as effective applications must take place first, before introducing the user to computer-aided engineering, such as finite element modeling, mass properties, and computational center of gravity.

(4) *Workflow*. This calls for prioritizing the work; establishing precedence; providing scheduling; assuring tracking capability; and developing a productivity baseline. It is the job of the engineering manager to establish the outline for the user manual and to elaborate the productivity baseline.

Productivity is intimately related to the definition of the workflow and is affected by many factors. For instance, if detailed work is done at the drawing level – with no conceptual and no modeling aspects – the resulting productivity improvement will not be as high. CAD dynamics help very much in simulation and modeling.

The definition of workflow characteristics should reasonably reflect the expertise of the end user – how efficiently he may be using the system. For instance, in the PCB world, if the company does not get a 3:1 ratio, it means that there is something wrong with the organization – not with the equipment.

(5) *Environment*. This is a compex proposition and involves human engineering. First and foremost, operator comfort must be ensured. The computer allows better working conditions, but the office environment must support them in terms of light, noise and partitioning. If the operator is not comfortable, he will not be as productive, and the company will suffer as a result.

Next to the user's comfort we must study the I/O media and integrate them with the job in hand and the environmental perspectives. Such media will typically be:

- Alphanumeric/hard copy,
- Alphanumeric/visualization,

- Graphical 2-D,
- Graphical 3-D,
- Graphics and color,
- Voice.

It is necessary to understand that the I/O capabilities at our disposal define the means we put to work for man–machine communication. Voice communication, both input and output, for command and information, will be a significant development in the coming years; they too will impose environmental prerequisites.

When we examine the man–information interaction within a given environment, criteria for choice are: *who* is the user? *What is* his work? The answers to these questions help define the scenarios to be followed; and the choices to be made condition the final system usage.

(6) *Personnel.* The able handling of personnel requires the setting of job descriptions and the associated career path development. If we move people about in CAD/CAM we should not use our resources casually.

One way to look at this subject is to define shift priorities. For instance:

- First shift: design
- Second shift: detail/drafting
- Third shift: CPU-bound activities.

Organization-wide it is not advisable to do CPU-bound activities in interactive design time, as this increases response time and the result is very frustrating. But in terms of the human resources, the setting of shifts should reflect personnel requirements.

Another way of examining personnel needs is the soul-searching decision about employing professional operators for CAD/CAM, or training all the engineering staff to do the job. Arguments and strong points exist for both approaches. The proponents of the former suggest that the typical engineer who moves in and out of the CAD unit may forget how to use it and not be able to log in again. 'The user/operator,' this argument goes, 'should be a professional in this job.'

The alternative is to train all engineers at different levels of expertise and also to have some younger engineers as part-time specialized operators. The former must study entry level operations for drafting and design. The latter must be trained as real experts to ensure a good level of support to all users.

Along this line, manufacturers offer a range of training courses oriented to:

- system manager at the VP level with basic concepts of CAD/CAM;
- system operation courses able to train in archiving, indexing, formatting (the disk), and software loading;
- end user courses, mainly oriented to applications training.

But the CAD manufacturer cannot and should not tell the user which strategy to follow. Management should analyse its own engineering needs and see how a given alternative fits in with the particular environment of the firm.

My suggestion is that the best policy is to train all engineers in CAD/CAM, without expecting all of them to achieve the highest dexterity. This will still leave room for one good user/operator per engineering function. The rationale for this approach lies in the fact that over-training in mechanics is spending money on a discipline the people may never use. Figure 4.7 presents a typical growth curve in know-how, and we should also note that, given the rather frequent changes and updates in hardware and software, the user may never become 100 per cent proficient on the mechanics of the machine. His goal should be productivity.

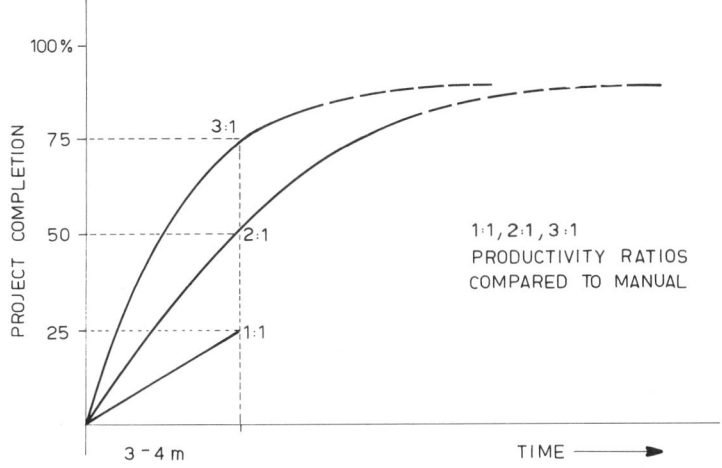

CALENDAR MONTHS, BUT UNTOLD HOURS PER DAY

Figure 4.7 The ideal training will include conceptual aspects, integration perspectives, the use of the engineering database, and some mechanics. Also a great deal of hands-on experience

While the typical engineer may never be as productive as an operator, unless he sits down on the terminal every day, productivity must be counted on the total job. Some parts might show a 10:1 improvement, but total product completion will never show such ratio: a 3:1 to 4:1 goal is pretty good.

(7) *Communications*. Goals must be established and communicated to the users. Management by objectives helps to get people involved and, therefore, to perform better. So do staff meetings, and the existence of open internal communication lines.

As a means of stimulating the imagination of the end users as to what CAD can do, external communications with user groups is one of the most useful methods. The exchange of ideas and experiences can really help towards a solution to the problem. But it is not advisable to send the VP to such meetings; it is better to send the design engineer. The same is true for international conferences.

Written communications too are a valid means – particularly for manuals and as a technique to improve the user's productivity on the system. Written communications must, however, be presented in a comprehensive way to be really useful.

(8) *Future applications.* Minds should always be open to future growth. This requires the active study of what CAD/CAM can do. We must look not only at the immediate end product – and the way to back it up through the right process – but also prepare for the next one.

In this sense, we should be asking ourselves:

- What steps are involved?
- How much of the manual approaches still exist?
- Can we automate them next time around?
- Can we integrate design steps with manufacturing? Assembly? Testing?
- What about quality histories? Feedbacks?

A great pay-off can come from planning and preparing for growth. But there are also prerequisites. What is involved in personnel needs? In CAD/CAM specialists? Analysts? Instructors? Archiving? Indexing? New applications requirements?

Both logical and physical issues must be faced: for instance, equipment updates from 16 to 32 bits per word (BPW); facility expansion; new software releases.

New terminals become available, offering the user a powerful interactive tool to put into his system. Or there may be a new release of easy-to-use software that cuts development time and makes system integration easy. A third case may concern a straightforward, modular design which ensures better flexibility.

Meeting the goals

Since performance calls for preparation, the projected improvements have to be studied in a cost-effective manner. Are the new terminals compatible with the existing software? Which are the most important features to weigh in the decision to adopt them? Are the projected results readily accessible? How much training is necessary to change user images?

Though the largest part of the training effort will concern the changeover from manual approaches to CAD, the training process in itself will not end at any particular time: *Training is the most fundamental ingredient in planning and preparing for growth.*

Yet training, although necessary, is not enough. To be realistic, it should go hand in hand with the preparation of the applications cases, and this calls for objectives. In a typical civil engineering application, for example, it is not enough to say that the projected CAD system will permit interactivity and pave the way for the reduction of errors.

We must demonstrate through concrete, convincing examples how and why design changes (the bugbear of every designer) can be instantaneously projected and visualized; similarly, that the output on video and on plotter effectively represents the structure for which the calculation has been done. Further, it must be documented through practical, day-to-day examples that this instantaneous visualization permits the optimization of the final product.

CAD affects both small and large firms, whatever the products and systems they develop. On a variety of structures it permits solutions to problems which so far have defied rigorous analysis. But until the procedures, the symbols, the semantics, the graphical normalization are decided, these ideas may remain only vague.

The preparatory steps we are describing require a certain maturity on the part of the organization having to carry them out. How can it acquire the needed know-how? The answer is through study and research. This is the policy followed through a recent equipment selection study and it gave significant results – technical and financial.

First, the engineering departments interested in the CAD acquisition described in technical terms the work to be done. Seven CAD manufacturers were then called in and given the specifications. This led to a preselection, with first five, then three CAD vendors remaining in contention.

Several visits to 'friendly' CAD installations and a number of working meetings followed the preselection of equipment. Though the primary goal of these visits and meetings was technical and not financial, it did result in concessions from the CAD manufacturers as they felt the heat of the competition.

One of them made a written offer to change the proposed CAD mainframe from 24 to 32 BPW (bits per word) – significantly greater computing power. The second offered a front-end unit to manage the terminals, for a token charge. The third added one extra megabyte of high speed memory, a communications controller for X.25 protocol, and extra man-days of CAD consulting assistance for start-up.

In the last offer was a provision for a new color graphics support package. It should be noted that the subject concessions followed other contractual advantages, including a flat 25 per cent cost reduction in the price of the software/hardware package, as well as important parts of software obtained cost-free.

What however really tipped the balance in favor of this third solution was the applications software leadership on its side. Interestingly enough, this choice was seen at one of the sites being visited, and one might say that had it been picked straight after the subject visit five months would have been 'saved'. If ever this argument is offered, it is wrong for two main reasons:

(1) A 'rush to solution' would have given none of the significant financial savings obtained from the manufacturer.

Most significant, too, is the following factor:

(2) The elapsed five-month period was not time lost but represented hard work by the user company's engineers, who devoted themselves to the task of system testing, thus acquiring important know-how for their coming work in CAD.

All engineering departments standing to benefit from CAD worked during this period with both dedication and concentration. They also altered their views on two aspects: color terminals and the need to implement a distributed CAD system.

Just as information systems for industrial and financial organizations have become distributed, so CAD equipment is in its way serving a distributed environment, given:

- steadily evolving users' requirements;
- smaller, more powerful, less costly CAD units;
- the developing data communications discipline.

Several computer-aided design users are currently progressing toward a distributed CAD environment, with the smaller computer systems to be installed on the periphery (still 32 BPW; but in the $25,000 to $30,000 range).

Equipped with X.25 datacomm controllers, the central CAD installed can operate online with the mini-CAD at factory sites. This course makes sense and deserves study for implementation by any user with distributed engineering resources – *after* the CAD installation is made and practical experience is acquired. CAD facilities should benefit every corner in the organization, or the implementation cannot be considered to be complete.

Chapter 5

A new design philosophy

While electronics, aeronautical, mechanical, and electrical engineering have been the big boosters of CAD/CAM in the 1970s, civil engineering and architectural applications seem to be edging up as key fields for this decade: the architectural/construction area is the largest single potential market for CAD installations. As a result, significant effort is now invested in civil engineering.

Architectural, civil and construction engineering (including mapping and plant design) represent a significant share of the market. Table 5.1 demonstrates this point, showing the current capability and worldwide potential market: it is considered that companies with annual revenues of $5 million or over are candidates for the use of CAD – and engineering companies of this dimension are mainly architectural offices and construction firms.

Table 5.1 Current capability and worldwide potential market

Engineering disciplines	Companies with over $5 million annual revenues
1. Architectural/construction	8845
2. Mechanical	3783
3. Electrical/electronics	2942
4. Automotive	1894
5. Aerospace	674
6. Others	6461
	24 599

The $5 million threshold may seem to be too low – yet there already exist certain companies in electronics and architectural design with a $5 million yearly business and having CAD units. Typically, such companies employ five or six architects and with a 30 per cent higher productivity largely cover the cost of a single-station computer.

Studies done in the United States demonstrate that an estimated 50 per cent of the businesses oriented to construction and plant design should be installing CAD. The economics are favorable for such development.

Figure 5.1 demonstrates that, on average, process plant design and construction roughly divides 50 per cent construction, 30 per cent material and 20 per cent design. (Finer detail for the design percentage is given at the bottom of the figure.) CAD can impact all three phases, though it is most often associated only with the design side.

PROCESS PLANT DESIGN

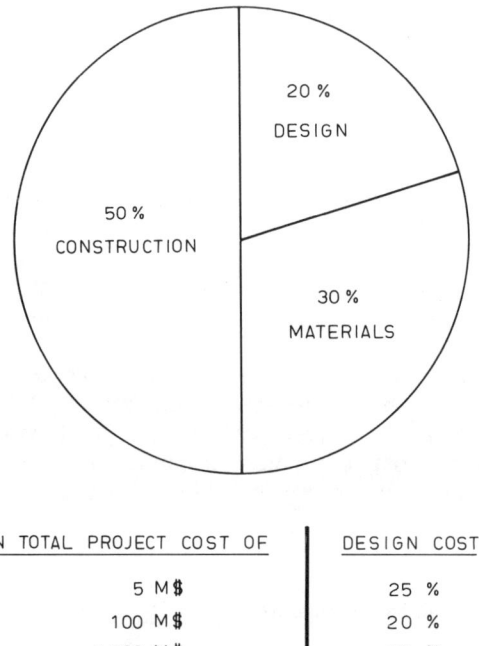

IN TOTAL PROJECT COST OF	DESIGN COST
5 M $	25 %
100 M $	20 %
1,000 M $	15 %

Figure 5.1 For large projects, the primary goal of CAD should be to handle complexity. In smaller projects it is cost-effectiveness which comes at the top

All the following factors force companies towards design automation.

- the large number of companies in plant design;
- the rise in capital spending on plant and equipment;
- the very substantial part of the investment devoted to design;
- the increase in the rules to be observed (environmental, legal etc.);
- the shortage of trained technical professionals (engineers, draftsmen, and so on).

However, as the preceding chapters have brought into focus, preparation is the key to success. On the one hand, the complexity of CAD/CAM forces specialization; and on the other, the general applications of the EDB and of the interactive approaches help to interconnect with a multitude of other systems such as office automation workstations.

There is a lot of money in CAD/CAM for all types of engineering applications. The real shortage is trained manpower; a reason why in the early 1970s turnkeys had such success. Typically, turnkey systems involve:

(1) the applications software;
(2) the means to structure databases;
(3) data management procedures;
(4) component libraries;
(5) efficient command languages;
(6) communications capabilities;
(7) interactive workstations;
(8) graphics tools;
(9) a host computer or similar resource;
(10) efficient reporting media for documentation.

A turnkey system must take all these issues into account and provide good answers to the user's requirements. More specifically, plant design support will include: SW (software), both basic and applications oriented; HW (hardware); databases; datacomm; manuals; and customer training.

A turnkey system for civil engineering*

What benefit does the user get from the implementation of a turnkey CAD system in civil engineering? Examples can be given from plant design, starting with the simplest applications – which, most likely, will be the first to tackle in a new implementation.

- 2-D schematic work involving, for instance, process flow sheets, engineering line diagrams, piping and instrumentation.

Significantly, such beginning work will be using the same DB 3-D modeling that will be required as the user organization gains CAD experience. Even a classical-looking 2-D process design is a very intelligent document, because of the EDB behind it. Such a CAD-based document can lead into a 3-D piping and instrumentation model as the EDB is 3-D oriented anyway. The system allows the drawing of different views on the screen in 3-D: isometric, views, sections, perspective views, and so on.

The outlined work can be supported on the screen (and through hard copy) on solid or wire frame drawing; and the same is true for modeling. Thus when, for instance, a pipe is routed through the model, the latter knows if the space is or is not occupied.

The system may be supporting a two-mode operation: the model mode, and the draw mode. If it is set in either mode and we make a change in the EDB, the system will update. However, for experimental engineering purposes, it can also offer the ability to disconnect the two modes; change the data; shift around, make a choice, reconnect; then update.

---

* This section is not intended to imply that this book supports turnkey policies; I am rather negative toward them. But it is useful to follow a turnkey example as this approach dominated CAD/CAM usage for over a decade.

The three ways of providing the designer with an opportunity to compare what he thinks he has with what he really has – and which is reflected in the EDB – are as follows:

(1) Dynamic rotation, through the image control unit. This will allow the structure to rotate.
(2) The use of color, at least through some of the workstations, preferably on a homogeneous basis. Color makes a big difference and helps comprehension.
(3) Hidden line removal. This facility permits the engineer to give one command and the system will then remove any line and/or sub-system. The designer can stop at any point and experiment. Through hidden line removal he can take any selected piece of information out of the complex design in the EDB, treat it as a separate issue and provide it with full documentation.

The examples given, however, underline the importance of the prerequisites we have been discussing. If the CAD system is to be utilized successfully within the engineering organization, it is vitally important to prepare all the people for action. We should consider all persons, including both the potential operators and those who may never get the opportunity. We have to try to create a positive attitude that will displace the fear that a CAD system might generate.

There are several fears to overcome: that of being replaced by a machine; of failure when they try to learn the operation; and more generally of the unknown. Indeed, personnel training is the most important and sensitive part of this mission. We must decide whether to train our people from the top down, best designers first; and whether or not we are going to reclassify our design people as CAD operators.

The most valid philosophy in this connection is that CAD is just another tool, albeit a very sophisticated one. Therefore, the best people would be more likely to learn faster and use the equipment most effectively in the design mode.

The elaboration of valid procedures should go in parallel with the training program. They should include file labeling; design station scheduling; work request forms; system protection, and so on. They must provide direction and guidance for the user, and also demonstrate that he really knows what he is doing. This is important for establishing credibility.

A key issue is that of facilities design; probably one of the subjective areas where choices should crystalize through observations made during tours of other CAD installations, as well from technical articles on the subject. Alternatives must be examined to determine the most effective facilities arrangement, providing a creative atmosphere that

- will attract the designers;
- make them want to use this new tool;
- assure an aesthetically appealing installation.

We have to ask ourselves questions such as 'Is this aesthetically right? Would we like to work in this environment? What do we dislike? What can be improved? What are the problems? Then we must address these problems in an effective manner.

Scheduling the job to be done

Everything should be done to ensure the ability to work on CAD in a dynamic way, with growing confidence for the future. This calls for a method of job selection. For chosing the particular work to be applied to the system, a number of specific criteria must be considered.

- The complexity of the job; this is one of the most important criteria.
- Job schedule pressures; they build up whether the work is old or new. If old, is there time to reconstruct the database on the system?

In the general case, job selection has three basic steps involving engineering and drafting: a listing must be formulated shortly before first application and continuously updated; engineering management representatives should be given the opportunity to review the list and input definitions of priority; and negotiations must take place to resolve any differences.

Above all, a valid methodology must be instituted and, as I never tire of repeating, there is simply no reason to re-invent the wheel. This is why, even prior to vendor selection, we should visit as many CAD installations as we can afford. Not only should we not limit our trips to vendor demonstrations, but also, for this installation survey, it doesn't matter if the CAD equipment is not from the same manufacturer we are considering, or if the application is not always the same as ours. What is important is to gain from the experience of others.

One organization with experience suggests the following methodology with regard to the preparatory steps.

(1) Idealize the project (conceptual design).
(2) Identify the fundamental parameters.
(3) Proceed with the definition of the general architecture.
(4) Ensure the detailed examination of all components.
(5) Effect the integration design.
(6) Do the proper testing on CAD.
(7) Relate to manufacturing engineering.
(8) Provide the documentation.
(9) Produce the drafting chores, and
(10) Guarantee the updated bill of materials.

Figure 5.2 relates the process under discussion to the three fundamental design procedures – abstraction, experimentation, concretization – to be supported through CAD. A valid methodology will see to it that the idealization of the project considers the functional issues.

The analysis, for example, may address itself to kinematics, dynamics, plasticity, elasticity, deformation, and the synthesis of these factors. The point is, however, that when these classical issues are being done independently of one another they do not necessarily lead to an effective integration.

CAD provides the basis for integration – thus leading to an online design and manufacturing engineering. In the case of mechanical industries, this involves:

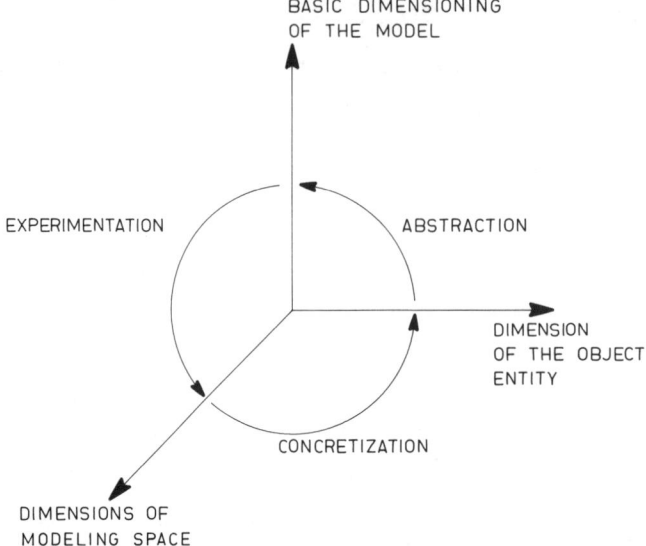

BASIC DIMENSIONING
OF THE MODEL

EXPERIMENTATION

ABSTRACTION

DIMENSION
OF THE OBJECT
ENTITY

CONCRETIZATION

DIMENSIONS OF
MODELING SPACE

Figure 5.2 Abstraction and idealization are very important in model making. So is experimentation, leading to a concretization of plans and designs

- final product design;
- production cycle;
- production machinery;
- quality characteristics and control;
- drafting and BOM produced not in general but by workpost.

With civil engineering comparable outputs are the construction documents and bill of materials. In both cases, this presupposes online access to the EDB and the existence of the appropriate applications programs.

There are a number of reasons for conceptual similarity among processes. In both cases, the ability to model, simulate and experiment allows one to test, evaluate, and optimize functionality, topology, technological characteristics, form and detail.

Proper choices call for a geometrically complete model. CAD contributes computer support for form description for lines, surfaces, and volume – as outlined in Figure 5.3. This can ensure a significant improvement over the classical, manual design which contains information relative to

- form,
- nominal dimensions,
- technical specifications, and
- tolerances,

by making this information resident in the EDB and, therefore, interactively available; no longer subject to repetitive input but accessible to modeling elaboration and polishing.

FORM DESCRIPTION FOR LINES, SURFACES,
AND VOLUME

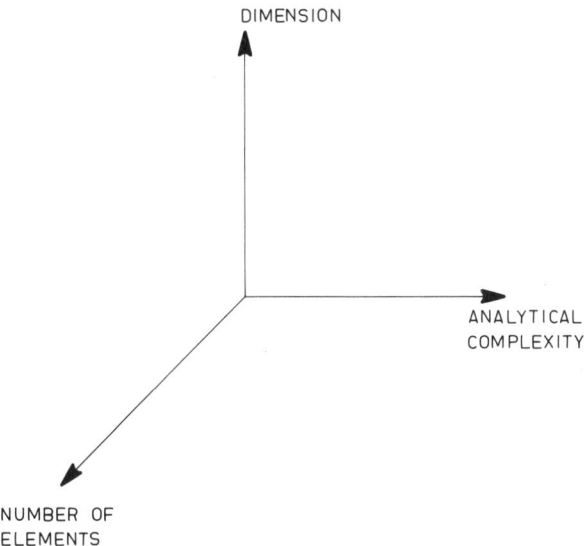

Figure 5.3 CAD makes feasible a multifunctional discipline of which we should always take advantage. From that comes the payoff

As stated in the earlier discussion, through CAD/CAM the resulting description, per line, surface and volume, can be done directly in 3D or through 2-D approaches – at the user's choice. It can be realized interactively (which provides by two orders of magnitude a better capacity than batch), and it can be achieved in graphical presentation and color.

Lessons can be learned on how to go about the CAD system in an engineering environment by examples based on experiences from other fields, such as mechanical engineering. This capitalizes on already acquired know-how.

For instance, in a mechanical engineering project, on manufacturing parts for the petrochemical industry and concerning proposals, part design, and subsequent passage to manufacturing – all supported through CAD – the following problems have been identified.

(1) Organization. The computer augmented and amplified the existing problems – which, with manual approaches, had many hidden parts. The lesson is that such problems should first be weeded out. If this step is skipped in the beginning, it will cost five times as much later on in terms of delays and confusion.

(2) Training. We have often underlined the wisdom of this activity, so we do not need to elaborate on it again.

(3) Forecasting the possible expansion of CAD applications. This has been found necessary in order to start, from the beginning, with an integrated

approach. Batch processing by computer left much to be desired in this respect: even if computerized, the different phases of an engineering project tended to be done in a disconnected, case-by-case manner. And this results neither in product quality nor in productivity.

The phases of a project

The different phases of an engineering project are very significantly interconnected. If this is not borne in mind from the start, the results will be disastrous: high cost, low integration, increasing difficulties and 'impossibilities'. Because it is online and interactive, CAD highlights such deficiencies.

The contrast between a 'manual plus batch' approach and an online approach is shown in Figures 5.4 and 5.5. The former presents the engineering cycle of the typical company, including bill of materials and the correspondence with the suppliers. The latter identifies a highly simplified data flow which is completely interactive.

It is quite understandable that the greater the level of integration projected, the more important the number of precautions to be taken. Standardization and interfaces are vital, because if they are not dealt with we necessarily come to the point where we have to spend a great amount of time in coding and decoding the different incompatible levels of information transmission – which, classically, have characterized manual operations.

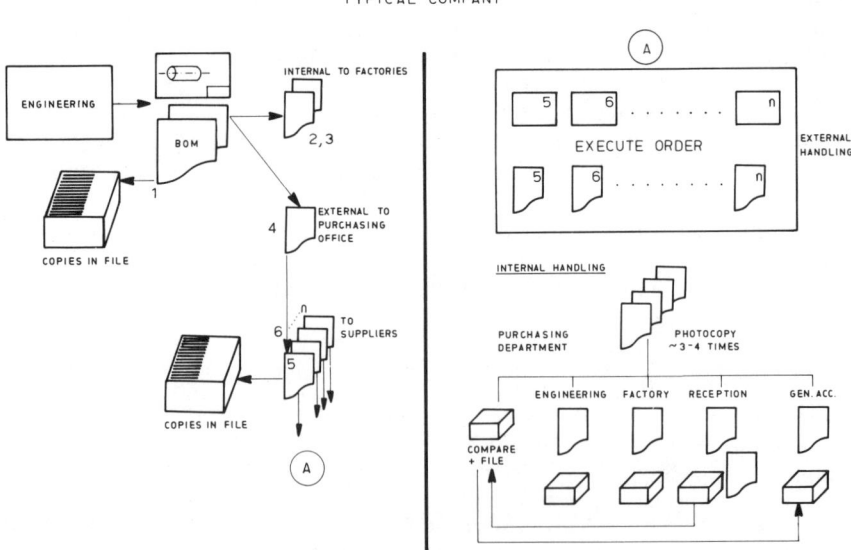

Figure 5.4 The 'classical' use of computers in engineering was a batch, non-integrated approach. Some companies kept this bad policy even after introducing CAD

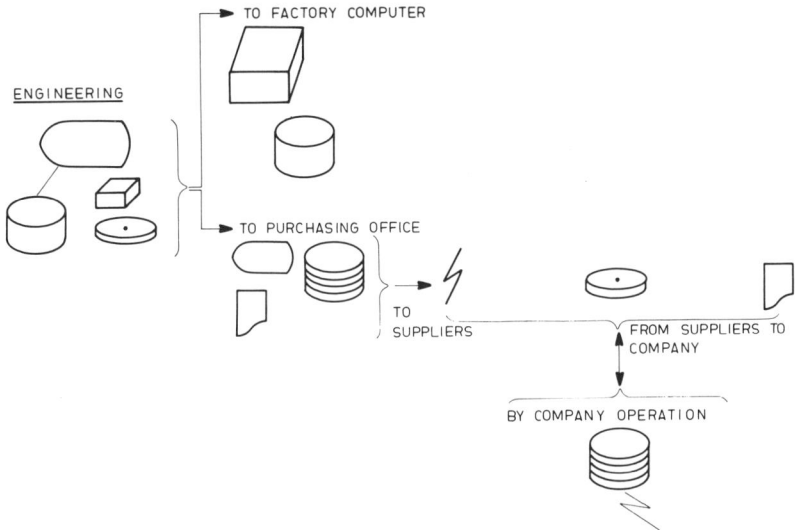

TO FACTORY COMPUTER

ENGINEERING

TO PURCHASING OFFICE

TO
SUPPLIERS

FROM SUPPLIERS TO
COMPANY

BY COMPANY OPERATION

Figure 5.5 The engineering workstations should be linked online not only to the factory, but also to the purchasing office. The purchasing office itself should be online to the suppliers

Quite evidently, whether we talk of mechanical, electrical or civil engineering, there is a need for good communication between the designer and the other specialisms which come into play. In the case of civil engineering and construction projects, the reference starts with the architect and demands correct and comprehensive descriptions of the proposed building, traditionally in the form of working and detail drawings, and specifications of required materials and workmanship.

Along this line of reference, CAD provides the architect with

- automatic drawing capabilities;
- the ability to create standard libraries of constructional details;
- database accessibility, with standard ranges of windows, doors or sanitary fittings;
- generic classes of component parts.

Characteristic design issues can be parameterized on insertion into the building model. CAD helps create correct and comprehensive working and detail drawings; ensures better coordination of product information; and makes design a truly multi-disciplinary affair, involving teams of professionals with diverse engineering specialisms.

In any and every project, it is important to coordinate the various disciplines in order to eliminate costly conflicts and ensure that any change made to one aspect of the design is reflected in, and accounted for, in all other affected areas of the project. The single-source database supported by CAD provides a unique master copy of the building and sees to it that change is consistent throughout all drawings and documentation.

The next most important reference is design evaluation. The CAD system helps predict how a given design is likely to perform after it becomes a completed building. Evaluation is enhanced by CAD-supported:

- interior and exterior perspectives,
- with hidden line removal, and
- with environmental simulation.

The system graphically displays the effect of lighting factors, heat loss and solar gain, even predicting the fall of sunlight through windows onto interior surfaces. It also helps analyze value factors much harder to visualize and quantify, such as weight distribution and the circulation of people in the building or factory.

Among the advantages to be derived from CAD in civil engineering design is the real-time evaluation of isometrics. They can be produced automatically, with the dimensioning done by the designer, while 'descaling' helps keep the written dimension right, but relatively shrinking or magnifying certain parameters at the designer's choice.

Isometric production can be sharply reduced, as needed work is automatically produced by the system. One reference claims to have cut design time from 12 hours to 3 hours. The online EDB will help create:

(1) *From–to report.* This links the different schemes together, and will also say if there is any discrepancy. From–to can be done for drawings, piping, steel T, and other components.

(2) *Cost control.* This is closely associated with design information, and project evaluation. Cost control relates to the total building design process and can be considered part of CAD from the early design stage, used to roughly estimate the cost, as well as at the ultimate value level.

Computer-supported routines help in cost control of construction projects since bills of materials and other references can be used as a basis for reasonably accurate and detailed forecasting. In cost control, CAD makes its greatest contribution in the measurement of the building fabric. Done manually, this would be an error-prone and time-consuming process; but it is reasonably straightforward when done by computer.

(3) *Bill of materials.* Not only BOM will be automatically produced by the system; software support also sees to it that the involved materials can be tested – for instance, through a pipe-stressing program. Furthermore, supported applications programs can lead into a transit file, as a gateway to mainframes or other computers.

(4) *Interfaces.* CAD will, as stated, ensure the working interfaces among different disciplines working on the same project; for instance, the program will evaluate

- pipes checked for, say, 4 inch clearance, and
- possible pipe interference with the drawings of the building.

As a result, it will discover all contradictions between given parameters or specifications. This is done fully automatically and will check any specified item against another.

Major gains can be obtained both in engineering productivity and in the quality of the outgoing product by dynamically evaluating all interferences.

If the CAD system says there are no interferences, there will not be any; if it says there are, they can be corrected interactively in real-time.

In the foregoing sense, a CAD system can produce a variety of views of the design which have been stored in the EDB; for instance:

- show the hidden parts;
- support a view for the installation engineers;
- show a variable view – for example, 2 meters above the ground.

There are, of course, implications from the earlier discussion on the design of interfaces and databases. The special needs and problems of architects and civil engineers must be understood by CAD software designers. Architects are more likely to think in purely graphic terms: they are less accustomed to communicating in mathematical languages; they have a keen awareness of 3-D form, but are more apt to conceptualize new graphic images with reference to other graphic images rather than coordinate systems with angular rotation.

In consequence, an architectural database will need more associative data. This is particularly true if the architect must obtain complex area or

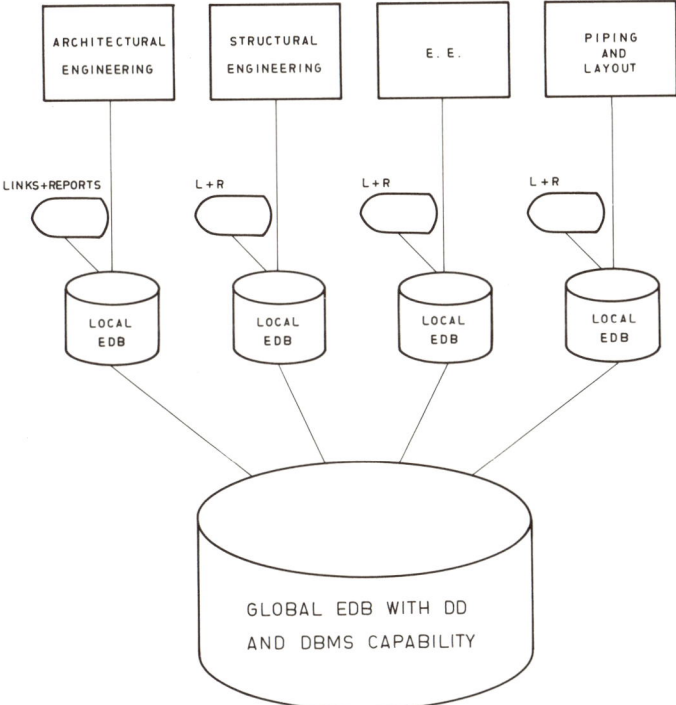

Figure 5.6 If a company has many divisions, and each has purchased its own CAD equipment, management is faced with a problem: the creation of a global integrated database

volumetric measurements of the building fabric for cost control purposes, or for design evaluations of rooms and spaces within the building. The building model should possess intelligent descriptions of 3-D views to help develop a useful architectural database.

The applications areas we have been considering will be further enhanced as the tools available to treat them become more sophisticated. the implementation of CAD in civil engineering is still in full evolution. Among the coming capabilities in facing, for example, the plant design problem, we can distinguish:

(1) *Software to handle complexity*. For instance, 20,000 to 25,000 pipes and associated fittings, for up to 300×10^6 data items.
(2) *Multi-disciplinary software*. Chemical processes involving ME, CE, EE, and all related issues for control and instrumentation. Also alternative costing – handling for each engineer his different views of the system.
(3) *More powerful archiving and retrieval,* holding in the EDB a thesaurus of as-built documents for future modification, extension, maintenance, disaster recovery, and so on.

The last is an EDB problem which can best be supported through evolution in the CAD system architecture. Figure 5.6 presents the new generation of CAD systems which will help integrate local and global features, providing the design engineer with polyvalent support.

Engineering analysis and modeling

To help exemplify the CAM-based process of engineering analysis, we can start with an overview of the building study and see how it can be radically changed by CAD techniques. Designing a building can be broken down into four separate phases:

- sketch design;
- detailed design;
- production information;
- on-site supervision.

Typically, the major portion of manpower on a project is allocated to the production information stage. Technicians and draftsmen must generate masses of information to meet contractual schedules.* This produces a pronounced peaking of the know-how curve: the manpower ratio between the design stage and production information is at least two to one. Yet the most important design decisions are made much earlier, during sketch design and, to a lesser extent, during detailed design.

It is at the earliest civil engineering design phases that critical decisions are made about overall building form, siting and orientation. Such decisions have far-reaching cost implications. On the other hand, the

---

* This chapter is based on a presentation by a civil engineering firm and on the references given by a CAD manufacturer.

production information stage involves decisions of a much more tactical, small-scale and local nature.

The contribution of CAD in the sketch and detailed design phases is typically being done through modeling (we will return to this issue). CAD introduces at the production information stage the ability to flatten the manpower curve, as shown in Figure 5.7. Even if CAD is used at this stage only, the results can be significant. A company can complete projects more quickly with less manpower, and more smoothly manage the on-site stage through better coordinated information, with the resultant productivity increases yielding substantial financial gains to the user.

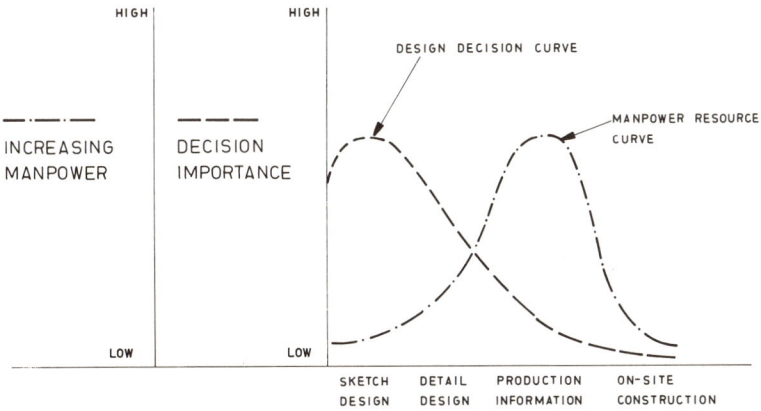

Figure 5.7 The automation of engineering jobs should be made both post-by-post and in a company wide sense. This is necessary to flatten the manpower curve

Thus, when we talk of engineering analysis, to start in the right way from the beginning we should focus on modeling – which means that we need to develop the model. To answer this need, software packages are available supporting dynamic modeling, multiple-view digitizing, and interactive menus.

The dynamics allow us to define an isometric view of the geometry if a plain view exists. Transformations are done through the graphics processing unit of the CAD system.

Multiple-view digitizing would allow, if there are different views of the part, the use of all views to help create the geometry. In this sense, all views – top, side, down, isometric – are active.

Interactive menus on the video screen make it feasible to scroll commands and develop a prompting/training/decision view format. This is a verb-and-noun modifier. It also constitutes a good training tool, particularly for new users, and makes it easier to operate, with less keyboarding.

With finite element modeling, we can effectively handle the user-defined elements, including as a subset:

- 1-D (beams); 2-D (plates); 3-D (bricks);

- mesh generation in 1-D (points on curves); 2-D (surfaces); 3-D (volumes);
- shrink elements, as defined by the designer;
- the ability to merge boundaries.

This last is an interesting facility. As Figure 5.8 suggests, when there is a grid on the screen, we do not necessarily know if the defined element edges with its neighbors or not. Just as for merge boundaries, we must study the coincident nodes for accuracy, and reconnect the pattern.

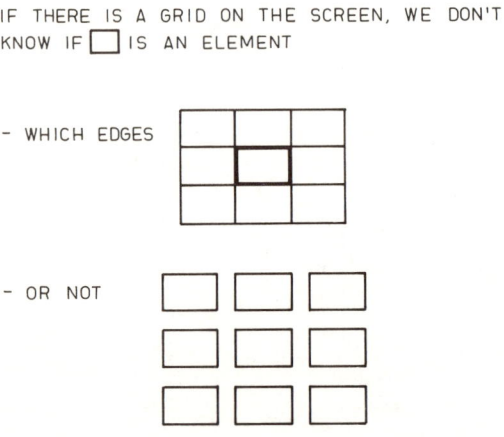

IF THERE IS A GRID ON THE SCREEN, WE DON'T
KNOW IF ☐ IS AN ELEMENT

- WHICH EDGES

- OR NOT

FOR A MERGE BOUNDARIES EXAMPLE SUPPOSE

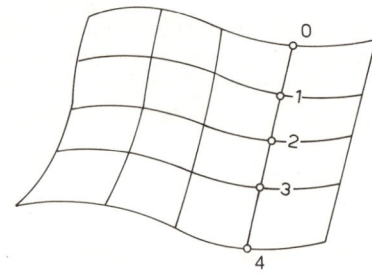

0, 1, 2, 3, 4 ARE COMMON, WE MUST STUDY THE
COINCIDENT NODES.

Figure 5.8 Software selection should be tuned not only to current but also to future development needs. The people with problems to solve are the best source for drawing up specifications

The models in reference will be converted in the EDB into a 3-D schema. The element connectivity can be outlined through a job control language, and technical as well as textual information can be stored in the appropriate file for extension and reuse.

Solid modeling has recently been much publicized for its ability to provide shaded pictures. CAD manufacturers have developed packages which:

- integrate with upstream design functions;
- assure user interfaces (primitives, building blocks);
- support the DB structure;
- enhance analysis/display through ray tracing and other analytical techniques.

(The 'ray tracing' approach shoots pixels at a given structure. The designer knows from where they come but now gets to know the approximate value. Shaded pictures permit better understanding of what the object looks like; the appreciation of hidden lines; and so on.)

This work is part of the integrated EDB and can provide dimensioning; NC tool paths; mass calculation; mesh generation; and perspective presentation effected through shaded pictures.

With the part geometry and finite element work well under way, the engineering department can use the geometric definitions already in the system to enrich the work in progress. In other terms, elements which are in the EDB can be addressed directly. There is no perpetual re-input. Furthermore, the designers can obtain cuts, views, and so on at their choice. (This phase is still away from drafting.) There is literally no loss of geometric definitions or associations.

Through such facilities, if the design engineer is in the process of studying a given complex surface, he can directly generate the mesh on this surface; all mechanical design features are available to him.

But, once again, the preparatory work must be kept in mind. Symbolisms, terminology and normalization are part and parcel of this work. The terminologies of the different designers and of the different professions tend to merge, but it is also wise to ensure in an explicit manner that the designers can use the same terminology.

This discussion identifies a step-by-step approach to civil engineering, using interactive computer graphics as a means of improving speed and accuracy through the power of a computer. The approach taken ensures quality and accuracy in drawings while improving productivity. In terms of an overall methodology, Figure 5.9 suggests the need to stress the part geometry under study, and the finite elements constituting this part.

Taken together, these two issues form the engineering analysis – that is, the pre-processing phase of the study. Its outcome will be stored on a transit file, and made available for processing either on a mainframe (through a package) or, preferably, online to the engineering analysis phase.

If the CAD system does not support online computational capabilities (for instance through an integrated 32 BPW CPU), it will typically provide a transit file capability. Then, when the calculation part has been completed, comes the post-processing phase. The latter will typically involve stress plots; the calculation of deformation; 3-D presentation from the EDB; and so on. It will lead to printouts and documentation through the drafting stage.

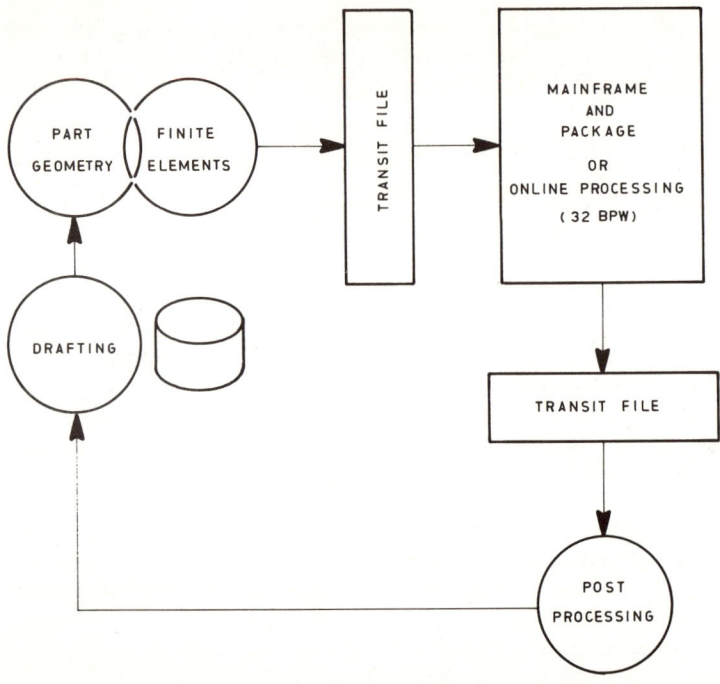

Figure 5.9 An implementation policy for CAD/CAM should be evolutionary in nature, always providing for interfaces which by and large regard database elements

Post-processing can bring up 3-D deformations, underline stress contours, and provide color-shaded plots for better understanding. The deformations can be flashed through static or dynamic runs, simulating the motion of natural modes. Taking eigenvector values, displaying them on screen, and animating them, is one of the developing approaches.

Packages can present on screen the deflection of a pole on the ground, making available for study all relative parameters. This automates most of the manual procedures – except the civil engineer's ingenuity.

Chapter 6

The experience of two engineering firms

We have spoken of the work which can be done through CAD: from assuring product quality to precise pre-processing procedures involving finite elements. We have also discussed the importance of the engineering database and the models elaborated to ensure data exchange.

But the employment of a CAD system, as has so often been stressed, demands much more than the availability of tools or the straightforward application of techniques. Each user has (or develops) his own approach and this can make one application system look totally different from another, even within the same branch of engineering.

The methodology proper to a given user can range all the way from the broader perspective of the implementation down to the level of exploiting the system's ability to take a group of lines and pivot them about a specified point. In one company this may be intended for checking clearance paths. In another to demonstrate the CAD's ability to position standard library components: nuts, bolts, keys. In still another, reasons and criteria may be different.

Accurate sectioning, view placement, cross-hatching are among the most closely examined capabilities by all users. The same is true of distance evaluators: true 3-D distance between points, sketching capabilities, command stringing and actual plotting of a drawing. Yet, while these are primitives of every engineering design, the implementation aspects may vary from one user organization to another, and with it the expected results.

Practically every user has his own checklists and methods of evaluation. The latter concern not only the way toward problem solution but also his view of system capabilities in terms of hardware and software requirements. This, too, is quite important: while vendors can conduct impressive demonstrations, the user should take particular care that CAD capabilities relevant to his own applications are shown in a factual and documented way.

From a simple part for design creation, to a complex part for design modification, the systems and parts library, the user-friendly programming language, and so on, the user wants to get results. Therefore, prior to discussing productivity issues and matters relating to equipment selection, it would be useful to consider some practical experiences in detail. This is the goal of the two case studies.

Most significantly, in the discussion that follows we will go through practical experiences which help document what an engineering and manufacturing company can expect from the implementation of CAD equipment. The statistics we will review, on the amount of change characterizing existing engineering designs in order to adapt them to new factories, are both impressive because of their nature and important for management decision purposes.

The Alpha experience

Alpha is a consulting engineering company. It works worldwide and employs some 400 people, with a good percentage of engineers and architects. For many years this company has used computer support in its engineering calculations, and in late 1979 it demonstrated interest in the use of interactive systems in design. Three areas of application first attracted management attention:

(1) mapping,
(2) electrical engineering,
(3) mechanical engineering.

They were quickly followed by two other domains:

(4) architecture,
(5) civil engineering.

The preliminary investigation in these fields was done in cooperation with a professional association on CAD and computers – hence, in a common project with other engineering firms. As a result, a report was written on the state of the art of all available interactive systems.

This common project quickly grew in scale. The initial list of participants featured some 20 companies – and they considered an impressive list of 30 alternatives. The options were too many and management decided to proceed with reduced numbers on both counts.

The first goal was the use of CAD/CAM in drafting; but three months of work on this issue proved that this orientation was too narrow. As a result, management decided to enlarge the CAD perspectives to the areas mentioned above.

As equipment selection constituted an integral part of the effort, the engineers entrusted with this mission made a list of critical questions for selection purposes. About 50 critical issues were raised and organized into homogeneous groups. They included:

- the graphics possibilities of the system;
- interactive approaches;
- databasing capabilities;
- accuracy;
- reliability;
- maintenance policies, and their availability in the country;
- clauses implied by the user – i.e. departures from the standard contract
- organization of vendor support;
- applications library.

Once the applications issue was cleared, the professional association agreed a benchmark, involving 25 to 30 machines. The tests particularly stressed the graphical possibilities of the system:

(1) dividing lines,
(2) line fonding,
(3) dimensioning,
(4) adding text,
(5) line drawing,
(6) response time for typical application,
(7) rotating,
(8) mirroring,
(9) copying,
(10) rescaling and part insertion.

This benchmark took roughly one hour per machine, for an experienced operator. In the evaluation phase, the analysts first thought of using some weighting factors on the results, but they dropped the idea as they found that this is very difficult – and dangerous too.

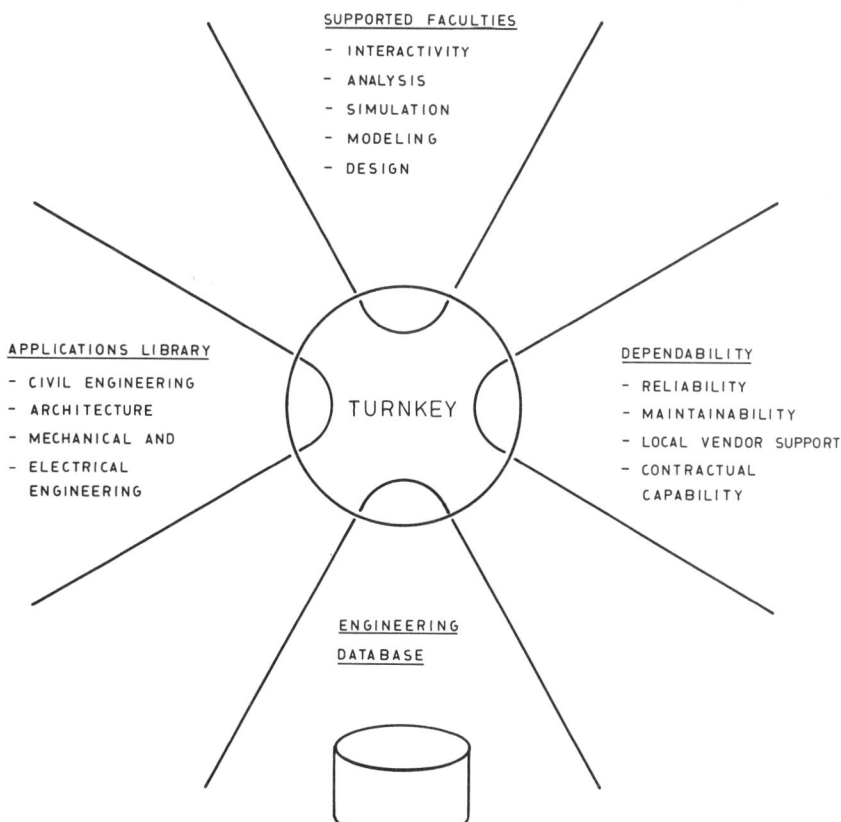

Figure 6.1 Many turnkey solutions are only partial, primarily applications oriented. They fail to cover all four areas characterizing a good CAD system

While much of this work was done in common with the other firms, gradually as the subject became clear enough and the criteria were established, management decided that Alpha would be better off by going it alone. Having decided on a turnkey solution and its key component parts (Figure 6.1), this company reduced the list of participating CAD vendors to six and conducted its own benchmark tests on five of these equipments.

The alternatives examined were: Aristo/IDI (US–Germany); Mac Auto; Applicon; Cablos/Medusa; Computervision; and Calma. The last was dropped because it did not have a local establishment at the time the choice was made.

Alpha's own benchmark stressed some of its typical problems, particularly building design work. The goals were to establish:

(1) how easy it was to manipulate elements in drawing;
(2) what sort of technique the benchmarked equipment used;
(3) how fast it was done;
(4) which different ways were possible to solve the problem.

To ensure that the end users were fully in the picture, the engineers responsible for the benchmark first discussed the issue with the users, and

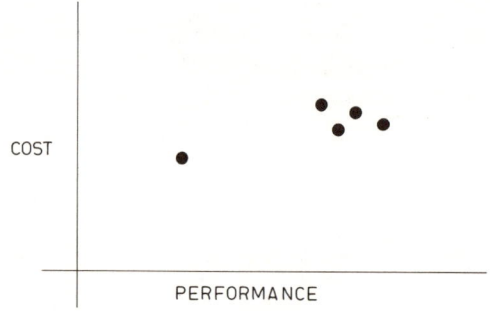

AS AN ALTERNATIVE, RESULTS MIGHT HAVE BEEN

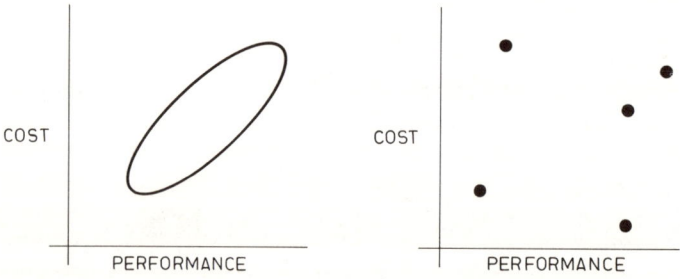

Figure 6.2 Cost/performance evaluations often provide surprising results. The more expensive equipment and software does not always have the higher cost/performance

clarified what the real problems were. Given the lack of CAD experience at the time, it was found that no system was *really* suited for the work on hand. Hence, they examined three criteria:

(1) Which CAD system has the power to solve the problem in the future?
(2) How can the results of tests be judged?
(3) What is the evaluation of the vendor organization in terms of customer support; training; technical support; applications libraries?

Based on these criteria, a plot was made of cost/performance, which demonstrated that there were no shocking price differences (Figure 6.2). Hence, a technical base was used for the selection process. For instance, Aristo dropped out because of 2½-D (not 3-D), rather low accuracy, and a narrow range of applications. Similar criteria were used till the final selection was made. Subsequently, the installation took place on 1 July 1981.

The selected configuration, a Computervision system, included a CPU with 300 MByte disk; the CADDS 3 software; and two WS, with slave digitizers for mapping purposes. Before installation, six people were fully trained: two project engineers, two from the structural department, and two from the building department.

A no-professional-operator approach was adopted; instead the company opted for the integration of duties and work. Particular attention was paid to the avoidance of gaps in know-how. Alpha briefed *all* of its engineers and designers on CAD through a two-hour presentation with visual aids and subsequent discussions on organization, procedures, and expected results.

Within the overall applications perspective, it is very important to underline management's decision to have as prerequisites:

(1) a wide range of applications, and
(2) the necessary system accuracy.

Range of applications

In defining the wanted range of applications, current organizational perspectives played a leading role. The first goal was to serve 80 per cent of the drafting work, which is done in two departments: architectural building design, and the structural department (concrete, steel, wood).

These are interdependent, and management felt that any valid solution should enhance such interdependency. There was no rush to get the maximum out of the machine. Instead, the company used the first six months to feel comfortable in building design, structural studies, and how to expand CAD into the infrastructure.

Mapping, cartography, piping, utility mapping, town development and 2-D modeling were the first applications to be handled successfully. Subsequently, the engineers moved into 3-D, which had already given results for drafting.

In cooperation with the vendor, Alpha started to develop a system approach to the manipulation of building elements (beams, windows, floors, doors) – not through lines but design-wise, including both data and text, and adding cost evaluation. The CAD system is currently used to help manage costs and budgets. Aso, in parallel with the CAD unit, Alpha uses another computer for administrative work.

A sound policy has been established that all work starts behind the CAD screen at the very earliest stage of the project: the architect, structural engineer, and draftsman sit at the WS at the very moment they begin projecting a given process. Say that the company gets an order for a new factory. Then:

(1) The architect, in cooperation with the engineers, designs a sketch layout. In a transition period this may still be done by hand, but it will be done on the CAD WS after the architects have had the necessary training.

(2) The structural engineer involved in designing a given structure fits it in the layout, through CAD. This stage is done on WS and is a typical CAD application.

(3) The draftsman gets behind the screen. This still does not happen for 100 per cent of projects, but for the large majority. 'If you get 75 per cent of projects this way, it's good,' said a senior executive.

(4) The structural design draftsman gets behind the screen. For projects run on CAD, this is done 100 per cent and permits building up the EDB. Although it is feasible for less profitable work with no EDB impact to be done by hand, management stressed the importance of being consistent.

This sound procedure established by Alpha allows its architects and engineers to plan layouts from concept through to completion on a computer graphics workstation. It works quickly and efficiently, recalling all the minor details that are often forgotten until the remedy is costly and time-consuming. The right guidelines see to it that, before the design is started, the steps needed for a successful operation are properly supported.

A good example is that of preliminary specifications. These may include architectural sketches, catalogs, process models, piping layouts, structural designs and civil engineering models. Using the information these specifications provide, a 2-D or 3-D layout model can be created. Means of model creation are available and the EDB access can be valuable, as it includes steel structure, storage tanks, pumps, generators and so on. There are various basic geometric shapes that may be utilized, and the degree of detail in equipment creation is totally user-dependent.

Detail may range from a simple building-block representation to a sophisticated model: during initial stages of plant development, the user is interested in space allocation and interference checking. As each component piece is constructed, it may be stored in the EDB with its associated properties of interest, and the performance specifications. The EDB may be accessed by several users simultaneously, as the need develops.

Any time a change is desired, the user may elect to apply that particular modification to any or all similar design references. This enhances the analysis phase of model development, eliminating time-consuming, repetitive changes when a particular unit is replaced at any point in the design process. Reports may be generated on request and range from a complete listing of all specifications connected to a given design to all listings of all occurrences in a particular model.

Annotations can easily be made, involving such items as name, number, descriptions or elevations. A model may be integrated with steel or piping designs, and supported facilities enable the user to standardize all layouts according to established in-house conventions.

Properly studied procedural steps and the online capabilities help avoid past manual and batch computer practices, which unavoidably lead to repeating the work three or four times prior to conclusion. Other facilities are provided through CAD that are not available with the manual method. Examples are cost evaluation and design optimization. Furthermore, the final presentation to the user is timely, well documented and very clean. All this work is done as the pre-project.

The structural calculation proper comes after the project is authorized. In Alpha this is still done on a Harris computer for 80 per cent of cases. Also used on a Service Bureau basis is the 'Stardyne' package (on CDC machines) and 'Strudel' (on IBM). The latter is employed for the more complex calculations.

Number crunching does not need to be done dynamically – it can be deferred – but modeling does require dynamic approaches.

Needed programming is done through Vapro, PEP, and FORTRAN. Programming by Alpha personnel concerned only minor key routines. Such effort started six months after the CAD installation and is not intended to produce more than two routines per month – mainly small ones to enhance the available software.

Results – amply demonstrated during this early application period – have led to an increase in user population among structural draftsmen and building designers. The CAD configuration itself grew, adding two WS in 1982, and another two in 1983.

Equipment growth is a vital issue. The maximum configuration of the Model 100 by Computervision is six WS for graphical tasks and another two for non-graphical jobs. Adding more workstations can inversely affect the response time. It is frustrating for the designer to sit for one minute behind the screen, waiting for the machine's response. Longer response time can also adversely effect productivity.

The productivity results Alpha has obtained are convincing. For the same job done manually and on CAD, the ratio was 1:3 in favor of CAD when the application started. With experience, because of learning, and the build-up of the EDB given repetitive work (some 10 per cent of all cases), this ratio has reached 1:6 to 1:8.

It is well to remember that this is the best case, because the company chose those projects most favorable to using the system. Though Alpha made the reference to 'repetitiveness' as a key ingredient, it also stressed that on rare occasions the architect has to deal with a unique design in his work on offices, small hotels, factories and power plants.

One can be selective in this work in starting with CAD/CAM. 'Selective' means evaluating very carefully the projects that are the most likely to lead to productivity and quality improvement. Both play a major role in the results to be obtained – and on management's appreciation of return on investment.

Indeed, one of the engineers participating in this meeting was to remark that fine-tuning a factory project – as a result of interdepartmental cooperation – makes it as if it *were* repetitive, even if it is a one-shot proposition.

At Alpha the next strata of 'favorable projects', representing 40 per cent of the workload in the structural department, have reached, after tuning, an overall ratio of: 1:3 for structural design, and 1:2.5 for building design.

A different way of saying this is that 50 per cent of the work of Alpha involving architectural and engineering premises has gained, on average, between 320 per cent and 400 per cent in productivity – which is an impressive factor. But management underlined that to achieve such results it requires very good planning and organization.

If this is lacking, one simply does not get the productivity results. A user organization is thus well advised to establish the use of the system properly for the projects it is to undertake, and for everyone to share the facilities. Orderly progress is the key to success.

I stress these points heavily in order to impress the need for preparatory steps to the introduction of CAD/CAM. Computer-aided design has been part of the engineering profession for some years. The addition of more fields – such as architecture and civil engineering – does not reduce procedural requirements: if anything, it adds to them.

Computer-aided design at Beta

Beta is a major engineering company involved in both design and manufacturing tasks. It is a worldwide leader in factory technology:

- 90 per cent of its business is for factory equipment and related to design tasks;
- 90 per cent of its yearly business is for export.

Typical studies start with raw materials and projects involve testing, analysis, design flow sheets, putting together proposals, negotiating, contracting, and the final projects. A major part of the work is done in CAD.

The company has chosen to use packages. 'We only develop small, specific programs and interfaces,' a knowledgeable executive was to remark. Because of the work done during the 1970s on the mainframe, Beta still has 300 major programs to be maintained. This, as well as new development work, is done by six people:

- one manager;
- one CAD specialist, oriented to the end user and the manuals;
- two calculation experts (FEM, etc.);
- one system programmer;
- one user programmer.

Asked whether the company adopted a structured method such as HIPO or Jackson, the systems executive responded: 'There is no consistent policy, because there exist no documented results.' And he added:

'We know what it is, but it is not applicable to work which has been done – and that's the true problem.

'We don't aim anymore to develop big packages – *we buy them*. It's cheaper.'

Cost analysis and budgeting are among the major CAD-supported features. They are done by the Commercial Department – not the Design Engineering Division – and they are based on both financial and technical premises. A fairly extensive online computer facility is run side by side with the CAD installation. (We will return to this subject.)

Whether CAD is used by the sales or the design engineers, at Beta the applications involve both the electrical and the mechanical fields in designing processes and equipment.

(1) Checking flow sheets and modifying them according to agreements. The design of flow sheets of electrical circuits, mechanical conveyors and kilns, was among the first applications to be undertaken. Applications with electrical circuits and mechanical conveyors have given very good results, less so the approach to General Layout because of the relatively limited size of the screens. We will look at these points in a more precise way when we mention their impact on the company's workflow.

Management duly emphasized that they are still at an early stage in their experience, using a rather limited number of WS at the start, while not all cement equipment is amenable to CAD. An example is the field of general arrangement drawings, which are too complex and in which the density of information is extremely high. Similar reservations apply to steel construction for belt conveyors – there is little repetition in the work.

Good areas, according to Beta, are those where a sizeable number of people are working on drawing boards and on decision projects – but management was quick to add that 'Development is rapid, even in areas where we originally thought it couldn't be done.'

(2) Transferring contract data from the project EDB to the contract DB, implementing the necessary updating. Specific data relating to equipment design are weights; dimensions; specifications such as throughput, kW, m^3/h; costs; engineering hours; and the delivery times of the suppliers. Beta has classically followed delivery schedules through a control system (Pert, Bar Chart) which will be integrated into the overall CAD procedure.

(3) Design proper. The company uses CAD to generate the BOM, and this can be done in two ways: manually, then inputting to the computer – for management reasons; or directly, through CAD.

Statistics based on experience

The CAD installation took place in early 1981. The original order involved four WS for the designers; a fifth WS was then added for training and development; and two more WS were ordered for delivery within the first year. While these units are primarily employed by the designer, 100 terminals online to a mainframe are available for contracting purposes and other studies. They are also handling bill of materials and alphanumeric-type applications.

Most importantly, these 100 online terminals are supported by a full organizational infra-structure as a result of original work which took place in 1978/79. The main sub-systems are:

- plant layout,
- pre-layout,
- electrical,
- kiln,
- mill,
- materials handling,
- geological,
- chemical.

Thus, computer-aided design was able to benefit from work already done. As the CAD practice progressed, management has increasingly found that much can be done with CAD. A senior executive commented that '30 per cent of the 350 people working on the drawing board can be immediately converted to CAD. The constraints are organizational and training. There are no terminal constraints.

Based on this experience, Table 6.1 presents the best applications areas as management conceives them. The first column reflects the situation as its stands after less than one year of CAD utilization; the second is a projection of percentage influence after fine tuning and the gaining of subsequent experience; the third presents an estimate of overall drafting operations. Notice the footnote on the general layout reference. It is however possible to work through windows on soft copy and have general layout view as hard copy.

Table 6.1 Areas of CAD interest

	Type of design work done:		Overall impact on company work
	Now	Later	
1. Flow Sheet: 2-D not to scale (incl. electrical plans)	100%	100%	100%
2. Pure mechanical drawings (kiln etc., to scale)	30–50%	80%	50–70%
3. General layout and arrangement drawings*	–	–	30%

* Screen size is the stumbling block. If the size is large, then the impact may be 100 per cent.

The statistics in Figure 6.3 are important. They reflect an analysis of a typical month's work. During this period:

- 34 per cent of the engineering and drafting use of CAD concerned new designs;

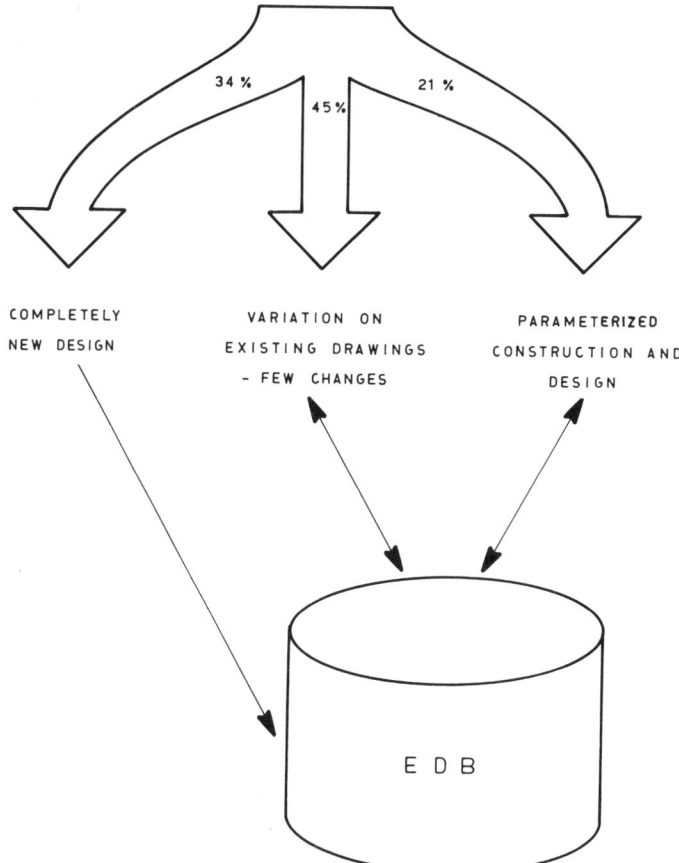

Figure 6.3 A wise policy for an engineering firm is to divide the CAD work to be done into these three categories. The percentages may vary, but the categories are always valid

- 45 per cent were design variations in terms of shape and dimension, including the use of existing drawings for special purposes – with few changes;
- 21 per cent was parameterized construction and design: same shape, different sizes.

A point to be particularly appreciated is the interaction with the database. This EDB contains:

- material data,
- suppliers,
- standard parts,
- graphic support,
- project management information,
- cost evaluation,
- commercial handling reference,
- customer file.

Its structuring and implementation have been greatly assisted by the organizational work already done on the mainframe, which has been integrated into the CAD. (Non-interactive computer-aided design approaches were started with the classical DP which had given this firm 3-D geometry through a program done with the local university. This program has now been transferred onto the 32 bit CAD machine.)

Other computing programs running on the CAD equipment are contained in in a specially bought package for finite elements, and processing calculations.

The user organization has established interfaces between the packages which it acquired or developed itself. In a systems sense, these are:

(1) 'Cablos-Medusa', whose goal is processing work – which however constitutes a pre-processing phase for package No. 2;
(2) 'Femgen' (Finite Elements Generator), an interactive design support for Fine Elements Mesh (FEM);
(3) 'Aska', a number cruncher with the FEM calculations as goal;
(4) 'Femview', which acts as post-processing to Aska, supports interactivity and presents the Aska results to the end user.

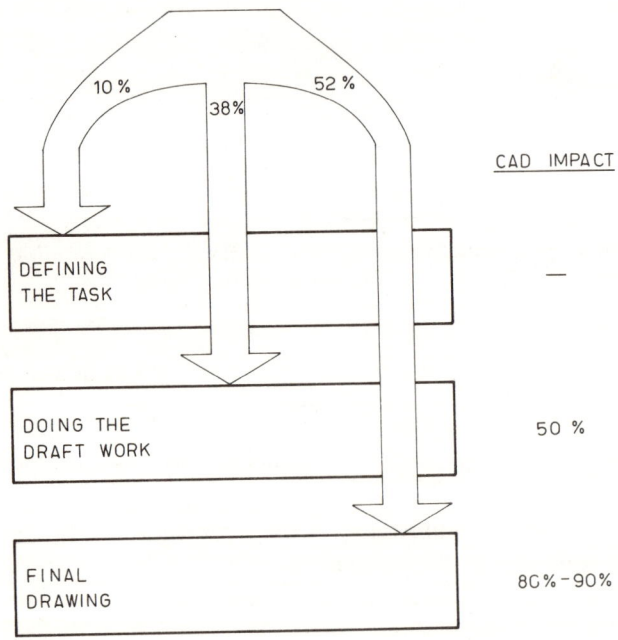

DRAWING HOURS WITH CLASSICAL WORK

10 %   38%   52 %

CAD IMPACT

DEFINING
THE TASK   —

DOING THE
DRAFT WORK   50 %

FINAL
DRAWING   80%-90%

THE OVERALL TIME SAVING IS 65% – OR A 300%
PRODUCTIVITY IMPROVEMENT

Figure 6.4 This is a specific case from the Beta company. Other engineering firms have found a significant CAD impact in defining the design task

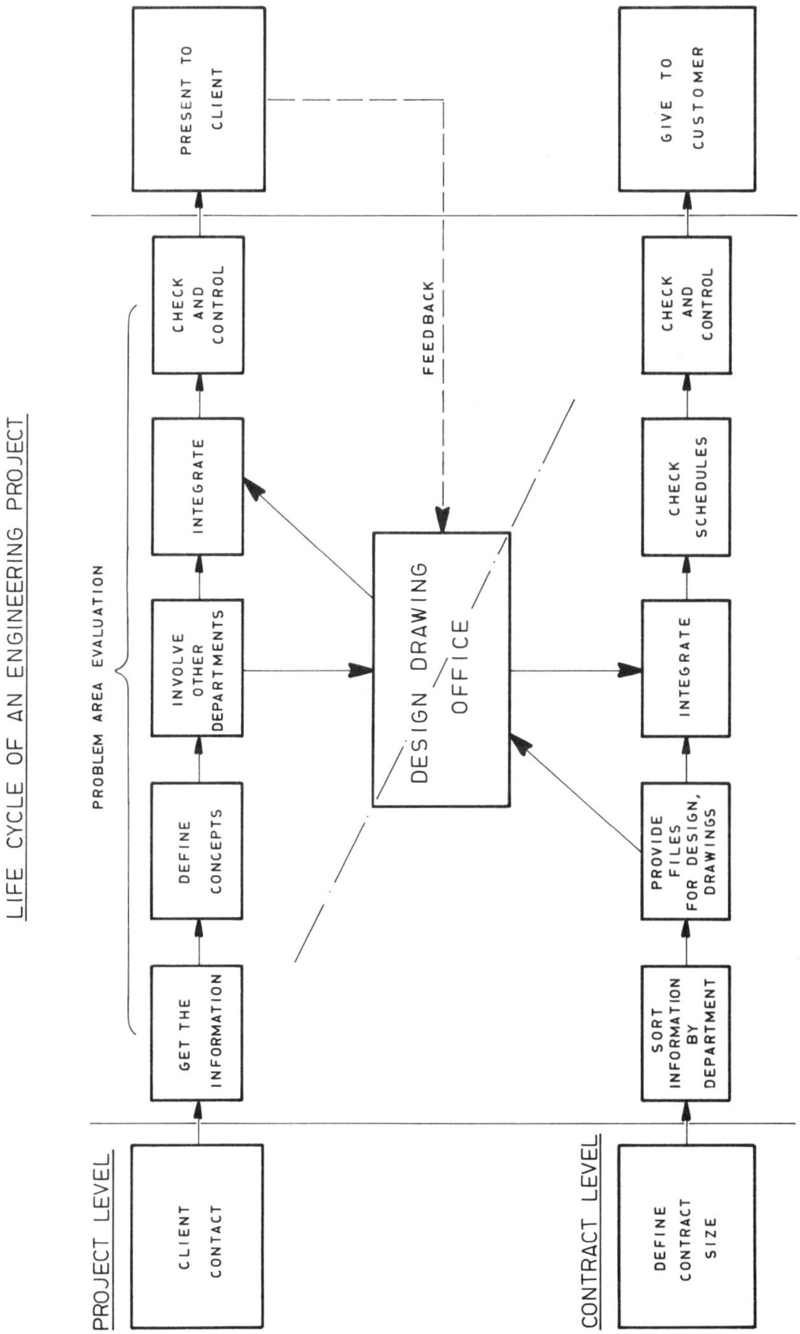

LIFE CYCLE OF AN ENGINEERING PROJECT

PROJECT LEVEL

PROBLEM AREA EVALUATION

CLIENT CONTACT → GET THE INFORMATION → DEFINE CONCEPTS → INVOLVE OTHER DEPARTMENTS → INTEGRATE → CHECK AND CONTROL → PRESENT TO CLIENT

DESIGN DRAWING OFFICE

FEEDBACK

CONTRACT LEVEL

DEFINE CONTRACT SIZE → SORT INFORMATION BY DEPARTMENT → PROVIDE FILES FOR DESIGN, DRAWINGS → INTEGRATE → CHECK SCHEDULES → CHECK AND CONTROL → GIVE TO CUSTOMER

Figure 6.5 Automation will give much better results if we take a life-cycle view of the design and engineering project. This means from client contact to client satisfaction – including all internal facilities

An office automation effort is going on in parallel with the CAD implementation; on both the CAD CPU and the mainframe, the company uses database management systems. In the former case, the DBMS is Medas/Power Plus with query language for the administration of the drawing. ADABAS is implemented on the mainframe.

The CAD CPU supports the stated graphic terminals and another 10 alphanumeric units. It is linked online to the DP mainframe through 3270 and 3780 protocols. The mainframe drives the 100 AN terminals. To the CAD CPU are attached a flatbed plotter and an electrostatic plotter.

The statistics shown in Figure 6.4 represent the overall drawing hours in terms of classical, largely manual work. Out of a sample of about 16,000 hours, the distribution indicates that:

- 10 per cent of the time is spent defining the task. CAD has so far been of little assistance with this.
- 38 per cent of the time is invested in doing sketches. Working on the video, the requirement in manhours has been cut in half.
- 52 per cent of the draftsman's time goes in the final drawing. Here the time requirements have been cut by 80–90 per cent.

An analysis of these statistics shows a weighted result of 65 per cent time savings, which roughly corresponds to a 300 per cent overall improvement. It is an impressive result indeed. In fact Beta has a rationalization factor of 1:3.

Cost-benefit evaluation is more impressive when we consider the overall life cycle of an engineering project as outlined in Figure 6.5. This diagram places emphasis on CAD assistance in evaluating the problem area, and on the interconnection of both the project and the design work accomplished by the Design Drawing Office.

Chapter 7

A mechanical engineering implementation

The task of developing metal structures presents a number of challenges to manufacturing engineers. In any process, different kinds of fabrication are dependent on full-size patterns of the product views. In sheet metal work, for instance, a pattern is used to lay out the cut lines so the cut metal will, after it is rolled, folded or formed, make the desired part. Such an outline laid out in one plane is the flat pattern development of the surface.

In a complete part outline, the locations of holes and slots in the flat do not need to be identical to their locations in the final part. Folding or bending the material causes a stretching and an expansion of the plate, which affects the final dimensions; the difference between the length of the flat and the length after bending is the bend deduction. A bend deduction is affected by:

- the bend radius;
- the thickness of material;
- the angle of the bend;
- the type of material.

As several fabrication processes require that the holes or slots be machined before bending, an operation is required to calculate the true hole locations relative to the dimensions in the flat; and a subsequent operation for the production of the appropriate drawing.

Gamma is a mechanical engineering/manufacturing company which has been faced by these problems. Beyond the purely technical tasks to be mechanized, management was interested in obtaining through CAD a significant improvement in turn-around time, the possibility of eliminating most calculation errors, the ability to move toward standardized tooling and design approaches, and accurate drafting documents.

Though this sort of implementation is far from being a highly sophisticated approach, it is a good example of the routines beginning CAD users must go through. Prior to the decision to adopt computer-aided design, and in order to ascertain the kinds of result that could be obtained, Gamma set a benchmark with a bracket made of three plates, representing a typical mechanical design. This was simple enough for an operator to comprehend without much effort and yet be able to demonstrate the ability to create geometric shapes.

The goal was to evaluate CAD's ability to perform different design primitives, and to observe the ease and/or difficulty experienced in the initial work. Once the basic geometry was created, the engineers asked to see alterations made in line with tasks they experience daily. This gave them an idea as to the system's freedom to move, extend, or trim lines.

They asked to transform a view from one drawing position to another, and checked to see if the new view remained orthographically correct. This demonstrated the ability to copy and move data by groups, and showed the methods for drawing formulation. They experimented by having the base plate thickened, and checked whether or not data modified in one view would be automatically updated in all other views. CAD demonstrated that it can edit and modify data that had already been created in 3-D. Finally, by separating individual sub-assemblies, they controlled dimensioning and labeling.

Looking forward to coming areas of application, the benchmark included a machine tool component consisting of mainly cylinders and cones. The purpose was to control the system's ability to edit designs. For this, they examined:

- surface definitions;
- intersection of surfaces;
- spine line generation;
- line trimming;
- hidden line removal.

To check on the CAD/CAM numerical control (NC) capability, tool path, profiling, pocketing, and the ability to alter a generated tool path were closely checked. An experiment checked whether tool paths could be verified visually, dry runs simulated and tool collisions essentially eliminated.

The results demonstrated that not only could these results be achieved but also cutting times and material utilization rates were optimized. The same numerical control package used to produce the tool paths was also employed for the subsequent nesting of the parts on the inventory. The outcome was convincing enough to management to authorize the acquisition of CAD/CAM equipment, but, rightly or wrongly, it posed one condition: CAD implementation in the engineering department should start from the drafting board.

The standard drawing form

A milestone in the procedure for creating an engineering drawing is the standard drawing form. The actual drawing is created mainly by inserting standard components, from a library of items, with additional information handled by using pre-established commands, as necessary. The information for the bill of materials is contained within files which can be inserted with the library parts or separately. Data extract procedures are used to create a bill of materials report.

Drawing sheets are held on the system in the standard sizes A0 to A3. Each sheet comprises two parts:

- an outline frame and certain other data, to be inserted into the engineering drawing as individual entities;
- fixed text and title descriptions, to be inserted as a single figure.

The part geometry includes: the outside edge and inside frame of the drawing (which may then be used for reference, if necessary); 'text nodes' describing the text to be added to the title box, defining its position, font, height and other parameters; and access to properties for use by the data extract procedure. The EDB contains the remainder of the drawing sheet, the internal boxing, the company name and other annotation, symbols and other information contained in the company's standard drawing form.

Depending on the policies of the engineering department, variations on the theme may exist; for example, the same fixed standard title box may be inserted in various sized frames, or there may be a completely different layout for each size drawing. Layering conventions must, however, be used, the particular requirements determining the complexity of the scheme.

Engineering drawing files identify the individual items on an assembly. Assembly drawings can be built up by adding parts which represent the items that make up the assembly. In many applications involving a schematic representation of the finished component, such as piping, the individual items can be added as figures to provide a pictorial presentation of the assembly.

An assembly drawing can be generated through the process of adding together items and sub-assemblies in the library. The library comprises the individual items and frequently used sub-assemblies.

Individual parts normally contain just the geometric description but sub-assemblies may include cross-hatching, center lines and hidden detail in the way in which they would normally appear in the finished drawing. The sub-assemblies and, where appropriate, the individual items also include the references suitably annotated and placed in a position convenient for the finished drawing. Other annotation may be included to assist the user.

Part of the library are certain standard sections and views which are required for the finished drawing; standard blocks or notes; data tables; and other similar items. In many applications, the majority of the library items are being constructed and stored as parts on the system. Other applications will make use of parameterized parts. Generally, the library is built up on an 'as needed' basis: the first time an item is required it is created and used, then it is filed as a library part for immediate use on the next occasion.

Whenever it is necessary, the bill or materials is obtained online, through a CAD package, providing the facilities for extracting non-graphic information from a drawing to build a file of textual information. Such software is quite flexible and may be used to create a variety of reports from a part or set of parts. The output from data extract can be restructured to provide:

- trailer lines for change information;
- double line spacing of items;

- a tally of the number off of each item from counts on the balloon, and other minor modifications.

The resulting report is typically output to a line printer in a way such that it can be cut into A4 sheets that closely resemble the existing non-computer generated forms.

Although this procedure is valid and applicable with new projects, a vital question remains: 'What do we do with the old designs?' The best answer is to take only the most important, as the work has to be done mainly manually. (We can scan a graph, but for dimensions and other elements we have to do it manually.)

Anyway, most of the existing documents are not vital to new designs, and the process can be costly. One user, who wanted to keep everything, needed one dedicated CAD system working three shifts for three years to put in all his old designs – while Alfa-Romeo found that the 15 per cent of existing drawings is all that is necessary, even for consultation purposes.

A demonstration of capabilities

The demonstration of equipment capabilities at Gamma, including software, hardware and end user functions has been fairly successful in convincing management that CAD/CAM is likely to be a critical factor in making the company work better and compete in more intelligent terms. CAD

- provided for more efficient design;
- saved the designer's time;
- helped improve the final quality of the product;
- created goods that are more producible.

It helped make structural information and parts specifications more accessible; permitted employees to do a better job; often provided job enrichment and upgrading; and generally tended to eliminate waste.

But CAD did not necessarily reduce labor overhead: as always with computers, savings come from the right preparation – not from the equipment itself. Time and again, experience teaches that computer improvements allow us to work faster and open the way for doing things we couldn't do before. One of the examples given is steel plate nesting.

This was not particular to Gamma. Nearly every manufacturing company that makes parts does some nesting. This involves a careful layout of the parts so as to make use of every possible inch of material. Yet, for optimization purposes, the number of shapes and sizes of metal parts required makes it impossible to work through manual or even batch approaches. As the number of parts goes up, the manual limitation creeps in, and so does waste. (One company known to use CAD for nesting purposes is GE – and management says that the company was able to increase utilization rates from about 60 to 90 per cent just through the use of interactive graphics, drawing on the computer to position parts for the plasma cutters to burn out of plate steel.)

A steel structure program application precisely focused on nesting cells together. The manipulations done on steel part design have been stored in the EDB with *one keystroke*, and recalled. This way, parts and structures were handled as shells or broken up as primitives.

The computer-based EDB also pointed to defects. A service tracking program has given one manufacturer the ability to put a finger more effectively on customer problems arising from design, engineering, materials, manufacturing, transportation or installation. Those problems might be defects or lack of compatibility.

Though pinpointing and correcting problems is not a new notion for many firms, manually handled error detection and correction is random: data consists of impressions from conversations – and there is no feedback to a CAD unit to be used in the next design process. Since interactive graphics showed tool paths and tool motions, they made errors immediately apparent, also greatly reducing the number of prototypes.

Using computers to assist in conceptualizing, analyzing and documenting designs, and to convert design information into the actual product, can help in increased productivity and profitability by eliminating the need for paperwork in the design process. In the case of Gamma, this has been well demonstrated through the transition from drafting to designing and manufacturing.

Particular attention in this transition has been paid to the development of tool libraries. All types of tools in use by the firm were defined, along with their supporting structure and links to fabrication processes. This concerned drills, bores, counterbores, countersinks, and also mills, lathes, taps, reams, and the like.

Interactive graphics permitted visual and dimensional checking of the layout and of the tooling design, fixtures and components. As the procedures available with CAD/CAM and associated software developed, tool-to-tool-path associativity prevented accidental omission of required tools. Tool path regeneration was automatically produced as original geometry was updated or path parameters changed.

Profiling boundaries were defined with both planar and non-planar part surfaces, including full control over:

- finish and rough cuts,
- tolerances,
- retracts,
- surface thick,
- part interference testing.

Pocketing boundaries were defined, including control over surface and boundary tolerances and step-over values. The three-axis surface cutting was provided with containment capabilities to all surface edges, to specific minimum–maximum coordinate values, and to multiple user-selected geometry boundaries. A five-axis surface cutting included surface normal approaches and retracts, thick values, and so on.

Tool display gave the operator a visual check on the areas and paths cut by a particular tool. This led to tool path modification capabilities, including:

(1) point addition, deletion, or replacement;
(2) machine control statement insertion and modification.

Lathe path generation was elaborated through machine cutting optimization. Numerical control calculations were executed with double-precision accuracy using floating-point operations on the CAD computer.

With accumulated experience it has been possible to optimize machine motion on surface preparation, also creating user-defined cycles and repeating circular bolt-hole patterns. Software-wise, standard machine control statements were used for controlling scaling, rotation, translation and circular interpolation records, and coolant, spindle and feed rates.

Management well appreciated that CAD/CAM gave the Engineering Department the flexibility and speed necessary to analyze several alternatives and propose higher-quality/lower-cost products. The path had been from drafting to design; from there it led to planning and scheduling information.

Once the final design was established, rapid access to text and data on the materials, parts and processes became critical. Bills of materials and manufacturing instructions were quickly and accurately generated through CAD.

Manufacturing Engineering became increasingly involved, from the product design phase to the prototypes and production. Computer-aided design provided accurate 3-D models and detailed design information, eliminating the potential for error and also reducing the time-scales. This allowed tool designers to group and check visually all the components needed, with their correct dimensions.

As stated in the preceding paragraphs, while interactively generating the required tool paths, the available NC program provided visual feedback from the tool motions, thus giving a dry run on the cutting of the part – including feeds, speeds and tool changes. In turn, this ensured that both prototype models and production runs were held to the design engineering specifications.

Tolerances, finish requirements and treatment processes were verified to protect product quality and enhance reliability. Each one of the steps outlined was important, and though none revolutionized engineering the results obtained permitted a valid approach to problems that have always presented particular challenges and called for efficient solutions.

Integrating plant layout

This is, in a nutshell, the general reaction to the applications perspectives seen during the demonstration of equipment capabilities. Some of the key points, addressed by another company working in civil engineering, have been technical schematics, localization on terrain, 3-D design – architectural, mechanical-oriented, piping – and control of interferences.

Mechnical and civil engineering have many areas of common interest. An important issue in their study has been model mode operation with *layering* used as a segregating tool. The chosen CAD system supported up to 254 layers, each having a homogenous group of information elements For segregation purposes, it was feasible to assign a color by layer. Let's see how the solution goes.

Line fonts are used for topographic presentation. 'Text Notes' can be added in a layout, and they are user-definable. It is also possible to put a foreground drawing or design in the background, then return to it.

As an example of the use to which the layering concept can be put, a public utility company is using CAD to incorporate the existing floor, power and service layouts into an accurate graphics database. The plant, which consists of three major buildings – two shops and one administration – was divided into equal parts with a suitably size for plotting and maintaining the database.

Each part contains approximately 1200 square meters of floor space. The graphic data for each part of the subdivided plant consists of a

- floor layout
- power layout, and
- service layout,

stored as a single file in the graphics database. An accurate database of the entire plant has been the primary goal, providing shop personnel, contractors and engineers with reliable, scaled drawings that can be easily modified. This design function saves considerable lead time for a variety of projects and has also led to a significant degree of standardization.

Floor, power and service layouts are the most important applications. For floor layout purposes, the plan view outlines all equipment and facilities, including bench-mounted capital equipment. Specific information about each item is specified in a call-out and contains name of equipment or facility, identification number and drawing number of applicable installation drawings. Electrical plug-in distribution bus ducts are shown on power layouts and are labeled as such. Power supply runs are shown from the electrical plug-in bus ducts to the point of service. This includes overhead and in-floor power runs.

Power layout runs are also shown from the electrical circuit breaker panels to the point of use. Information contained in a call-out includes square duct or conduit size, number of wires and gauge of wires. Plan views of electrically serviced equipment and facilities show main components, such as control cabinets, main disconnect switches, motors, starters, heating elements, transformers receptacles, and so on. Wall- or column-mounted distribution panels show incoming service, service runs from point of distribution to point of use, and a description of the distribution panel. Standard power symbols are used and stored in a parts library.

Service layouts mainly regard the plan view of equipment and facilities requiring mechanical services. Associated with this equipment is a call-out which contains similar references as in the power layouts. Service loops and supply piping runs from the service loop are shown, along with the service drops to the equipment. Information involves pipe sizes, drop sizes, elevations of horizontal runs, and pitch of runs (if applicable). Return and drain piping from the equipment or facility to the return loop is included along with the same call-outs.

The graphic presentation of the individual layouts within a single file is determined by layering procedures. Line weights and plots of specific layouts are also conditioned by layering, as is the case with floor layouts, power layouts and service layouts. For instance, layers 10 to 19 are reserved for entities which appear on floor layouts only.

Equipment and facilities that do not have electrical or mechanical service requirements are shown on layer 12 and plotted with a medium line weight pen. Fine lines and dashed lines are on layer 11. Layers 9 to 49 are reserved for entities which appear on all three types of layouts. Equipment and facilities that require both mechanical and electrical services are shown on layer 42, and plotted with medium line weight. Fine lines and dashed lines are on layer 41; and so on.

In general, each plant layout file on the interactive graphics system contains the data required to produce a floor layout, power layout and service layout for a single building part or half-part. The plant layout file name consists of the building number, part or half-part number and the issue numbers for the floor layout, power layout and service layout drawings. The files are stored in catalog form with each of the items mentioned being treated as a sub-catalog.

Such examples further document that, through CAD solutions, plant and facilities layouts can be made more easily, faster and more efficiently. Many tangible benefits are the result of a well-developed program: up-to-date plant and facility drawings save time and effort in plant rearrangement or incorporation of new facilities. Changes made to any one of the layouts allows the revision of the remaining layouts with minimum effort.

Revisions may be visually checked and cross-referenced from one layout to another to ensure completeness. This minimizes the time and effort required to generate new drawings. Fast, accurate plots and checkprints are made possible with the use of the appropriate plotter and printer.

Such examples are valid throughout the applications domain, and particularly so when we deal with architectural, steel, piping, concrete, layout, and space planning opportunities. Crucial in each and every case is the systems management facility, including

- logging in and
- file structures

in order to assure the proper user interactivity. Data concerning piping, steel joints, layouts, and macro-operations are resident in system memory, but the end user should

- load the files,
- input the different commands,
- edit to bring into a base file,
- call in the proper grid.

Since input activity consumes the time of the engineering user, we must study carefully ways and means of inputting to the system.

(1) *Plain typing* does not save much time.

(2) *Menus* – through a graphics tablet – can do a better job. Such menus are fully definable by the user, while CAD programs offer prompting and

help. The menu can be assisted through the keyboard, requiring only a very limited number of strokes as opposed to full keyboard entry.

(3) *Functional keyboard* (for instance, 8 × 8 keys). The functions are user-defined through the No. 1 and No. 2 type entry. The control information is normally in English, but other languages can also be employed, as the user desires.

(4) *Tablet symbol recognition* Going through a teach mode, we can create graphs to be handled by the computer through a memory search. Twenty commands go into the system as a start, but the user can create and add his own.

In this way, a steel structure design, through parameter input by graphic tablet, can be presented in 3-D. Training is straightforward: learning to work with the system takes about one week to become interactive; and one month to learn to generate own commands.

Applications are assisted by basic software, with the system structure and file manager transparent to the user/operator – whoever he is. The same is true of access to and usage of the EDB – whether global or local.

Let's return to the fundamentals. As underlined in preceding chapters, every engineer in the department should learn CAD and use it in his daily work. But the system also has some very sophisticated parts and for these we must train people professionally to know more than the typical user.

A demonstration of capabilities for the end user population in working with a CAD system will essentially follow the basic facilities:

(1) taking a comprehensive view on the equipment of the project under study;
(2) breaking the design into primitives;
(3) zooming-in on part of the design;
(4) putting the dimensions on the design;
(5) changing the dimensions of one of the components;
(6) labeling, after selection of names;
(7) automatic spacing of partitions, after defining how many;
(8) taking a front view, top view, side view, down view, front rotated, scaling;
(9) efficiently accessing and enriching the engineering database;
(10) using the plotter and printer to produce drafting documents and bills of materials, as required.

As experience accumulates, more functions can be added to this basic list: for instance, revisions to be done by entering changes into an edit program, thereby updating the component file; making changes to the drawing at the graphics workstation and entering them into the computer; automatic scaling of the drawing to fit onto the drawing border, while not de-scaling the components; and so on. As with all engineering and computer work, development and improvement will continue with the addition of new functions – which, in turn, will call for another set of programs and lead to better know-how and more powerful production features.

The preparatory work

Obtaining the best performance from our investment in CAD means proper preparatory work, personnel training, and construction of a solid understructure. The design and engineering interface should not suffer from the problem of incomplete understanding of capabilities, requirements and constraints.

Neither should there be insufficient data exchange in the applications phases. CAD must be viewed, within engineering, as the opportunity to bring about an aggregate of methods to assist the organization in performing the design and drafting process through the application of interactive computer-based graphics.

Computer-aided design is no longer the isolated applications tool it used to be in the early to mid-1970s. It is the means of linking the engineer to an integrated system that organizes and shares all design capabilities across the company. CAD technology addresses system integration through a series of phases, each of which becomes the foundation for the next technological step.

Such evolutionary development follows the concept that design – civil, electrical, mechanical, and any other – should be considered as a single, unified, composite process in order to achieve overall productivity increases.

A computer-aided engineering development can be viewed as a series of phases, as shown in Figure 7.1. These range from the one-shot, single-design usage, through interdepartmental engineering cooperation,

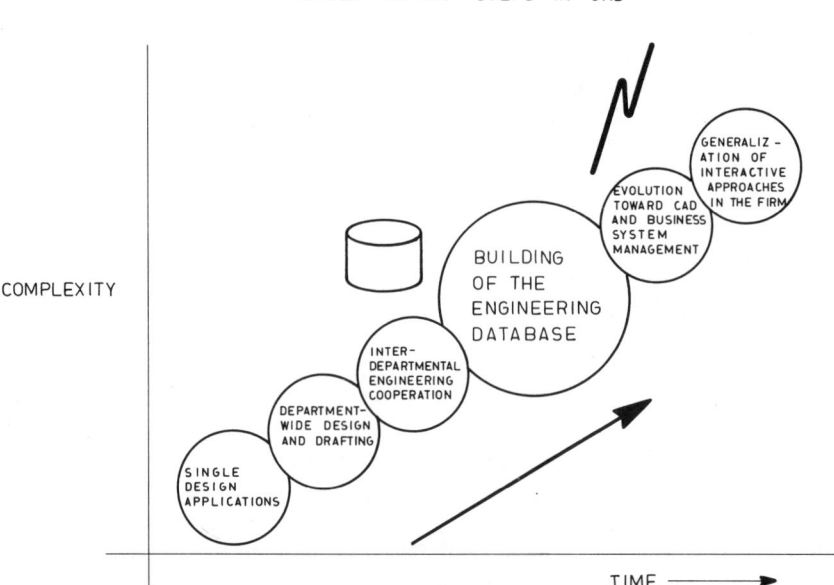

Figure 7.1 The building of an integrated engineering database is mid-range between prehistoric CAD and present-day sophistication. At which level does your company stand?

the building of the engineering database, the datacomm capability through an integration of CAD and business system management, and the generalization of interactive approaches in the firm.

We must offer the engineering end user a well-rounded approach with which he can work in an interactive but also friendly manner. The problem with many solutions in the past was that the people associated with the centralized computer bureaucracy wanted to stay with their machines and their little empires.

Machines are easier to deal with than end users. Adjusting something, debugging code, interpreting numbers – that's what makes many of the centralized computer people tick. Their own technical orientation and excessive specialization is causing them to shun user problems.

That's the sort of spirit which has reigned for 30 long years and has given computers and their specialists a bad name. Much of the current problem is centralization in physical and logical resources, which persists because of the lack of updating in skills and self-confidence by the traditional computer people themselves. They think they have to keep what they do a mystery, to hang on to what they have got. They do not realize that they really have the best position if they modernize their approach to doing business.

There is a new opportunity offered to all – users and specialists alike. Because of the user-level orientation, they no longer have to speak a different language from one another.

For this to be successful, the whole DP mentality must change. As an executive commented: 'Nuts and bolts guys get nowhere. They often stifle their own growth because they don't use analogies that business feels comfortable with.'

The need is pressing because:

- the new generation of managers and younger engineers is increasingly comfortable with computers as an integral part of day-to-day operations;
- they expect to use this tool to monitor more closely their work and to aid decision-making and/or design work.

Logically, everything comes together in information services and we have to look at it from this angle. We must aim steadily to increase the people involved with information systems at the user end.

To do so, the best way open to us is the use of intelligent workstations, local area networks, file servers, and online links to mainframes. That is, personal computers with graphic tablets hooked by communications to a more powerful CAD/CAM resource able to process standard software and do number-crunching when necessary.

Once we set up the environment where end users do the lion's share of the communication, it spreads like a brushfire through the organization. The message is passed very rapidly from one user to another, and they all want to get rid of their paperwork and build their own computer-based facilities.

Facilities at the WS level should certainly involve a dual soft-copy capability:

(1) scratchpad,
(2) reporting,

with an optional low-cost hard-copy facility. Typically, such a facility should be microcomputer-based: one personal computer per designer, executive, or other professional.

Workstations must intercommunicate through a local area network, the latter having:

- a local database,
- gateway(s) to the CAD and, as the need dictates, the mini or mainframe.

Connections must be decided on the basis of existing applications software and file residence as, for instance, bill of materials.

These choices must definitely consider the wider strategic issues facing the firm. A CAD implementation is only part of this broader perspective of company needs, for which information systems support must be provided.

For, nearly two decades, the trap many computer managers have found themselves in has been that they have been trying to design and develop computer systems without knowing how their company is doing business. Whether we talk of CAD or other systems, their implementation will be more successful the better the understanding of the business philosophy and objectives.

Computer-aided design is a good example of the movement of computers out of the predominantly financial type of processing and across the whole business. Thus computers achieve a better visibility – a fact instrumental in changing the DP budget from just another overhead to a key part of corporate plans for growth and survival.

Evidently, direct user applications support must have the accord of management if it is to succeed. Experience demonstrates, however, that as soon as top management begins to realize that this is technically possible, and that other firms have done it, this accord is easy to obtain. There is a whole set of techniques that relate to self-support activities, the best example being applications.

Getting end users and management to specify their own objectives, their own IS requirements and their own design needs helps tremendously in obtaining better results. It also helps to draw out the knowledge of the specifics of information requirements which end users have – and which typical computer professionals do not possess.

These developments will not just happen. They call for a strategic planning approach, able to analyze the company's interactive, datacomm, and databasing technology, and steer it in a way to obtain cost-benefit. With CAD implementation, a company requires substantial investments in systems, human resources, and structure.

Productivity gains are dependent on many factors: management style, work procedures, and personnel. Not only the obvious fall-out but also basic quality improvements, such as the reduction of errors, must be considered. The by-products of CAD, such as production of a bill of materials and the sharing of information among engineering disciplines, must be brought into perspective. And all parts of a company's operations must be made aware of the new facilities.

Chapter 8

Product quality and engineering performance

We have said that product quality and engineering productivity are the two pillars on which rests management's interest in computer-aided design (CAD). The portability of information and its accessibility are the key reasons for the extension from CAD to CAM (Computer-aided manufacturing).

Reference has also been made to the fact that computer-aided engineering (CAE) is regarded as the integration of analysis and design into one computer-based, well-knit system. While in many instances analysis is not integrated into the design cycle, with experience we come to appreciate that this is how it needs to be.

For any product the continuity in text and data from specifications to production leads both to higher quality and to reduced costs. Yet machines alone, though necessary, are not enough. Procedures and norms are needed for transferring product definitions:

- to serve as input to the production system;
- to allow the exchange of information within the firm, and also to and from suppliers and customers;
- to provide long-term recoverable storage of text and data in the engineering database.

Engineering means analytical studies, and analytical studies rest on documentation. The role of CAD/CAM should thus be seen not only as a computer-based design tool but also as the means to propagate increasingly precise information into all phases of product design, manufacturing engineering, and a robotics environment.

This implies the existence of a standard for communicating drawing and geometric information between CAD/CAM systems, and between suppliers and customers utilizing different graphics software and databases, to produce

- a format that permits the communication of basic geometry, drafting, and structural entities,
- an open-ended facility able to facilitate the communication of new material – while
- minimizing the burden imposed on pre- and post-processing, and
- gathering input from the interested community of CAD/CAM.

Though these goals will be easily recognized as those of the Intitial Graphics Exchange Specification (IGES), it should also be appreciated that their implementation imposes a significant amount of preparation which should characterize the use of CAD/CAM. Machines alone, though necessary, are not in themselves the solution; this always depends upon the amount of work we do while preparing for the use of machines.

Creating and managing the engineering database

We have been speaking of the preparatory work necessary in preparing to implement computer-aided design. Such procedural design work does not come packaged on any hardware system, but every engineering department has the basic experience to see this prerequisite through. The approach should be analytical, with two aspects characterizing the procedure:

(1) What we do in a design? The premise here is that a drawing is a lot more than most people think it is.
(2) How do we manage the engineering database? Which are the essential requirements?

As with military weapons systems, the one-at-a-time or one-shot solutions are of no value to CAD/CAM. The keyword is continuity. From a design we must be able to derive lots of essential information leading to a dynamically maintained bill of materials – but also opening the way to the integration of the design, which is the present object, with other designs in the EDB. The same is true of its parametric manipulation.

To derive full benefit from a system, CAD has to do a lot more than drawing. Also, a drawing has to be interpreted by other computer-based systems and not just by humans – whether engineers, draftsmen, or manufacturing construction people.

This concept starts at the level of the fundamental characteristic of any project: there is much more to a line than there seems to be. Let us take as an example the elementary electrical diagram in Figure 8.1.

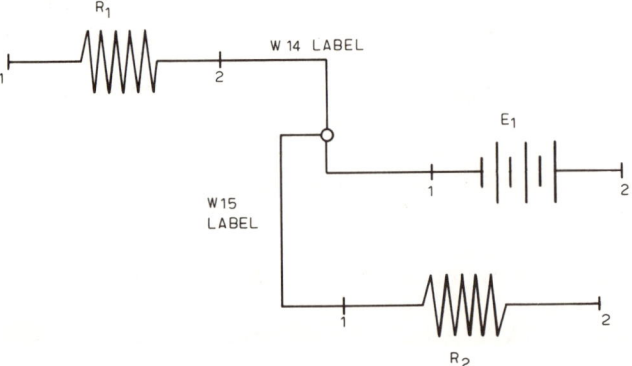

Figure 8.1 Even an elementary electrical diagram can benefit from a CAD solution. The text tells why

This is a very simple electrical diagram. Yet there are many more associations in this picture than appear at first sight. If CAD is worth its salt, resistors, capacitors, line labels and lists must be done by computer. Essentially, this means the need to automate all processes connected with the design. And this leads to the creation of a consistent data structure. A data structure is made up of elements:

(1) text elements;
(2) lines (the primitive element is an 'open polygon');
(3) primitive drawing elements; little pictures; icons.

The essential issue is to uniquely identify the elements holding basic information; then to decide what we should do with the resulting information elements. Text, lines, prims have attributes and other properties which are specific to them. For instance, a prim is a length, a line, a picture.

Having established the character of an IE, the next question is: How are all the associations represented? The answer can be given when we know the basic explicit structure: this may, for instance, be a tree structure.

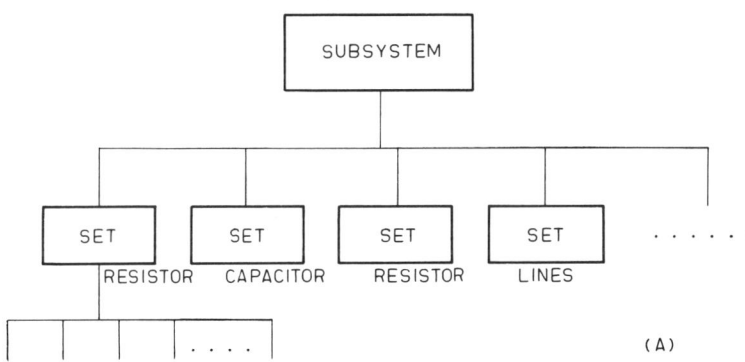

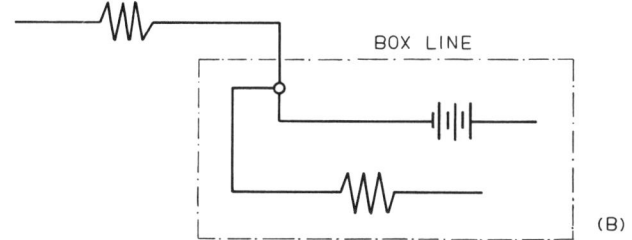

Figure 8.2 The information elements (IE) involved in a CAD study may reside in a hierarchical, networking or relational database. Both explicit and implicit associations are advantageous for interactive approaches

Let us make the hypothesis that a hierarchical approach characterizes the structure. What stands at the top is the sub-system we are about to design (Figure 8.2a). Such a sub-system will be composed of parts (or sets); each set will also have its component parts. Integrating upwards, the sub-system under design is part of a larger system, or of another sub-system, and so on.

The very essence of an engineering database rests on this notion. The EDB is nothing more than the total of the information elements composing it. The procedures for IE manipulation and the computer-based supports expand this total well beyond the sum of its individual parts.

In reaching this aim of an expansion in facilities, the description and structural organization, while necessary, are not enough. We also need the concepts of association and listing. When all elements are defined, the structural approach helps to obtain:

(1) the association characterizing the drawing and its parts (sets);
(2) the listing of the parts themselves.

Let us recall that the parts of any system or sub-system under study must be defined and stored in the EDB. As the latter builds up, the chances are they will be in the EDB from other CAD projects. What is then necessary is a software routine able to scan the drawing and establish the parts list.

Another basic point concerns the man–information communications aspects. Here, the challenge is to make the CAD system work fast enough for interactive approaches. An answer can be obtained through a dual solution, the use of *explicit* and *implicit* associations. Explicit associations are of a given, well-established type: for instance, tree structure or line structure. Implicit associations have to be searched for. Box lines or matching texts exemplify this approach (Figure 8.2b).

Box lines can be labeled and searched thereafter; a matching text capability will associate, for example, all wires labeled 5 V. Depending on the power of the software available to manipulate the EDB, such association can span different drawings.

The points just made support the basic principle we outlined at the beginning: if we look at a drawing we must be able to infer what it means, and it should be possible to do so whether we 'read' that drawing by human eye or by machine.

Different approaches can, of course, be taken; one of them requires no explicit structure. That is what the relational database is all about; but relational solutions are not yet fully supported in data processing at the current state of the art, with the exception of some query languages. It will take some time before we have relational solutions in CAD/CAM.

What are currently supported are features of database management systems (DBMS). The IE type in the EDB can be used in a number of ways, enabling the system to process it through the use of a data definition language (DDL) put at the user's disposal.

Quite simply, the approach works as follows. Every information element has stored how it should be drawn: color is one manifestation of this; shape is another. The DDL contribution is to say which elements are allowed within a clam (or set). Its three basic functions are:

(1) List of element types. This is necessary to tell if the system knows the type or not; whether the IE looked for is allowed or not.
(2) Which type is the IE we need? For instance, is it text or line? What are its characteristics?
(3) In which context may it be used? This provides both assistance to the end user and control. Can the IE be used within a symbol, dimension or text?

A man–information interaction must characterize the process, and this is shown in Figure 8.3. Significant, though not always appreciated, is the fact that once this streamlined approach is taken other important uses can also result, for instance the bill of materials. Both product quality and engineering productivity depend highly on the ability to extend the design perspectives without appreciable further effort.

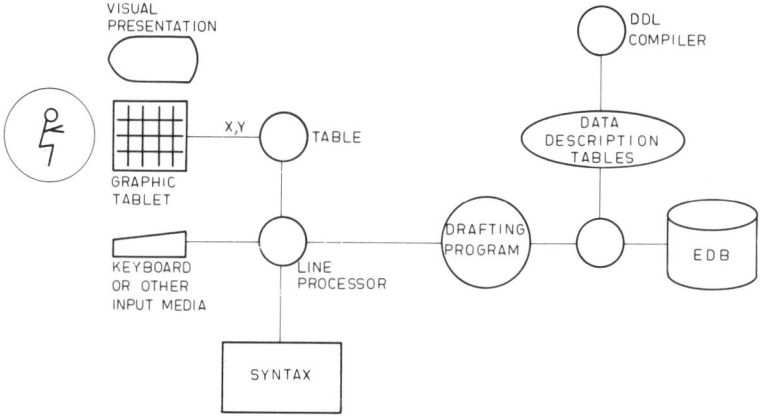

Figure 8.3 CAD facilities should be designed around a man–information dialog. The bridges to bill of materials, quality control files etc. should be unobstructed to the user

BOM requires the existence of a property file able to provide, for each part, name, type and description.

The mechanism will typically handle identification/classification numbers; associated text; properties linking this part to other parts and/or expressing issues of interest beyond the pure design stage. Among the properties may be, for instance, an on/off switch, used as means of reflecting design conditions.

A data extraction capability should assure tallying, sort/merge and rearranging features. Other properties may also be called for, such as accounting information and the drawing's update.

Since the BOM is the result of engineering design, the CAD software should proceed in sequential steps reflecting the basic procedure being adopted. Typically, after the design phase is completed:

● a 2-D drafting system will produce a set of drawings;
● these will be handled by resident software routines to produce a *text file*.

As an intermediate procedural step, the text file is an unsorted listing of all part numbers and quantities in drawings. Processing through text format (a control file) the system should produce a BOM complete report.

The latter must be sorted and formatted, ready for use. As Figure 8.4 outlines, a CAD-oriented data dictionary (or catalog routine) must be online to help in controlling and in formatting. It should contain a complete description of what is in the text file.

A BOM PROCEDURE

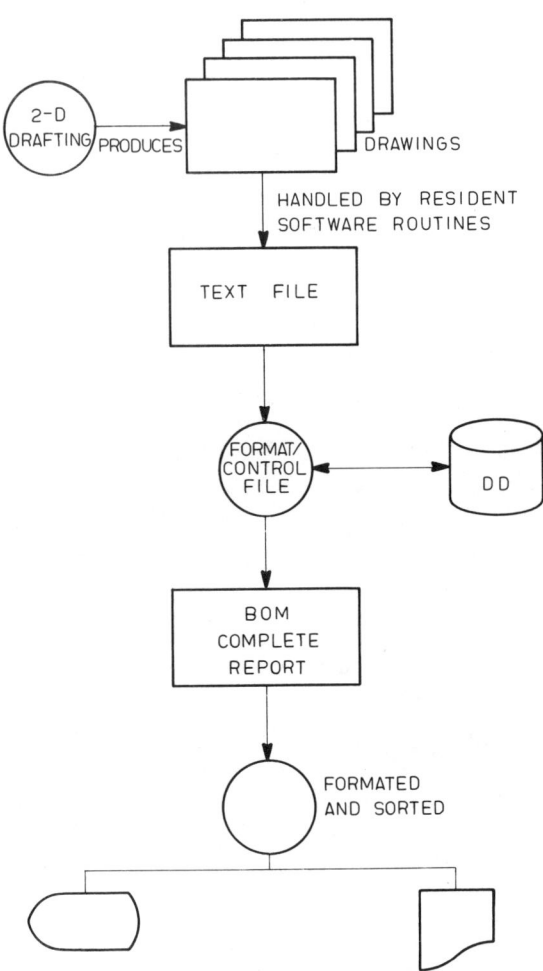

Figure 8.4 Computer-aided design is indivisible from a bill of materials implementation. Design specifications, design diagrams and BOM should be part of the engineering database

Furthermore, the system and its implementation must be flexible enough to allow the complete report to be inserted back in the drawing, if necessary. This will permit a two-way approach to the handling of the bill of materials, making it feasible to all authorized parties to communicate with the EDB.

Modeling

By definition, a model is an idealized representation of a real situation. It can be physical (such as a scale model) or algorithmic, hence logical. In either case, its goal is

(1) to help in improving product quality, by making it possible to pre-operate a product or system; and
(2) in contributing towards engineering productivity, by simplifying the job but also by flashing out errors, omissions and inconsistencies in design.

Modeling is based on analysis; that is, on a similarity of properties without identity. When analogous systems are found to exist, observations and measurements made on the one system can be used to study the other – including the prediction of its properties and behavior.

An important point is that the product (or system) and the model under study do not need to be analogous in every respect. What is critical is that they exhibit analogies on the variables and functions which are of interest. This reference to analogies should not be confused with the type of the model, which can be analog or digital.

Scale models are physical and they work on the analog principle. Logical (algorithmic) approaches may be either analog or digital – and both rest on analogies governed by:

- attributes,
- measurements,
- parameters.

The existence of these analogies (whether analog or digital), and their description by means of equations, sets the stage for a computer-based study of what may otherwise be unrelated phenomena. This is of significance in three ways:

(1) It helps us visualize the behavior of unfamiliar systems and parts, on the basis of familiar ones.
(2) It assists in setting up convenient, and often inexpensive, calculating devices simulating the characteristics of the system under study.
(3) It assists in ordering our approach towards engineering problems, which grow increasingly in complexity as the fund of scientific knowledge and experience accumulates.

The rough approximations used in the past in engineering design are no longer satisfactory. Modern practice makes stringent demands on materials, processes, performance results – and on people. But analytical approaches are impossible without advances in computers, mathematics, modeling – and in the rational organization of our thoughts.

The goals of computer-aided engineering, to:

- reduce design cycle time,
- cut costs while improving quality,
- help the designer understand quick modifications,
- assist in estimating production runs and specials.
- serve in debugging and the reduction of errors.

can be best served if we have an overall approach and we are able to express it (then implement it) in a concise, comprehensive form. Figure 8.5 provides a structural solution. Any CAD project also needs a basic philosophy and corresponding methodologies.

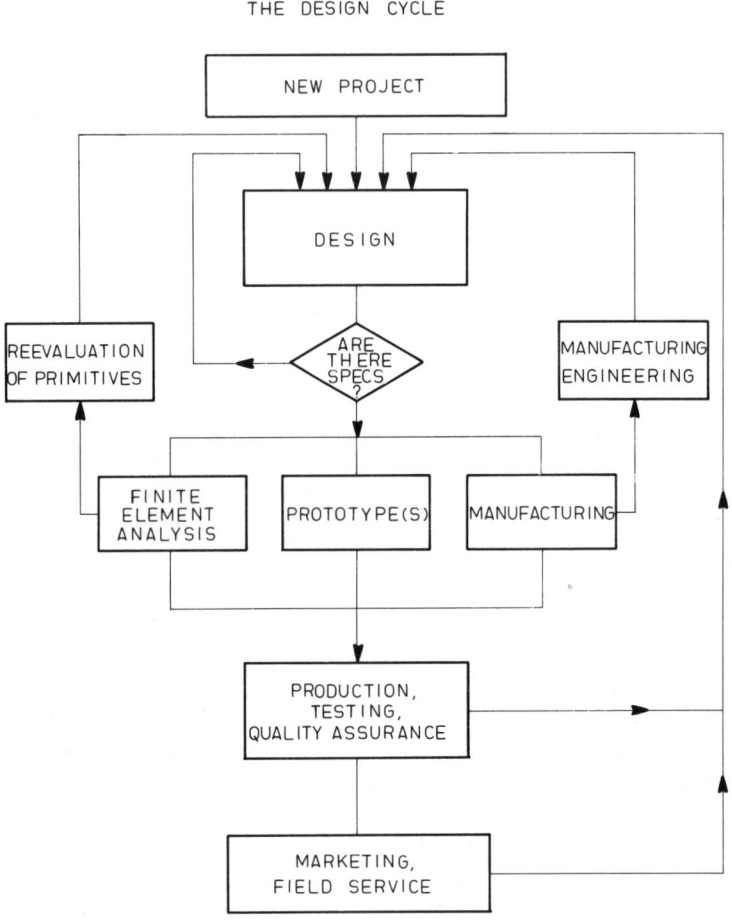

THE DESIGN CYCLE

DESIGN IS THE PIVOT POINT IN THE FEEDBACK

Figure 8.5 The design cycle of a product does not start in the laboratory. It starts in the market place. This should be reflected in CAD implementation

Let us take as reference general modeling for solid design. The philosophy here is to make a geometric model, while providing for the interfaces. Then comes the specialization.

For instance, within the perspective of mechanical engineering and associated drafting, the aim is to give, through computer-based approaches:

(1) descriptive geometry;
(2) dimensional analysis: clearance, interface, location, fit;
(3) definitions of finite elements;
(4) an interaction with the EDB and its upkeep, including annotations;
(5) drafting and technical illustration;
(6) ability to follow the manufacturing needs in a comprehensive way;
(7) service capability, for after-sales/maintenance purposes and for reliability support through remote diagnostics.

This fairly broad range of implementation suggests the wisdom of integrating, then modeling, not only the more classical design characteristics but also BOM, materials take-off and fabrication perspectives – all the way to delivery. However, to reach that level we need to start from the fundamentals.

The fundamentals in engineering design begin with the handling of line primitives: straight line, arc, conic, spline, and their combinations. From 1-D lines we move, in terms of modeling, to 2-D surfaces. There are three basic types of surface – whether plain or irregular:

● ruled surface,
● tabulated cylinder,
● surface of revolution.

The next step is handling solids, and there exist two approaches:

● surfaces enclosing a space, or
● building blocks.

The latter define solid primitives, then build through boolean (logical) operations.

Solid modeling essentially means representation of 3-D geometric information in an unambiguous and complete form. Other solutions we will be considering do not exactly support this approach. Wire frame has its limitations, while surfaces may or may not be fully described.

The aim with solid design is to support an integrated engineering database with interactive capability. This means that we can work in solids but also in subsets: wire frame; surface; and in 2-D representations if we so choose. (2½-D is a rather corrupt expression coming from numerical control of machine tools.)

The reference to *interactivity* must be properly underlined. It means that the designer has a step-by-step feedback of everything he performs, through direct access to the EDB and short response times. This provides a display flexibility:

● wire frame look,
● mesh surface,
● edge picture with hidden lines removed,
● shaded picture (color or monochrome).

Interactivity also means *ease of use*. Sweep operations should permit the user to go, for instance, from boundary representation to end result both more quickly and more safely than in a batch, remote-batch or classical time-sharing mode.

Sweeping is a basic reference in modeling as it permits one to define a section, then work along this section to produce the corresponding solid (Figure 8.6). Another facility is *deformation* (twicking). It sees to it that, if we have a boundary representation in the EDB, we can take it and deform it to fit our design goal.

TO DO THIS

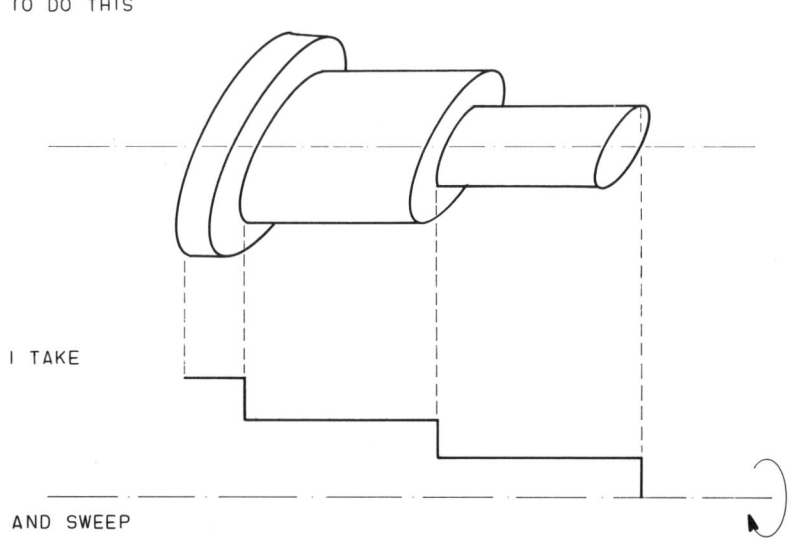

I TAKE

AND SWEEP

Figure 8.6 The CAD facility which we have availabe should satisfy a growing number of design requirements, including modeling. Sweeping is an example

These are examples of possibilities we can realize if we have the right methodology and are equipped with the proper software. Sizing the information in the EDB to fit our design aims permits all parts (and graphical data) to be presented in the right size, handled in an effective manner, and used in the final product design without repetitive efforts or accumulated discrepancies.

In conclusion, when we talk of modeling approaches in engineering design, key topics involve:

- how models are built;
- the purpose they serve;
- the engineering disciplines for which they are useful;
- how computational tools can be of help.

Both continuous and discrete event modeling must be considered, along with model structure identification techniques and deductive procedures. Both a tool and (at times) a limitation is the availability of modeling software constructs.

A fundamental though not always appreciated principle is that in CAD we should aim to answer 90 per cent of our needs through software packages. That is why the emphasis on ready-made software is so important, right from the initial choice.

A parametric system

To attain product quality, engineers have tended to heavily rely on direct experimentation to obtain numerical results. Yet we all know from experience that, though desirable, such experimentation is costly, slow, and at times impractical or even impossible in terms of measurements needed, as feedbacks.

Other ways have to be found, one of the best being the indirect experimental approaches we are describing. Accuracy, speed and use-factors relating both to product quality and engineering productivity point that way. The approach must, however, be methodological. Since an analogy is based on the similarity in form of algorithms governing the design, a vital first step is to prove that the analogy truly exists.

Once the analogy has been established and the algorithmic description made, other concepts come into play to enhance productivity. One of them is the parametric system. Its use rests on the premise that the physical systems with which the engineer gets involved are usually characterized by a distribution of properties which can be:

- discrete (best expressed in a digital form). or
- continuous (the subject of an analog implementation).

The method of solution often depends on the type of equation involved, but if we are careful enough in its production the incorporation of key parameters will allow us to go well beyond the classical sense of experimentation. It may involve the ability to check for missing dimensions in a design as well as for contradictory measurements, which do not add up to a coherent total.

Problems addressed by a computer-based parametric system may involve any or all of the following areas:

(1) *Families of parts.* If we assemble components out of a library in the EDB, the chances are that they will vary parametrically.

(2) *Design changes.* Quite often design changes and updates center on one or two parameters. Much more can therefore be gained if it is possible to describe a given system, product or component in a parametric sense.

(3) *Mechanisms.* The definition and movement of a mechanism can be generated by a parametric system. The same is true of rotation, zoom and all normal screen manipulations.

(4) *Tolerancing.* This is one of the most commonly felt needs, as all engineering designs, and subsequent drawings, involve dimensioning and many of them call for setting tolerances.

A parametric system can permit parameterizing from the drawing. It can, for instance help define the intersections of the construction lines, as we go on drawing the part; an experimentation on the consistency of dimensioning definitions; and the appropriate abort action in case of inconsistencies.

A complete tolerancing system can go much further than these references. Its kernel should involve the ability to check one dimension against another, and to check for tolerances (Figure 8.7). Three value-added features can be defined:

- tolerance analysis,
- tolerance build-up,
- tolerance statistics.

TOLERANCING SOFTWARE

KERNEL

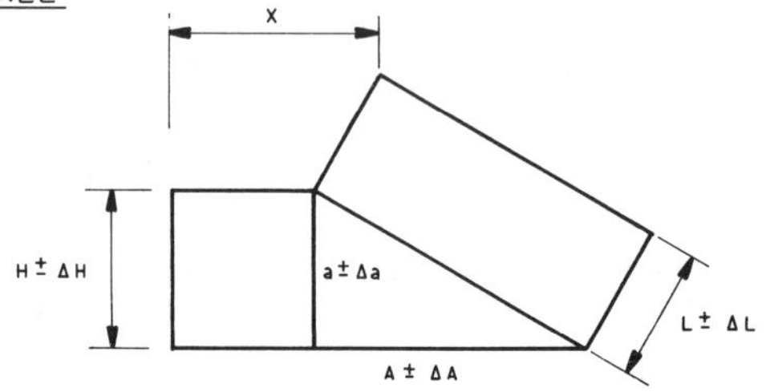

1. WHAT HAPPENS TO X ?

2. SET VALUES TO TOLERANCES

A + ΔA

H + ΔH

L + ΔL

a + Δa

AND EXPLORE WHAT HAPPENS TO X (UP TO SEVERAL HUNDRED DIMENSIONS)

VALUE ADDED:

1. TOLERANCE ANALYSIS

2. TOLERANCE BUILD-UP

3. TOLERANCE STATISTICS

Figure 8.7 Tolerancing software is important for quality control purposes. Expert Systems in CAD can offer valuable assistance in this area (see also Chapter 13)

In the value-added side of the software, *tolerance analysis* permits the study, variable by variable, of all the others in the product or system. This is a prerequisite to a matrix form presentation and subsequent parametric tolerance calculation.

Tolerance build-up permits the study and analysis of the *worst case*. Typically, the computer-based system should be producing a table with design dimensions and their tolerances. It should also allow the examination of the product's sensitivity to changes in dimensions and tolerances.

Tolerance statistics essentially refer to *variances*. Their importance can best be understood if we recall that often we design products or systems too precisely, setting tolerances much smaller than they need be. This increases the cost of the product.

The premise with this add-on parametric feature is that if we can incorporate into CAD the concept of a 'tolerance variable', then we can successfully experiment on the proper tolerance(s) through a statistical analysis of variance.

As CAD/CAM systems acquire experience and get more sophisticated, we can use both the parametric features and other qualities to ease man–information communications, improving both the product quality and the productivity of the design engineers. An example is the ability of injecting color to help in

- interference checking;
- parametric variations;
- the control of aggregates by drawing different objects in different colors.

Thus, while observing drafting conventions at all times, we can use modern technology to avoid redundant data, edit out ambiguous expressions and make it feasible to interpret automatically the content of design drawings and their specs.

Though necessary and welcome notions, product quality and engineering productivity are not abstract issues, to be obtained through wishful thinking or the simple acquisition of equipment. A steady, well-directed effort is necessary, which, apart from hardware and software tools, involves a medium to long range perspective starting with the rational organization of the engineering database and progressing through modeling toward more complex subjects such as solids and experimentation on tolerances.

Chapter 9

Assuring greater productivity

While greater engineering productivity is a goal sought by every CAD/CAM user, as stressed from the first chapter of this book, few organizations establish the right infrastructure to support it. This infrastructure starts with management's attitude toward CAD, as we will see in the first section, and continues through an impressive array of issues.

These issues range from personal training to the avoidance of the common practice of throw-away software. The proper procedural preparation will see to it that in topography, for instance, design data observes the principle of 'one entry, many uses', all the way from computation or digitization into complete land property maps.

An advisable procedural approach, in this particular example, would be to show the ground plan graphically on the terminal screen, effecting subsequent operations through simple commands: correction by deletion, insertion and change of points, and by matching of sheet edges: completing the drawing, its buildings and their cadastral numbers; and storing the completed plan.

Increased productivity should characterize the complete work cycle and guarantee high reliability through: approaches subject to monitoring; representation of information through interactive dialog; rapid access to randomly stored text and data; and significant user convenience. CAD should totally obviate the need for the manual preparation of maps, as far as our example is concerned.

As always within the perspective of the engineering productivity issue, CAD should answer not only problems connected with text editing and data analysis, but also those connected with adequate representation for the end-user. It should also take into account the fact that bottlenecks are likely to arise whenever graphic data have to be evaluated if there are no standardized procedures to rely on and the prevailing procedures involve time-consuming manual interventions. Mixing manual and automated procedures is always counter-productive.

Management's viewpoint

The Beta company we considered in Chapter 6 presents an excellent example of proper preparation in order to reach productivity goals.

Starting with some fundamental information elements to build up a complete CAD system, it expanded these into a network covering its area of operation. From the beginning emphasis was placed on management's viewpoint.

The network of basic functions was established as experience with CAD accumulated. A member of the Board remarked: 'Until you have worked with the CAD system for one year you *can't* say anything definite about savings and about quantitative results. It's a matter of faith. But with the proper organization, that faith pays dividends.'

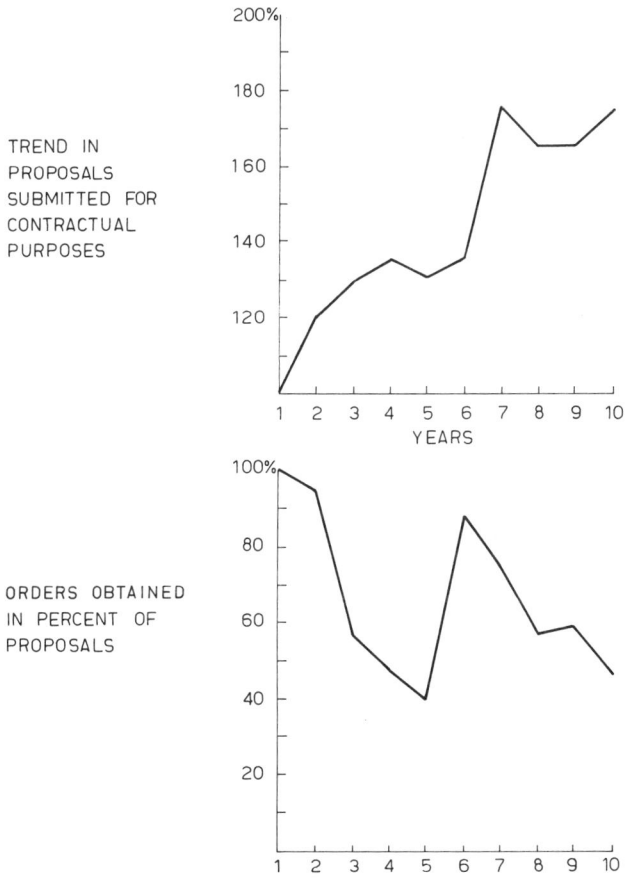

Figure 9.1 The number of proposals being requested (and submitted) is on the increase while the percentage approvals tends to drop. CAD and expert systems are very important in increasing productivity to face both trends

The urgent need for productivity enhancements and the financial advantage to the properly organized CAD user are demonstrated by two diagrams. Figure 9.1 spans a ten-year period in terms of the number of proposals made for obtaining business contracts and the decreasing probability of getting contracts relative to the number of proposals.

In simple terms, this means toughening competition. As a result, either the proposal preparation must be automated to save significantly on labor costs, or the financial position of the company will suffer. The curve of the commercial expense involved in contracting must be bent, without impairing business. The use of CAD by sales engineers has this as an objective, and it is complementary to the utilization of CAD for design proper, which aims to improve productivity and help control costs.

Figure 9.2 distinguishes between the accumulated *product (investment) cost* during the five key phases of a contracted project:

(1) sales and administrative overhead,
(2) planning and control,
(3) development,
(4) purchasing,
(5) production,

and the *financial commitments* being made in each of these phases.

In the first phase, that of the sales engineering effort (to which is added for accounting purposes the company overhead), the financial commitments made represent a meager 2 per cent of the cost of the product – while sales and administration activity consumes 20 per cent of the budget.

Planning and control eats up 5 per cent of the budget – but its impact on the company's financial commitment in terms of the end product is an impressive 13 per cent. So a tough P&C policy can produce major savings.

The star performer is, of course, development and engineering design. Here the impact of the commitments being made reaches a very impressive 70 per cent of the end cost of the product or process – while design and engineering consume only 10 per cent of the budget. This underlines the fact that results must be as much qualitative as quantitative: an astutely used CAD installation will focus much more on the 70 per cent than on the 10 per cent.

Another way of looking at the same issue is to say that while manufacturing usually 'makes the cost', the financial commitment has long been established in the design phase: the better the engineering work is assisted and controlled, the tighter the budget and the more profitable the results.

This point again stresses the need for preparation. As a senior executive remarked: 'A necessary precondition for implementing CAD is the proper classification and identification of all machines, assemblies, and pieces. In this company we were very lucky that we had already done the classification work prior to introducing CAD.'

The classification/identification scheme is based on three pillars:

(1) The classification number, organized in matrix form with families, groups and classes.
(2) The identification number, which closely resembles the <basic code> structure (see Chapter 11).
(3) The departmental code with drawing indication.

The classification (MC, or machine code) is *universal* and reflects a unique way of coding. It emphasizes 'Part Family', and as a result it is related to each machine or part, not on the drawing. This code is always

115

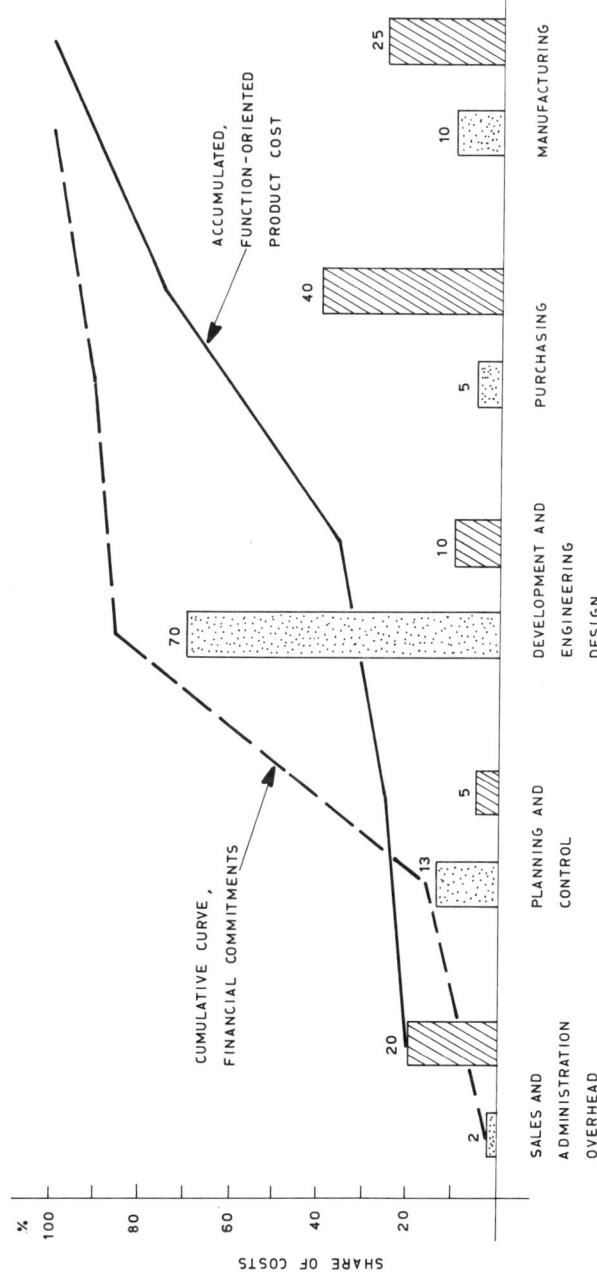

Figure 9.2 There is a discrepancy between accumulated product costs and financial commitments. Management can capitalize on this fact by looking at it as an opportunity to use high technology

stored in the computer, and it can be retrieved interactively when necessary. It is not carried on the drawing.

Importantly, the implementation of the classification code is a standard departmental responsibility. But its design and upkeep is a function of the Standards Department, just like the ID number, which is seven digits long plus a one-digit index to indicate drawing change. This suffix accounts for variations. It is therefore centrally kept and it is also universal. The ID code appears on the drawing (bottom right corner) just below the Drawing Code. The latter is also a seven-digit number, made up of three parts:

XXX.XX.XX

where: XXX department number

   XX drawing group or plant part – different by department

   XX sub-drawing number; machine group or sub-assembly.

Let us recapitulate. The total system is composed of three parts. Two of them, the classification and identification codes, are universal in the organization and are kept up by the Standards Department. The department/drawings code is run by the particular responsible department but it must have a one-to-one correspondence to CC and ID.

An important company-wide policy is that each part must have one and only one number; and that for each part there is a unique number to be assigned. This leads to efficient handling of the bill of materials. The BOM contains:

(1) Drawing number
(2) <bc><s>
(3) Clear text and dimensions
(4) Observations
(5) Material specs
(6) Quantity
(7) CC

While the engineering database is being developed, the draftsman fills the sheet manually and it subsequently goes to data entry for keying to disk. But with CAD all this is done automatically. Graphic tablets are used effectively in the CAD environment: the parts are in matrix form with graphic presentation. Each symbol in this matrix has the CC, <bc><s>, and design number references. Figures 9.3 presents similar classification work I did nearly 15 years ago with another engineering and manufacturing company.

This polished organization ensures that, even from the drawing, we can arrange BOM processing. In the typical drawing, all parts have a 'Position number' which uniquely identifies the part. Correspondingly, the EDB includes a shop drawing description.

As Figure 9.4 indicates, through the unique part number and the shop drawing description which are in the EDB, each aggregate is fully identified in terms of its assemblies and components. Subsequently, the BOM is produced through CAD.

The computer can get at the dimensions, materials, and so on, relieving the designer of the routine work. Through the Classification Code (CC)

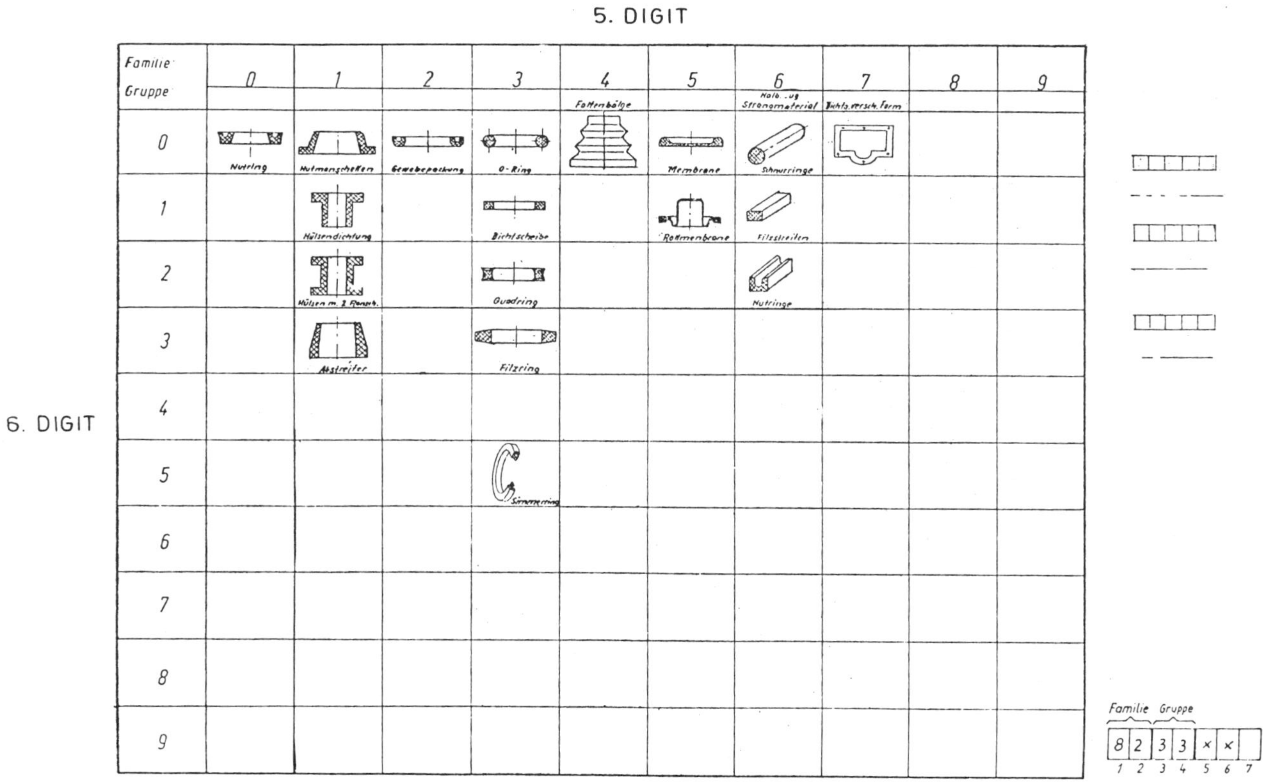

5. DIGIT

6. DIGIT

Familie Gruppe

Figure 9.3 A classification of parts done in a taxonomical way helps bring order to the engineering drawings. Fifteen years ago this was performed manually. Today it can be done by expert systems

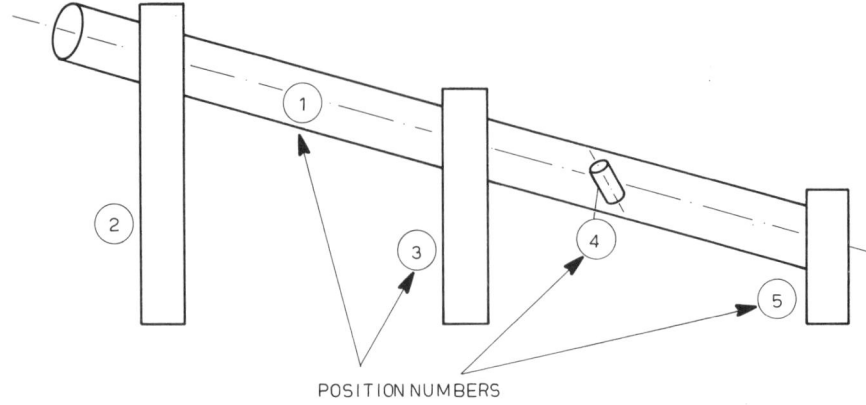

POSITION NUMBERS

EACH POSITION NUMBER HAS A UNIQUE
<bc> <s>, CC AND DESCRIPTION DATA IN
THE EDB

X ———————— X	
DEPARTMENT / DRAWING NUMBER	
< bc > < s >	
X ———————X	

Figure 9.4 The classification of drawings should be made with reference to aggregates (complete systems). In the classification, the latter must constitute a family of their own

can be found groups of parts, and all parts in that group. This is accomplished at different levels of reference. It is a hierarchical structure, with a taxonomic organization highly dependent on the classification code.

CAD productivity: real or imaginary?

We have said that if we wish to measure the productivity effects of a CAD system, we must prepare for this task. Such effects would typically comprise:

- tangible elements that can be quantified, and
- intangible factors difficult to monitor.

The first group, the tangible elements and the associated productivity measurements, is mainly associated with the rate of production or the overall cost savings. The higher quality of the final product, the increased satisfaction of the end user, and the ability to design a product that could not be practically designed manually are included in the second group.

As far as the first group is concerned, CAD productivity should be defined as the *quantity of work done for a given cost*. Manual productivity must be recorded and CAD productivity compared with it.

- Productivity ratios of the manual method versus CAD can be calculated for the volume of output, and cost of production.

- Productivity ratios for products that cannot be designed without CAD are impossible to measure – but, for work classically done.
- Productivity improvement ratios of output, quality and cost can be computed, using a certain point in time as a reference base.

Management references such as effective use of resources, employee and customer satisfaction should be reported on a scheduled basis. Such issues, however, cannot be as rigorous as quantity, quality and cost.

The impact of CAD on quality must be given the proper weight. Computer-aided design has shown great quality improvements in many areas, but success in product quality issues requires the integration of approaches among many departments. Management must be aware of the capabilities of CAD in terms of resulting product quality prior to obtaining tangible results.

Measurements – of whichever type – must take into consideration the level of application, in the relative scale of CAD sophistication the organization finds itself at a given moment (Figure 9.5). The simplest solution, along a scale of increasing complexity, will be that of a local design graphics system, which helps to display and analyze some engineering solutions in order to reduce time for visualization.

The more interactive this tool is, the better it provides the engineer with the flexibility to study the different facets of his problem. An approach of greater complexity is that of a design graphics system which helps to integrate some typical design processes in order to reduce analysis and development.

- Such a system may consist of interactive color graphics, and a local database providing module-to-module exchange.
- Commonality and standardization are achieved through the design concepts of shared data, a modular program library, and selective control.
- With communicating capabilities added to the last point, information generated by one system is available to other areas via databases accessible through interactive terminals.

The effects of this approach will be greater the better able the engineering database is to provide an exchange of information for design engineers via a company-wide structure containing related data. Such a system can effectively unify design and major manufacturing functions, with part descriptions built step by step using graphics systems.

Once the part geometry is released, designed, and transferred to the EDB it can be accessed by different functions in a way that is both interactive and continuous. This leads to a CAD network: a system which allows a number of computers (usually minis) to be integrated together in order to best meet the application needs of the engineering users.

In this environment, users would get quick response for interactive local processing, accessing a host computer for processing power, data exchange, storage, and retrieval. CAD networking includes installation-to-installation data links supporting computer communication not only among designers but also to customers and suppliers. The customers can receive

120

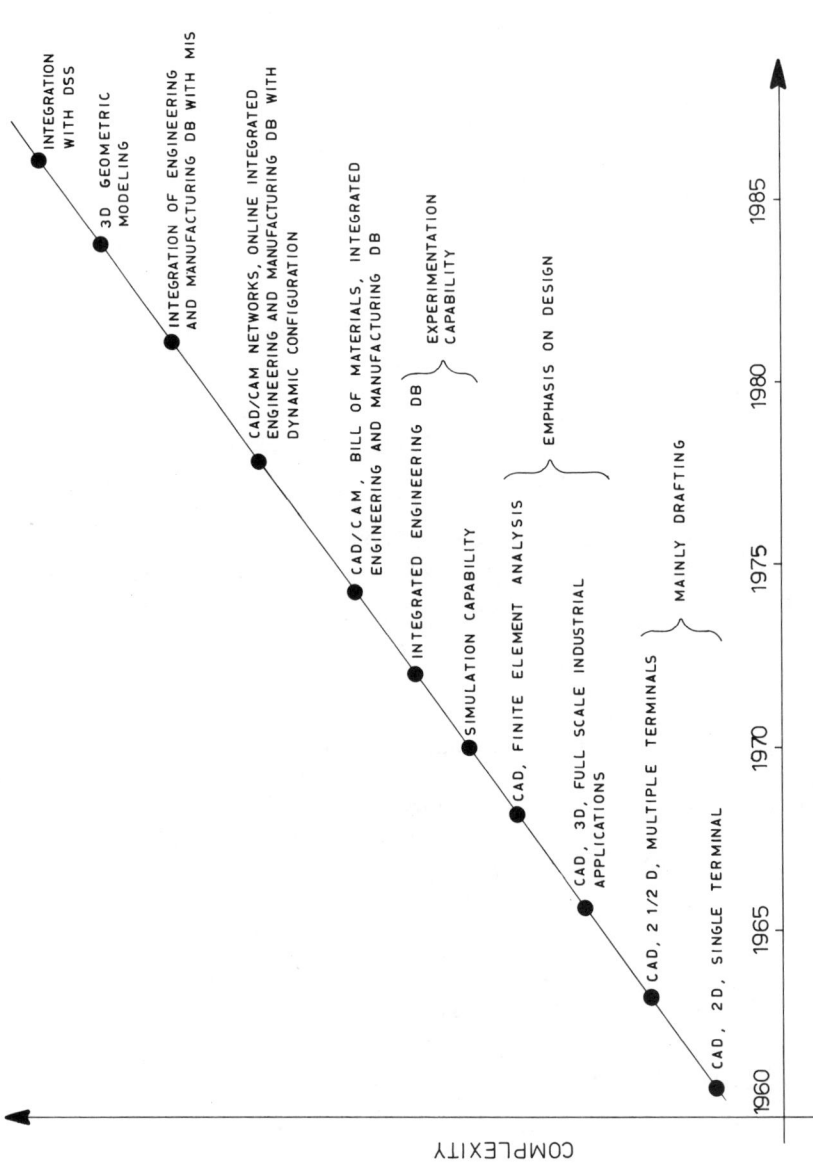

Figure 9.5 There has been an increasing amount of complexity, over 25 years of CAD implementation. In the future, complexity will be even greater and hence, the wisdom of using expert systems

performance data and manufacturing vendors can gain quick access to released part descriptions.

Further, by way of complexity, a CAD Management Information System provides an interface between technical and business applications, characterized by a high level of integration with scheduling, materials, inventory control, testing and quality assurance. Including Decision Support System capabilities, this solution will assist design and manufacturing departments by dynamic interactions between all computer-aided company systems. This approach considers all the design and manufacturing processes as a single unified aggregate.

Serious productivity measurements require that at each level of implementation:

- work units,
- quality standards and
- cost elements

are well defined; otherwise the resulting productivity ratios are not meaningful. For instance, possible work units are drawings, FEM analysis, and mechanical components are drawings, FEM analysis, and mechanical components handled through CAD. Feasible quality measurements are:

(1) number of revisions required to issue a document;
(2) errors found during checking;
(3) number of projects handled by one operator;
(4) adaptability of product for different applications, and
(5) number of repeat business orders from same end user.

Measurement ratios of volume of production, quality of work and cost of operation should be plotted against time. From such graphs, the relationships of

- quality versus volume,
- quality versus cost, and
- volume versus cost

can be calculated. Adjustment to the operation, to improve volume or quality, can be made using the critical factors identified during the work with CAD. Eventually, once we understand the relationship between quality, cost and volume, a single productivity index can be calculated.

Productivity results tend to be more pronounced if rational changes are made to the old procedures. An example of missing the possible scope is that of technical documentation. When no procedural changes are made, then documents issued with the help of CAD still require the same sheer volume as documents produced manually. What is more, without the appropriate procedural changes management has no better control of the engineering, design, and drafting CAD operation than it does of the equivalent manual operation. Ironically, more paper can be generated with CAD than without.

In conclusion, the productivity of CAD is greatly affected by how the overall operation is managed. The following issues have the most impact on productivity:

(1) *Management.* For a CAD operation to become successful, management support at all levels is a prerequisite.
(2) *Training.* Proper training of users and operators in CAD perspectives and application is the second most important productivity issue.
(3) *User reaction.* The success of CAD largely hinges on user approval. This is true of all new technology. End users must be convinced that their work can be done more effectively with CAD.
(4) *CAD organization.* To implement CAD technology, with the required changes in work procedures, we must assume the right organizational responsibility.
(5) *Operator background and attitude.* For a successful operation, all CAD operators should have a positive attitude to computer-aided design. Productivity is dependent on the technical background of the personnel using the equipment.

Other organizational and procedural issues can be just as important. Shift operation is an example. Many installations require that the equipment be used on more than one shift, to make the use of CAD cost-effective by better utilizing the hardware. Yet, while a two-shift operation is considered better than one, a three-shift system has often proved to be unacceptable.

Still another example is configuration management. These are logical consequencies from a lack of appropriate:

- configuration management,
- capacity planning, and
- implementation procedures.

For configuration management, an analysis of the expenditure curve should be done with respect to the company's ability to utilize the acquired resources. Management aspects become very important because of the nature of CAD and basic ideas about its utilization, such as the integration of design functions.

Sometimes a company begins to implement CAD technology without a management entity to direct such an effort, and relies upon voluntary cooperation between the participants, but this can create problems. An integrated effort will typically look into the following issues:

- *Software.* Command language and compilers; specialized applications packages; graphic language; 2-D software; 3-D software; database capability; distributed processing; vendor applications support.
- *Support services.* Documentation; training; maintenance; users' meetings; hand-holding capabilities.
- *Hardware.* Processor capacity; response time; supported terminals; flexibility; online storage; operational availability/reliability.
- *Cost.* Overall cost of first acquisition; incremental cost of additions; software costs; maintenance costs; overhead factors.

Each one of these issues plays a role in the effective use of resources. The possible idle time of the equipment results in idle time of personnel. The effectiveness of projects managed is a function of easiness to schedule. In the last analysis, increased user satisfaction is a basic ingredient of success.

Elements affecting the productivity effort

In the preceding section we considered the basic issues affecting productivity that should be taken into account when using CAD. In this section we will list some critical productivity performance factors. This is written in the full understanding that no standards or guidelines yet exist to calculate productivity in a unique way.

Furthermore, as stated in the last section, intangible benefits, such as the production of more legible drawings, should not be included in the productivity factors because they are too subjective and difficult to measure. We should be interested in calculating productivity factors that are objective and that require easy calculation to identify them.

Though companies with experience in this line of activity underline the need for productivity evaluation, they also suggest that it is difficult to quantify the benefits of CAD into one single factor. For this reason, productivity improvement factors have to be looked at with caution.

1.0 *Work process*
    1.1 *Turn-around time:* engineering man-hours; design man-hours; drafting man-hours.
    1.2 *Work methods:* reduction in the amount of paper generated; use of standards; integration of graphics and data.
    1.3 *Performance:* better legible documents; ease of revision; ease of new issues.
2.0 *Quality of product*
    2.1 *Product flexibility:* better functional design; possibility for design optimization; opportunity for developing complex products; products which could not be designed manually.
    2.2 *Database:* reusable information elements; improved material control; consistent data among groups; avoidance of repetitive data entry.
    2.3 *Quality:* better reliability; fewer errors; higher accuracy; better product finishing.
    2.4 *Simulation:* experimentation on alternative design possibilities; scaling calculations; parametric changes; product pre-assembly and testing.

If these are some of the basic references let us briefly examine the five most popular methods of recording productivity.

(1) *Manual hour estimate/actual CAD hours.* This is the most common and also the easiest to tabulate. Alternative approaches can be used; for instance, the manual estimate can be done by a supervisor not related to CAD, or by the CAD supervisor. However, the manual estimates are usually not very reliable. The CAD supervisor (and CAD operator) have a tendency to give a high manual estimate, while the line supervisor usually estimates low.

To avoid such bias, one approach for the manual estimates is to use a set of standard work units with predetermined estimated hours as the base line to calculate productivity gains. The elements included in the CAD hours still vary widely. Some approaches include all times such as downtime, plot time, file management, and overhead time. Other solutions only include the CAD hours worked while the operator is at the workstation. As such, the results are more fundamental, at least with regard to professional operators.

(2) *Output from CAD/output from manual.* This approach is quite general; it is usually based on comparing production rates of different groups. The production rate of the CAD team is compared to that of a manual group doing equivalent work. As the use of CAD becomes more general, the difficulty with this method is to find truly equivalent work.

(3) *Total project comparison.* Cost is the best common denominator. The total cost to complete a project with CAD is compared to the total cost to complete an equivalent project manually. This is used often, yet the way manual costs are distributed does affect the final magnitude of the productivity factors.

(4) *Benchmarking.* A number of CAD installations perform benchmarks on a regular, scheduled basis. Certain tasks done on CAD equipment are duplicated manually and the time/costs are compared. This solution is used when the tasks are small and manpower is available, but as the CAD experience progresses few installations are satisfied with this method.

(5) *Improvement over time.* Provided the right statistics are kept from the beginning, this approach ensures a valid and fairly inexpensive basis for comparing output from CAD with output from manual, also making it feasible to tabulate production rates. Through the proper statistics, past manual rates of production can be compared to the present CAD production rates for the same group; for example, number of FEM designs or number of piping analyses per man-month.

Each of these methods can be improved by introducing a cost factor, essentially accounting for:

$$\frac{\text{Manual cost estimate}}{\text{Actual cost with CAD}}$$

The difficulty with cost estimates is how to distribute the CAD cost equitably to general overhead. Solutions usually attribute all the CAD costs to the specific CAD work being done. Such charges are often dependent on the number of years over which the equipment is being depreciated and what is included in the cost. Certain installations include all direct and indirect costs, such as expenses in developing special software, while others take only the direct charges. A choice must therefore be made at the beginning and kept consistent.

At times, there are also poor solutions employed for monitoring purposes and they should be avoided. An example of a poor solution is the calculation of the number of square feet of paper generated; another, the monitoring of the man-hours per ill-defined units of measurement in design work.

One installation records the number of equivalent A0, A1, A2, A3-size drawings plotted over a fixed time period. To arrive at such a number, all the different size drawings produced were converted to an 'equivalent' A1 size. This however does not calculate a specific productivity factor by application: overall rates are monitored giving a general measurement of how the installation is 'producing' over a period of time.

A subjective method is that of using abstract judgement and experience without setting any concrete standards. In this sense, the CAD supervisor reports the productivity of the operation based on his judgement. Such practice is not consistent and should therefore be avoided.

We have seen that several basically objective factors can be applied to the different phases of CAD utilization. Qualitative criteria should only then be added to the results. For instance, it is relatively easy to observe that the drawings produced by CAD have consistent line work and lettering:

- the line quality of the drawings plotted is not dependent on the experience or ability of the CAD drafter.
- The drawing is always clean, with each new issue replotted giving a good original document over the entire life of the project.

Something similar can be said of finished products. The products that are designed and engineered with CAD have a better inherent quality than the products manually designed, and value engineering can be effectively applied in their design. This is just as true of quality. With the use of CAD, the designers are developing a better product.

Another point that affects both the quality and the quantity is turn around time. The time taken between the start of a concept and the delivery of the final product is decreased by using CAD. Thus end users are pleased because they see their work done faster, better, and in some cases at a lower overall cost. At the same time, as they learn the system, CAD operators are more satisfied doing CAD work than doing manual work.

We have underlined the impact of the engineering database. Here again the fall-out is both qualitative and quantitative. The overall system of documentation is improved as documents are stored in computer memory; they can be easily retrieved and/or duplicated directly to microforms through computer output microfilm. Original documents that are accidently damaged can be recreated with little trouble.

Reusable software

Right from the beginning of computer applications, one of the factors greatly affecting costs and productivity is the spoilage associated with software. This is particularly true of an engineering environment where most programs are one-shot propositions. However, even programs written for one-time use do contain repetitive subroutines which should be properly identified, classified, and reused.

The best policy by far is that of adopting and using packages. For those programs which *need* to be written by the organization itself, reusable software concepts must be employed. By applying the reusable design and code technique, engineering concerns have found that the redundancy in application development can be eliminated. This translates into a significant gain in productivity and the reduction of development/ maintenance costs.

Stated in a different way, while it is a common belief that each application, each program, and each information element is unique and must be written from scratch, this is very far from the truth. Functional area routines can also be prewritten and identified for interchangeability.

By properly identifying the redundant functions of the program, we can produce logic structures for each class of requirements. This can be easily achieved if a proper study is undertaken, which verifies the importance of using the reusable design approach.

Engineering firms who at first applied this methodology only to technical problems subsequently also found benefit in using functional modules with business problems as well. The significant statistic to recall in this connection is that 60 per cent of all business application code is redundant. As many data descriptions and functional routines appear in more than one program, the use of functional modules can be significant. The two major benefits are realized in reusable software.

An example is the requirement to access a particular project segment in a part number database – involving a typical two-level edit and data call as exemplified in Figure 9.6. To perform this task using traditional methods, an average of 150 lines of code must be written. By using reusable modules, however, only 10 to 15 lines of unique code need be developed.

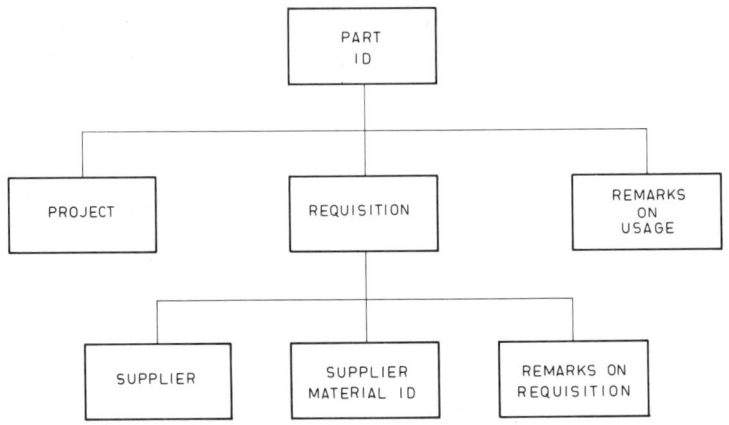

Figure 9.6 The part identification should be the pivot point around which the engineering database is organized. In a similar way, in banking the pivot point is the client identification

The reusable code approach can be effectively applied to both application development and maintenance. In the former case, the impact is significant because a library of previously written functions is available to the programmer. As a result, a good portion of each program has already been designed, coded and tested before the specifications are received.

For instance, the one-time investment made by a leading electrical/ electronics manufacturer in storing over 2500 reusable modules, composed of 80,000 lines of code, in a centralized library, has resulted in a payback of over 950,000 lines of reusable code – representing a saving of many man-years of effort.

Less evident may be the savings in program maintenance. However, since each functional module is copied into the program at compilation time, maintenance is isolated from the program. Thus, if a module is used in 20 programs and a modification is required, it is modified in the library only once, not 20 times. A methodology is however necessary. Typically, it may recognize basic utility categories such as:

- select or edit
- edit/sort
- update
- update/sort
- report/sort
- report.

The *Select* logic structure can be of great help in the editing of input records, the selection of records from a file, and runs against a master file. An *Update* function is of great help in situations where the transaction record contains fields such as add, change or delete; and in accommodating multiple transactions per master record. The *Report* logic structure provides for multiple levels of cumulation.

A supporting technology is fundamental. It should involve a reusable code index system able to reference reusable modules. No module should be written if there already exists code that fulfills the same function. Just as important are quality standards. They call for certification procedures.

A centralized library of reusable code should exist, facilitating the use of reusable modules and providing quality assurance for reliability. Access to this library can be assisted by a system of cross-referenced reports that shows the relationships between reusable modules by programs within a reusable module *and* by reusable modules within a program.

Solutions by eliminating redundant code through the structuring of standard routines not only help avoid redundant effort but also facilitate walkthroughs, testing, debugging and maintenance activities. They enhance communication between the analyst and the user relative to system requirements; eliminate error-prone areas; and reasonably reduce program preparation time.

Properly done, this work leads to a consistent organization of redundant logic; the possibility of reusing significant portions of the program; standardization of programming styles, names, labels; a wider documentation standard; and easier maintenance work. Substantial benefit is realized when the user requests modifications or enhancements to a program.

Let us recapitulate. Greater productivity can only be assured if the management of computer-aided design is done the right way from the start. This involves dynamic approaches, to be provided by strategic planning and management control, but also the right mechanics. As Figure 9.7 demonstrates, the latter range from operational control to packages, reusable code, and the training of the human resources. Every step is significant in reaching an interactive capability with the engineering database.

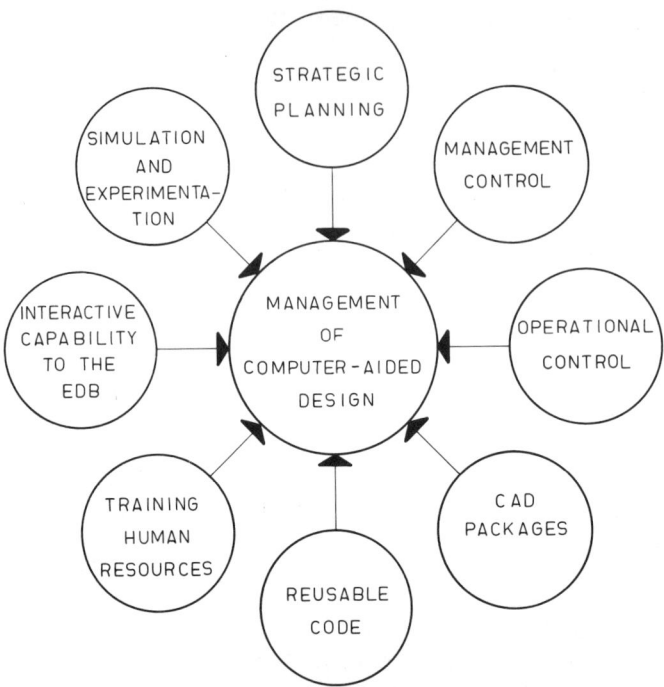

Figure 9.7 The able management of computer-aided design is based on eight pillars: software is one of them, human resources another

The basic advice, then, is to plan for and support reusable software. Implementing such a policy calls for:

- life cycle evaluations;
- quality code;
- robust software;
- programs designed to be portable.

The last point can be enhanced through parametric approaches simplifying the transport of a system from one application to another. Programs that can be transported without degrading their capabilities are fundamental in engineering design where a large number of needs are characterized by one-time processing.

In a successful conversion, the target application fulfills similar processing tasks to those of the source usage:

- it accepts the input;
- produces the output;
- stores the data necessary to complete the functions that comprise the original capability.

Most importantly, the converted AP is no less reliable, maintainable or enhanceable than the original – provided the proper attention has been paid at the design stage.

A number of tools can be useful. Static analysis, for instance, would produce statistics in terms of statements that violate certain standards or the language of architecture itself; possible non-observance of programming conventions; information on the syntax of instructions as they appear in target environment; a dictionary of fields, structures, files, and their usage; called-calling relationships among the programs of the system; as well as parameters and data passed between programs.

A dynamic analysis includes tests on the ranges of variables; evaluation of the control flow; data flow information; data sensitivity; and environmental information, including parameter passing and procedural testing. The goal is that of comparing asserted behavior to actual behavior, thus obtaining a history of program execution and facilitating the tracing of control flow dependency.

A quantitative program evaluation would produce a picture of the program's structure. The program's quality itself can be ascertained through a dynamic analysis. Polyvalent usage of parametric programs is successful if program quality meets accepted standards. Program portability verification is necessary in that sense.

The problems of program verification can be eased by employing a set of tools automatically to perform program quality evaluation – provided that the tools developed are reliable, portable, and economical. If so, they can help reduce verification of labor costs by an impressive margin.

In its totality, the suggested policy helps ease the programming pressure facing many engineering organizations as they expand their business beyond the classical processing chores and into broader, more fundamental design perspectives. It also simplifies program maintenance, which classically absorbs a very significant share of programming resources – and it helps bring the end user into the picture on man–machine communication.

Chapter 10
The systems study

A systems study should see to it that the *background* factors are properly studied and the *foreground* supported in an able manner. Vitally important is the need to provide the design engineer with *product visibility*.

If the designer cannot see where his project is going (in technical and economic terms), he cannot be effective in his work. More than ever with engineering studies, *forward looking* and *forethought* are basic pre-requisites.

In this sense, computer-aided design can help not only in attaining technical perfection but also in value-analyzing the product under development prior to final commitment. It can significantly improve object quality; shorten timetables and assist in meeting them; help improve the performance of the professional staff; and provide the necessary understructure for further developments.

One key reason why engineering companies (in all lines of business) are attracted to CAD/CAM is productivity. Productivity improvement averages range from 1000 per cent for such functions as inspection and control, corrections and update, engineering change orders; to 500 per cent for parts lists, bills of materials, circuit routing and placement on printed circuit boards, component packaging, and manufacturing drawings of all types.

Users have obtained an estimated 400 per cent productivity improvement through CAD/CAM with assembly drawings, wiring diagrams, and sheet metal drawings (mechanical engineering). They have reached some 300 per cent in work such as detailed mechanical drawings, piping and instrumentation diagrams, as well as preparation for numerical control.

Invariably, however, the prerequisite to obtaining results is preparation. This demands clear ideas about what we wish to obtain and the goals we are after. It also calls for proper analyses, which may themselves be assisted through computers and Fourth Generation Languages (4GL).

The failure to do the right preparatory work when we automate a certain job leads to paying the cost of electronics, which is high, while obtaining the results of a crowded paperwork, which are low. That's why it is so important to do the right systems study.

Failures are rarely accidental. Usually they are planted by man through his unwillingness (or inability) to work in a rational manner. Engineering problems come from lack of system integration perspectives; a wanting analysis; faulty or non-existent database design; deficient dialog capabilities; poor communications choices; obsolete programming tools; and, above all, lack of methodology.

Computer-aided design provides the opportunity to correct these deficiencies. Yet, if improperly used, it can instead magnify them.

A discipline for systems analysis

Science is characterized by a *methodology, rules,* and a *store of knowledge.* On these three pillars rests the whole scientific foundation. We could, therefore, reasonably expect that engineering studies and design approaches would move along in a structured environment. This is not so. The reason rests in the difference that exists between *describing* and *defining* – a fine, important difference, but one appreciated only rarely.

Defining is not describing. Defining only considers the major procedural milestones, including a statement of intention. This leaves great latitude to the individual design engineer in structuring the individual steps he will follow – and the manner of executing them. The result is that design has become more an art than a science.

Contrary to the degrees of freedom hand-based approaches permit (in hand-based approaches I am including the use of slide rules, calculators, offline differential analysers, and batch processing on number-crunching computers), online computer-aided design solutions imply a discipline to be observed. This discipline is in the origin of homogeneity CAD helps us obtain in:

(1) detailed design procedures;
(2) the establishment of an engineering database;
(3) the ability to test our design and experiment in terms of reliability functional features, also the observance of low cost; and
(4) the continuity to be provided from feasibility, through design, into manufacturing and field maintenance.

Detailed design procedures are to a considerable extent established by the methodology employed by the software we use. That's one reason why companies going for turnkey CAD projects in engineering should be very careful in choosing their source of supply.

The main point here is that once a certain CAD system has been chosen it should be used uniformly within the firm. It is a bad policy to take different CAD systems for different engineering departments and/or between engineering departments and the factory CAD/CAM installations.

Another reason advising homogeneity of equipment is file transfer. The importance of the engineering database can hardly be underestimated. In fact, in the longer run the No. 1 benefit from CAD/CAM is the development and use of a complete, detailed, properly structured EDB.

A properly structured engineering database is one that is integrated, no matter how many machines it resides in. Though such a database may be distributed to a number of equipments working online or offline with one another, its component parts – the information elements (IE) – must be integrated, which means:

(1) properly classified,
(2) unambiguously described,
(3) correctly identified, and
(4) easily retrieved.

Furthermore, getting CAD/CAM equipment with incompatible file structures is counter-productive and should be avoided. Though standards for file conversion and file transfer have been developed at different levels of the file creation process (see Chapter 2) it is silly to let oneself be trapped into the need to use them within one's own organization.

File transfer standards are very helpful in working with the external environment – customers, suppliers – in terms of online engineering file exchanges. We cannot expect the whole world to use one standard – but *one file standard* should be the rule in our own organization.

Regarding the role of an engineering database, we should recall that roughly 80 per cent of our processing is done against 20 per cent of our EDB – but the less often needed information elements should be there. When we have properly identified the critical 20 per cent we can look at how to distribute the whole IE population:

- at the personal design workstation level;
- the local EDB (department, factory);
- the corporate large text and data warehouse.

It is also good to remember that within a distributed design environment every IE at every post should be accessible by every design workstation (WS) in the system – in a way transparent to its user.

The homogeneity of file standards and of graphic sets (including semantics, syntactics, primitives, down to the level of characters and signs) is one of the objectives of systems analysis in engineering studies. Another object is to assure the ability to experiment with the elements in the database.

Computer-aided design needs systems analysis. Its technology is vital not only as a background reference but also in providing tools for:

- understanding,
- modeling,
- experimenting, and
- designing new systems.

Human intuition is not always present to catch abnormal behavior and handle special cases. If there is a design oversight, the system will malfunction. Abnormal situations cannot be detected by informal or manual techniques. There is a need to prototype:

(1) component functions,
(2) aggregate characteristics,
(3) composition and flow of materials,
(4) processing steps,
(5) coordination requirements,
(6) quality and cost goals, and
(7) the overall structure of the system.

Systems analysis must be instrumental in examining and in assuring control procedures. As we will see in the following sections, computer-based modeling is instrumental in amplifying our design perspective.

This amplification has come in steps. Whether we talk of engineering or business computer applications we have experienced successive generations of systems analysis tools and concepts. For the first twenty years (1950s, 1960s) systems analysis was done with totally unstructured environments. The early approaches largely rested on paper and pencil – though it was supposed their products would run on computers. It is therefore no surprise that the work was rather near-sighted and the results full of miscomprehension.

The only significant development to the credit of a system-analytic approach during the *first period* in project management was PERT (program evaluation and review technique). Though of limited capabilities by today's standards, it offered possibilities for engineering–supplier–manufacturing coordination when it was first implemented in the early 1960s.

The *second period* of systems analysis was that of the 1970s. Here again, whether we talk of engineering or business environments, the methodology used was structured through computer-based tools. But the image of using them was not there.

Furthermore, these early computer-run tools tended to use difficult languages even for professionals and they presented total discontinuity from analysis to programming. No significant results were therefore obtained at the user's end.

This reference does not concern CAD/CAM in its design aspects. It focuses on the analytical side. To a substantial extent the tools available in the last decade – and the concepts behind them – are responsible for the fact that over long years CAD was mainly seen as a means of fast drafting.

The *third period* in CAD implementation is the 1980s. It emphasizes prototyping through real-life programming, made possible through 4GL. It provides full continuity with coding, compiling, and testing; and it is able to ensure first-class documentation.

As systems analysis in CAD/CAM comes of age, engineering workstations are characterized by ease of use. They help obtain high productivity from designers, and offer possibilities of design optimization without disruption. The same is true for the passage from design to manufacturing.

Project management

While systems analysis is the fundamental tool of the designer, the manager of an engineering taskforce will typically run a product project. Such a project must be a well-defined activity set up to produce predetermined results. As a consequence, it involves resources:

(1) *know-how*, hence personnel;
(2) *money*, therefore budgets;
(3) *time,* projected in timetables;

(4) *performance* goals to be attained in terms of embedded quality and functionality;

(5) other resources, such as *computers and communications*.

As an organizational unit, the project is dedicated to the attainment of a precise, short-to-medium term goal. Projects must never be permanently structured: they must be dismantled upon completion.

Design projects should be organized by task (diagonal structure) rather than by staff or line. in a diagonal structure the control of performance rests on management capabilities. This implies major responsibilities because the project manager runs a higher proportion of professionals than any other manager in the organization.

Without the proper computer support to help in design perspectives, experimentation, component selection, integration and testing, project management will see development timetables extended beyond aceptable levels. Coordination will be wanting, with results failing to meet the ever rising standards. Modern, efficient management is based on four basic concepts:

(1) The project manager: a single point of authority and responsibility that is designated and upheld throughout the project's life.
(2) Planning and control: exerted by the project manager through the able use of computers and communications.
(3) Organizing, staffing, directing: organizational perspectives; staffing requirements involving the best of the available personnel.
(4) Computer-aided design approaches that range from conceptual activities to design, manufacturing and field maintenance.

The project manager's mission is to create a product or service, as specified in his job description. He must be responsible for design reviews; appraisal; corrective action; and factual, documented recommendations.

Included in the qualifications a successful project manager must possess are: a working knowledge of many fields; a career molded in the systems technology environment; a good understanding of general management problems; and familiarity with the concept of profitability.

Embedding low cost in product design must be a cornerstone of his thinking. The same is true of his ability to control timetables; the will to establish metrics and use them; and the existence of a strong, continuous, active interest in teaching, training, and developing subordinates.

A profile of the ideal project manager should include:

- the ability to foretell, plan, and estimate trends;
- an analytical penetrating mind;
- knowledge – to appraise alternative approaches;
- eagerness to quantify and qualify product design needs;
- willingness to put in writing (preferably in the engineering database) all project documentation;
- appreciation of product qualities, yields, costs, and human reaction;
- an iron hand in implementing orderly discipline;
- the ability to make up his mind as to the course to follow when faced with difficult decisions.

While *goal setting* is the job of senior management, the project manager must interpret these goals in clear, comprehensive, structured terms. Such interpretations must be explicit, precise, and set in the EDB. They must be understood by all members of the project.

Goals should not be changed mid-term as the project proceeds. A project should be closed down if:

(1) it fails to reach its milestones,
(2) it overruns its estimated costs,
(3) it misuses its human resources by periodically diverting them to secondary issues, or
(4) it gets out of control.

Many projects drift aimlessly because no one knows what the goals are – or how to control deviations. A related problem is the continual addition of new goals to the same project.

Organizational decisions made by the project manager affect the cost of the project. This reference includes its size, duration, extent of personnel and equipment needed.

Most companies have found unpleasant surprises if they have failed to control budgets, timetables, personnel and equipment to be acquired. All four issues call for the exercise of better cost control.

Winners in engineering design projects apply more management to the design phases and the passage to manufacturing. They see to it that tasks and budgets are properly defined – that changes are rare and more rigidly controlled.

Performance of sound design projects is closely watched. Management initiates action to prevent or correct problems without delays. A valid way to initiate corrective action is the institution of regular *design reviews*. A design review is the acid test of the project. It should be held at regular intervals (bi-weekly, monthly) and regard both the managerial aspects and the technical details.

This leads to the concept of *project control*. The heart of an engineering design project control should be designed to highlight cost, schedules and technical status. It should enable management to make an assessment of progress. It should also give a sound basis for determining where special attention is required.

Project control is appraisal of performance, and it cannot be exercised unless the seven phases of a project are properly observed from the start. These are:

(1) initial planning;
(2) logical system design/prototyping;
(3) physical system design;
(4) construction and documentation;
(5) testing and evaluation;
(6) implementation and operation;
(7) life-cycle maintenance.

Only when there is initial planning it is meaningful to talk of the execution of plans in accordance with the established standards. The same is valid for the initiation of any corrective action required.

The best project control rests on participation and on commitment. It is one thing to obtain senior management commitment, another to arrange for broad-based participation, still another to identify objectives, alternatives, constraints.

Therefore, the person to be selected as project manager must be experienced in product (and systems) development, know well the organization, and be motivated toward improving productivity and getting results. His well-defined responsibilities must include: maintaining awareness of development productivity tools and techniques; identifying potential areas for improvement; promoting the need for computers and communications in design.

Management should also appreciate that the anticipated changes in corporate-wide design methodology will affect many in the organization, not just the engineers. By having managers and professional users participate in the planning phase, major advantages can be achieved. Their enthusiasm and support are stimulated. Since they are part of the picture in building the plan, they commit themselves to carrying it out. Also, a more accurate assessment of costs and timetables is obtained. This is important in establishing a valid working basis.

Organizations must have the tools to coordinate projects; check the impact of the new products and automated production technologies on the existing structure; understand the implications; and plan in advance the life cycle before committing vital resources to a project. Those that lack these tools and/or the associated spirit experience the largest number of failures.

Prototyping: from product characteristics to robotics

A *prototype* is a working model. It is built to assure real operating conditions, making feasible experimentation, modification, and validation. Computer-run prototypes are built fast, thus saving manpower. After validation, they can be optimized to save machine time.

When a working model is functioning in a satisfactory manner, it is time to demonstrate the system to the end user. At the prototype level, changes can be made at little cost, as little effort has been invested in the making of the rapid prototype.

Prototypes can be easily modified to adjust to better defined user needs and requirements discovered during an early stage. However, the results to be obtained from the user's response will be that much better if education and guidance are given to users not familiar with prototyping.

During demonstration, it is important to emphasize that the user is not viewing a production system, but only an early approach on how that system might look. Just as important, it is advisable to agree on a review and approval schedule with the user, from the beginning of the project.

The implementation checklist should ascertain that a valid version of the prototype has been approved by the user who, in the best case, would also be the designer. Proper procedures should ensure that detailed specifications are complete, and that all documentation has been approved by an appropriate review process.

With prototyping, a flexible, readily modifiable system is in place. Both optimization and adaptive maintenance requirements can be performed using the same prototype. In this broader frame of reference, prototyping concerns:

(1) *The system context:* where text/data will be obtained and information delivered.
(2) The *essential functions* of the system; that is, design specifications, graphics, visualization.
(3) *Engineering database design*, distribution and access by all parties working on a given project.
(4) *Program development,* particularly by forms/by example for those parts intended to complement design proper.
(5) *Menu* form *and routing* structure (that is, the nesting of menus) for all issues associated with an engineering design: from bill of materials to manufacturing engineering and documentation.
(6) *Functional control*, including the invoking of functions at run-time from the appropriate menu.

Implementation and presentation should be keen in ensuring the user gets what he really needs throughout all the phases of his work. This should be done online, without mixing computer-based tools with manual steps.

Along this line of reasoning in system-analyzing an engineering project, there will be:

- a graphics core system,
- a system for procedural support, and
- information elements enriched in the engineering database.

In the best case, the graphics core system is fully three-dimensional, able to model all components as 3-D solids. Whether machined, welded, forged, cast or moulded, engineering components tend to have a large number of faces taking different geometric forms. Though planar and cylindrical faces are common, many others include cones, spheres, toruses and general sculptured surfaces.

In the computer-based design system, solid shapes will be stored as explicit representations of the bounding faces, edges and vertices. Carefully structured representations will separate topology from geometry.

- Topological data gives relationships between faces, edges and vertices.
- Geometrical data gives the form of each face and edge.

A valid graphics core system will model several disjoint objects simultaneously. This makes it feasible for different parts of a single component to be built up separately – subsequently the various components of an assembly are handled together.

In integration work, the system ensures consistency of the model, contributing to system robustness. At the same time the system must integrate procedural components, materials specifications, links to production processes, and associated managerial forms.

There is absolutely no doubt that the nature of the engineering workstation is changing. This is valid both in a physical sense (the hardware it employs) and in a logical sense (procedural objectives and software).

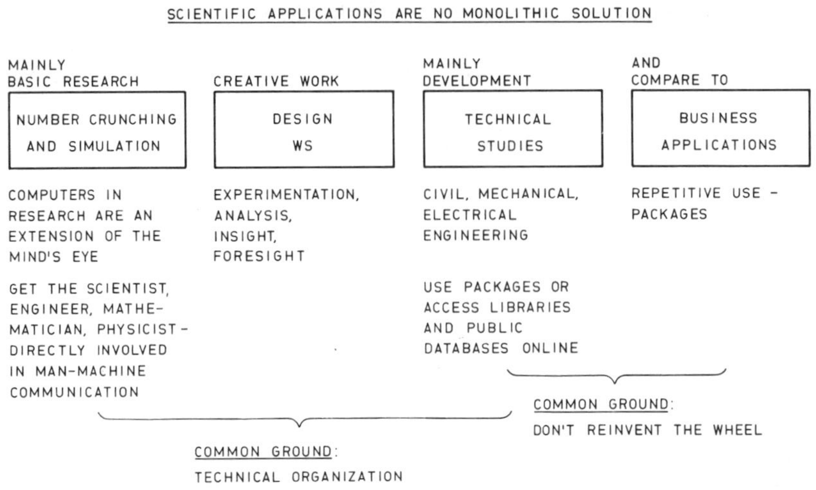

SCIENTIFIC APPLICATIONS ARE NO MONOLITHIC SOLUTION

MAINLY		MAINLY	AND
BASIC RESEARCH	CREATIVE WORK	DEVELOPMENT	COMPARE TO

NUMBER CRUNCHING AND SIMULATION	DESIGN WS	TECHNICAL STUDIES	BUSINESS APPLICATIONS

COMPUTERS IN RESEARCH ARE AN EXTENSION OF THE MIND'S EYE	EXPERIMENTATION, ANALYSIS, INSIGHT, FORESIGHT	CIVIL, MECHANICAL, ELECTRICAL ENGINEERING	REPETITIVE USE – PACKAGES

GET THE SCIENTIST,
ENGINEER, MATHE-
MATICIAN, PHYSICIST –
DIRECTLY INVOLVED
IN MAN-MACHINE
COMMUNICATION

USE PACKAGES OR
ACCESS LIBRARIES
AND PUBLIC
DATABASES ONLINE

COMMON GROUND:
DON'T REINVENT THE WHEEL

COMMON GROUND:
TECHNICAL ORGANIZATION

Figure 10.1 Scientific applications are flexible and dynamic. The vital concept is integration, not number crunching

Figure 10.1 highlights this change by identifying the switch that has taken place from number-crunching to business-oriented applications. Currently, this transition is more visible in the integration of manufacturing requirements into the early design process.

Experimentation through prototyping can lead to the restructuring of engineering designs, while the successive steps of development (and annotations associated with them) can be preserved for future reference. Often in design activities we are interested in equivalence-preserving transformations which can be performed at the workstation level, in order to review desired design goals.

Computer-based procedural steps describe a form and/or design instance before or after processing. Specifications can be expressed in templates of the form instance being described. This goes well beyond strict design considerations, making feasible engineering office restructuring.

In the coming years, with advancements in technology, the emphasis on the direct linkage of engineering design features to manufaturing and materials specifications is scheduled to increase. Such an emphasis is itself a reflection of *profound changes taking place in manufacturing*.

In the old mechanical fabrication plant, labor costs accounted for 75 per cent or more of product cost; 15 per cent was materials. In the new electronic products plants, 55 to 75 per cent of production cost is for parts and materials; labor accounts for 20 per cent or less – and is on the way down.

The share of labor and materials in the cost of goods sold has been reversed. Furthermore, companies are increasingly switching from large centralized metal working and assembly plants to smaller, dispersed production units. On the production floor, information technology makes feasible a better coordination:

- shorter manufacturing lines;
- non-labor-intensive operations;
- a sharp reduction of buffer stocks between manufacturing stations;
- a consequent cost-control capability.

In other terms, robotics not only displace labor and alter the classical manufacturing chores, but also make feasible significant cost improvements through computer-based production planning and control – including scheduling, inventory management, quality control, and the purchasing activities. These are 100 per cent integral parts of a CAD/CAM system.

Any engineering design system developed today should keep open exits toward the robotic factory. Robotics make feasible improvements in productivity through the automation of diversified, small-lot production. Their programs can be easily modified to cope with model changeovers, variations of working and movement paths, and other matters requiring flexibility. Robots can be programmed to meet substantial changes in production volume.

Industrial robots are capable of 24-hour operation and thereby greatly enhance capital investments. They are free from fatigue; can help reduce the number of defective products; increase the service life of tools; economize on paint; prevent industrial accidents and occupational diseases; obviate problems caused by a decrease in the number of workers willing to engage in simple, monotonous labor.

Typical applications range from press processing, casting, die-casting, forging, glass handling, furnace, arc welding, machining processing, spray painting, assembling, palletizing, tool changing and plastic moulding, to voice recognition systems.

The next generation will involve 'thinking' robots able to integrate sensory systems with more sophisticated computer software that will enable them to make decisions. Instead of having to look at parts individually, discretionary robots will:

- pull parts from the jumble of a bin,
- examine each part for defects, and
- use or reject a part after analyzing any defects observed.

If analyses of long-term defect rates indicate the need for corrective action, the robot would communicate with a computer overseeing the manufacture of the part, its quality control, warehousing, and inventory handling. This should be part and parcel of the CAD/CAM goal.

While plausible, such a goal demands certain prerequisites, one of them being the fault tolerance approach. Computer-based design should stress fault avoidance, making the occurrence of faults highly unlikely. Such considerations should include the reliability of available components and focus on the complexity of conceived systems.

Fault tolerance, for instance, stresses the use of protective redundancy to achieve the desired level of system reliability. It does not attempt to prevent the occurrence of faults but rather to provide the means for the system to continue to operate in a useful manner after specified faults have occurred.

Thus, from the early stage of prototype build-up, the designer must be keen to identify the causes of faults. These may be design flaws such as imperfect or incomplete specifications, unexpected component failures due to intended environment conditions, or other disturbances.

In elaborating on the characterization of possible faults, the prototype must account for

(1) duration (permanent, transient);
(2) extent (local/global; minor, major, catastrophic);
(3) type (stuck, unidirectional, bridging undetermined);
(4) nature (logical, physical).

Fault tolerance is very important in all processes, but particularly so with sophisticated visual/tactile robots whose sensors detect size, shape and required pressure – to attain a sensitivity almost equal to that of the human hand. A visual/tactile robot has multiple arms and camera eyes.

There are today robot welders using microcomputers and built-in sensors to detect weld lines automatically. There are spray/painting robots capable of remembering thousands of instructions and performing 100 different painting tasks.

To account for the new sophisticated requirement of robotic production lines, it is necessary to accomplish significant steps forward from past, more limited design practices. The prototype must extend beyond strict design engineering considerations into manufacturing. It must also involve the *new* industrial engineering perspectives. This means costing capabilities, and considerations related to sustained productivity. CAD-oriented solutions must be seen from an overall effectiveness viewpoint.

To remain competitive, industries figure that they must improve productivity by a 6 per cent annual rate. And the strategic plan for reaching such a goal calls for the wholesale installation of robots wherever technology allows. 'For every dollar spent on robotics, you save $3 annually,' says one of the users.

But profits will not come as a matter of course, just because we are making high technology investments. Throwing money at at a problem will not solve the problem. *If we don't understand what the problem is, we can never solve it.* That is why systems analysis is so important.

Chapter 11

Classification and identification

Classification and identification are management tools. Their able use makes it possible to promote a better utilization of existing resources – particularly machines, spares, materials, products. They provide accurate descriptions of all items and articles used or held within a company.

Classification is the systematic arrangement of similar items into suitably selected categories. Suitability is the foundation of the homogeneity of these items and of their final utility. *Identification* is the attachment of a code uniquely identifying an article or item. *Coding* is the symbolization of the classified descriptions of these items.

Properly done, classification and identification are crucial in assuring effective control, to prevent the accumulation of unnecessary varieties of products and parts, which tie up money with little return. The same process is also a precondition for forming sound foundations for industrial standards.

Full, thorough, documented classification helps in establishing a common language throughout Technical Divisions, sales operations, factories and other departments of a company – as well as between companies in a group. It is also instrumental in assuring accuracy of input data for processing purposes, and that output formats from computers are universally understood: the information which they can carry will be unambiguous to all executives.

This is the sense of the remarks made in Chapter 9 on assuring greater productivity. It cannot be repeated too often that significant improvements in engineering productivity, able to pay for the CAD equipment and leave a profit, will not come just because money is spent on machines and software. But they can be the result of the appropriate preparatory effort.

Proper classification, identification and coding are based on five fundamental principles:

(1) Only permanent technical characteristics must be selected and used in designing the classification.
(2) In the classification matrix there must be one place and one place only for each item.
(3) Item location within a classification matrix must be taxonomically organized.

(4) The essential requirements of each particular user must be satisfied.
(5) Adequate space must be allowed for future expansion.

This leads to the parallel setting of classification and identification.

Classification must be done by the engineering people, because research, development and engineering have full responsibility for the definition of product, semi-manufactured goods and materials. In this process, manufacturing should also collaborate – particularly in all matters concerning machines, assemblies, spares.

Another contributor is the sales department, since many technical products have variations from a marketing viewpoint. A similar point can be made about administration which, in many companies, manages inventories.

Thus, within an industrial organization, classification and identification is a cooperative effort. The outcome, if successful, will favorably affect all managers and professionals working online with computer resources – not just the engineers on CAD/CAM units. But while marketing and administrative people can still work (albeit limpingly) without a neat classification, it is the engineers' work that will be most negatively affected.

What is the point of classification?

Classification is the organization of knowledge. Since knowledge and experience, interpreted by reason, are the most reliable bases for action, classification is an act of intelligence. The first prerequisite of systematic classification is the accurate and unambiguous qualitative *entification* of each item according to its permanent, technical characteristics. Only after entification is it possible to classify all items within logically and technically correct categories.

Fundamental to any organizational work pertaining to the Technical Division, and computer-aided design at large, is the ability to establish *addressable entities*. During operations, this will be possible only if the proper development work has been done in a preparatory phase – starting with classification (Figure 11.1).

A classification system has three purposes:

(1) to facilitate communication;
(2) to enable efficient handling;
(3) to eliminate errors in dealing with items.

Such a system must respond in a flexible manner to the problem of comprehensiveness. This suggests taxonomic organization.

A taxonomic classification is by its nature an orderly systematic structure. The design of a classificatory structure must satisfy two basic requirements:

• comprehensiveness;
• mutual exclusiveness of its categories.

In designing a taxonomic classification, the scope has first to be wide enough to bring in all the items that need to be included. Second, the

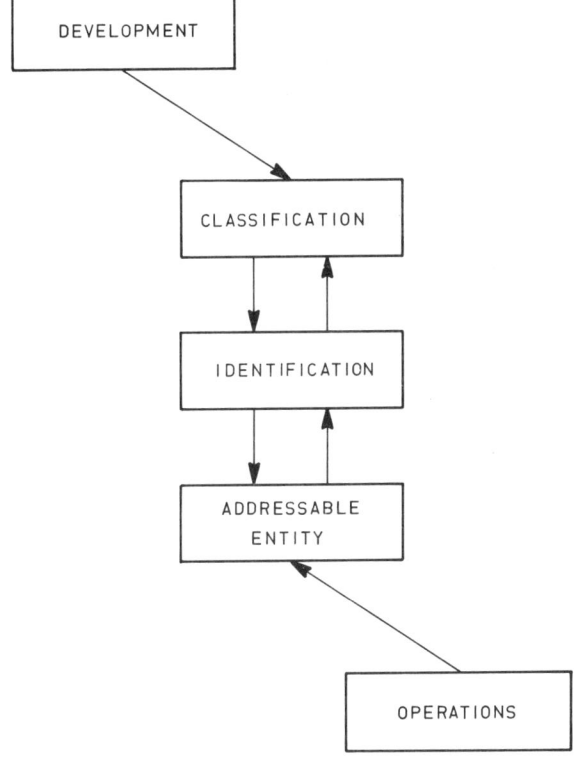

Figure 11.1 There are two ways to look into classification and identification: one is from a development viewpoint, the other from operations

definition of the categories must be exact enough to ensure that there is only one place for every item and that that place is the same for every user of the classification.

The underlying logic is simple. Every question must have a unique and unambiguous binary answer: yes or no; true or false; present or absent; included or excluded.

All data in an industrial or financial organization can be classified under general 'Family' headings. Each of these families is subdivided into lower levels of classification, the 'Groups'; and each group into 'Classes' (Table 11.1). This taxonomical organization reveals inherent similarities and duplications which exist in a subject population – therefore serving for location and sorting purposes.

Three basic criteria should be used to effect classification:

(1) technical characteristics,
(2) frequency of use, and
(3) the need for comprehensive coverage.

The effort should include research, evaluation, and documentation. It should rest on practical data.

Table 11.1 The taxonomical code X_1X_1. X_2X_2. X_3X_3. (X_4)

X_1X_1	Family
X_2X_2	Group
X_3X_3	Class
X_4	Norm evaluation

Suggested assignment of X_4 digit:

$X_4 = 0$	Norm not known. Not in Company Catalog.
$X_4 = 1$	Catalog part without known Norm.
$X_4 = 2$	Catalog part without known Norm, with modifications by this company.
$X_4 = 3$	Reserved.
$X_4 = 4$	ISO Norm.
$X_4 = 5$	ISO Norm, with modifications by this company.
$X_4 = 6$	Reserved.
$X_4 = 7$	This company's own design production specifications.
$X_4 = 8$	Reserved.
$X_4 = 9$	Reserved.

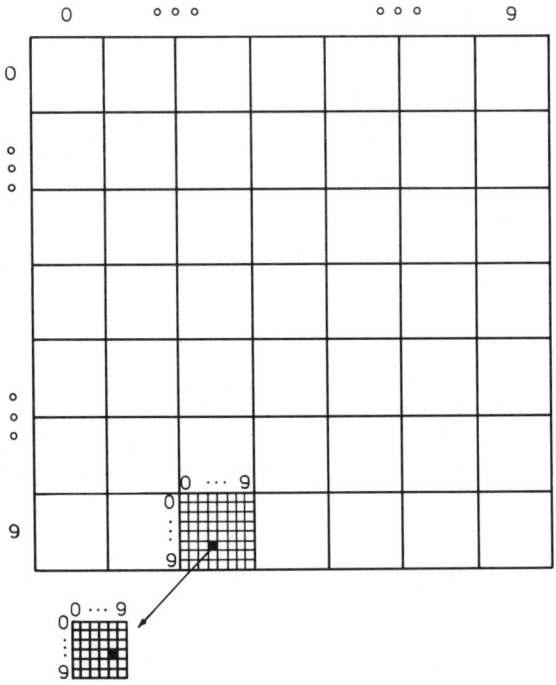

THE TAXONOMICAL CLASSIFICATION IS:

$$XX.XX.XX_{11\ 22\ 33}$$

Figure 11.2 Classification should be taxonomic. The database should be organized as flat files in a relational manner

Quite important is the structure of the taxonomical effort. A suggested approach is a relational-type matrix organization (Figure 11.2). The 100 cells of the Family matrix are exploded into 100 cells of the Group matrix; and each of the latter cells into 100 cells of the Class matrix.

Families, Groups and Classes designate the places to which things may be consigned and where they may be found. An individual article or item after being classified must be identified by means of a unique 'identifier'.

Let's repeat this point. Following classification, a code, wholly numerical, endowed with parity and of constant length, must be assigned to identify every item by a unique set of digits pertaining to it and it alone. Typically, this is a running number.

Identification is a precision process. First, we must clearly define an entity with which we wish to deal. Then, we must fit it into the classification scheme which we have established. Thereafter, identification is simple, provided we use a linear, expandable, and reliable system – hence the suggestion of using a running number.

There is a fundamental difference between a classification code and a running number. A number leads to an item of information isolated from possible contexts and dissociated from related items of information. Hence, identification must correspond to a classification code. The latter leads to an area of information, where the required reference is found in a context of related cells.

Codes are organically connected with the classificatory structure from which they are derived, and they have no meaning outside that structure. Each digit in a code has a value and a significance in the context of the other digits in the code.

Running numbers identifying the already classified items must be *short* for efficiency in transcription and transmission. They must also be endowed with parity for error detection by the equipment handling the inventories.

This dual system, based on two parallel code structures, has not been characteristic of engineering studies in years past. In terms of chronology, the first designations used in engineering design were purely descriptive sentences, words or initials. As time went on, it became customary to distinguish similar or successive items by including a number with the description.

At first the numbers held very little useful information, having perhaps not much more than chronological significance. Later, the numerical portion of a designation became partly meaningful, and played a more active role in sorting out engineering objects.

Such simple and fairly incomplete systems may serve when we deal with a few items, but they are totally inefficient with large populations. For large populations of items we need a fully structured system.

Discrimination against unnecessary variety is possible when all existing variety has been clearly recognized. Then it can be examined critically, and the superfluous types and sizes weeded out. This reduction of variety is a simplifying process which leads eventually to standardization – and it can be promoted through the classification scheme just described.

A code may consist of characters such as letters; punctuation marks are the least suitable for general communication, databasing and data processing. Letters have a greater capacity per character-position than numerals because alphabets consist of more than 10 different letters.

The radix for a numbering system based on the English alphabet would be 26. Codes composed of letters alone can thus be shorter than purely decimal numerical codes, but, even better, we can develop and use a radix 32 code which

- is expressed in a binary form,
- uses a strictly numerical basis, where the pseudo-alphabetic characters, A,B,C . . . X,Y,Z serve strictly as numerical signs, and
- further shortens the field size in terms of storage and transmission.

Thus, in terms of the numbering system to be used, the decimal code can nicely serve the classification requirements. Here, there is no particular reason to use short numbers. In fact, as we will see in the following section, within the classification code it is usually necessary to enrich the taxonomical digits with *Further Definitions*, in order properly to classify an item to its last detail. (We will return to this issue.)

To the contrary, as stated earlier, the identification code must be short and protected. Here, a hexadecimal or radix 32 system is advisable. By dissociating identification from classification we can choose for each the number system which best suits the goal we seek.

Organizing for a classification effort

An *overall plan* is the first requisite of successful classification. Such a plan must be designed to satisfy definite needs of a known organization. The finiteness of the classificatory structure is indicated by the Family matrix. The direction of the work to be done is identified by the management principles to be followed.

A sound principle is to look at classification as the means of simplification; a preliminary to standardization. Where an efficient classification exists, standardization can be embarked upon in full knowledge of what is available and of the consequences following action. The result is a viable set of standards. So often one finds a collection of company's specification and design data presented in a haphazard way. Users soon tire of such a collection and it falls into disrespect and disuse. However, classification is no substitute for standardization.

A collection of sources such as books, drawings, reports or abstracts will not by itself originate research or invent anything. But, if efficiently classified, it will save that time which engineers and designers must otherwise waste on seeking buried or widely scattered information. This is where the economies come in.

A sound procedure is outlined in Figure 11.3. It presupposes computer-aided design tools and also the appropriate organizational policies, which should be corporate-wide.

Choices are necessary in establishing such policies. If a classification had to reflect all the special interests of all its individual users, it would have to embody information of no interest to most of them. The answer is to have a prime, taxonomical classification with the highest common factor of

A CAD PROCEDURE
FOR CLASSIFICATION AND STANDARDIZATION

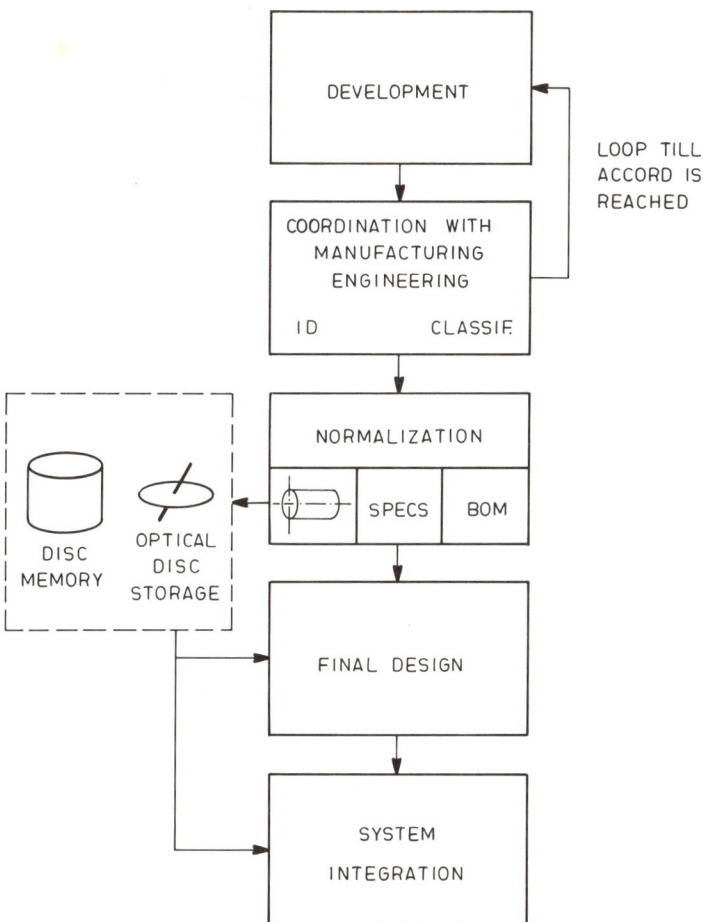

Figure 11.3 It is not enough to introduce CAD/CAM. The whole organization and structure of technical operations should change

interest, relegating the individual users' special concerns to a secondary classification made by means of *Further Definitions*.

Let me repeat this. What I am suggesting is an organization-wide taxonomical code applicable to all departments: in design as well as in manufacturing. All products – systems, machines, assemblies, parts, spares, semi-manufactured goods, down to raw materials – should be subject to this taxonomical classification, which is managed centrally by the Database Administrator.

No research, design, manufacturing or maintenance engineer should be permitted to introduce a new product (at whichever level of the product pyramid) unless he accesses online the engineering database and queries its availability in what is already defined and normalized. But a product cannot be fully classified through the six digits for Family, Group and Class. Many more are necessary to reach the highest level of detail for proper classification and subsequent identification. These are the Further Definitions.

My experience suggests that it would smack too much of bureaucracy to assign *all* Further Definitions to a central department. Besides, the best people to establish them are the designers working on the product. So let them do this work through CAD, immediately making it available online to all departments.

Different methods predominate in the classification of components: some are based on nomenclature, others on design features. All methods start from a recognition of the fact that undisciplined identification is a cause of unnecessary variety, because identical and closely similar parts remain dispersed and unrecognized.

Misclassification causes waste in a multitude of ways; waste which can be avoided by establishing standard nomenclature – but this approach is not generic enough with the majority of components. Not only does it become unreliable when the names are allocated by more than one person, but names alone describe – they don't define.

Classification by design features is a better approach as it depends upon the permanent characteristics of a product: machine, assembly, component, material. Being more objective than nomenclature, it is almost immune to individual interpretation. It is carried out in three essential stages:

- correct entification;
- systematic classification;
- significant coding, hence identification.

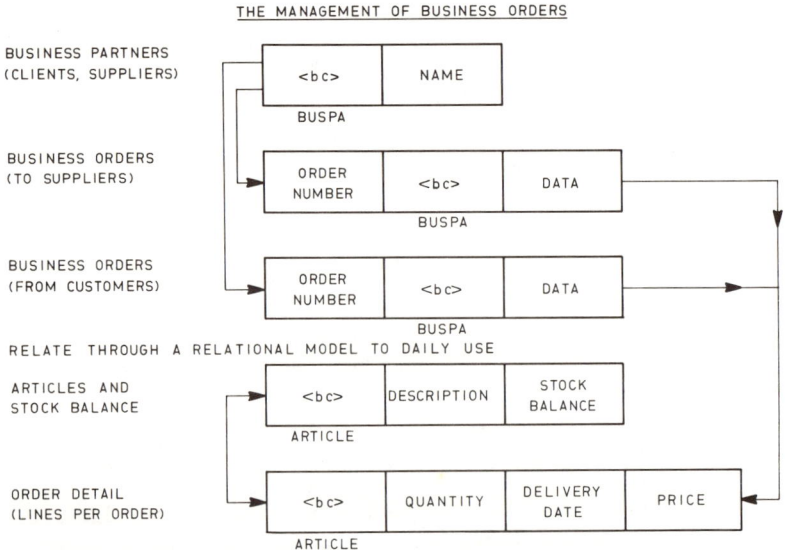

Figure 11.4 This figure identifies a database organization with pointers. Multiple pointers are also advisable in a tree or matrix form

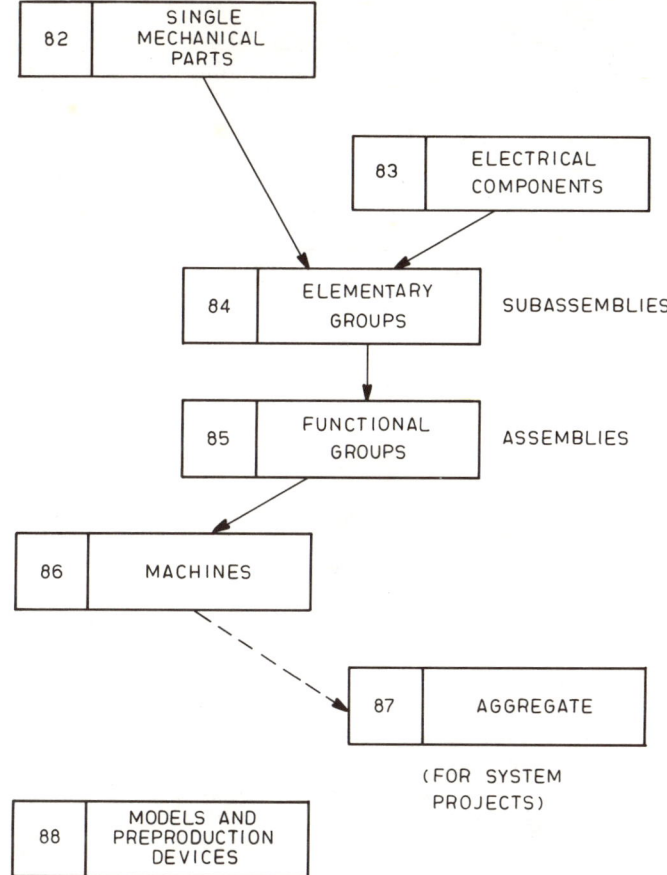

Figure 11.5 The advisable hierarchy from the bottom up, is parts, subassemblies, assemblies, machines, aggregates. More pointers can be established for parts directly integrating into machines

The best base from which to work is the engineering design, not the commercial references. For products of science and technology, only the engineering design can be a proven, controllable reference – but the method which we are describing is also applicable in other fields.

Figure 11.4 presents an example of the implementation of classification/ identification principles in commercial operations: more precisely, the development and use of a *business partner* (buspa) number for clients and suppliers. Whether in engineering or in business, the proper classification is beneficial. Existing similarities are revealed and future duplications prevented. Where existing entities meet new demands unnecessary expenditure is avoided.

Not only products but also the machines that make them should be subject to the classification/identification procedures, making feasible orderly management. New designs can replace one or more existing and similar designs, meeting both the old and the new requirements.

Special tools, jigs and fixtures for making current or obsolete parts can be examined, with the obsolete weeded out. Essential features of many parts may be embodied in a new design in order to simplify and standardize drawing-office practice, production and manufacture. Proper classification leads to system-building in a manner efficiently handled through CAD/CAM. Figure 11.5 is an extract from a study with a mechanical manufacturer where Families 82 to 88 were allocated to machine classification.

This orderly approach to organization opens many implementation avenues, modeling being one of them. CAD-based modeling approaches start from the premise that the physical implementation would be identical to the logical model, the association between entities being performed dynamically. The design of the physical product is subject to a number of performance considerations which can be elaborated to match the logical model.

In its fundamentals, a modeling procedure incorporates several steps:

(1) Information elements (attributes) are listed with their definitions.
(2) Entities are identified.
(3) Attributes are grouped under the entities.
(4) Repeating groups are identified and removed.
(5) The dependence of attributes is established through proper steps.
(6) Entity association diagrams are constructed, and the model implemented.

This process can be performed using a data dictionary – and it is very similar to the classification job we have been discussing.

To work properly with a classification and/or modeling process we must enter all the data elements and their definitions into the data dictionary. The IE should be identified both by their full names and by code abbreviations. Codes must be created and monitored by the Database Administrator, who should also ensure that uncontrolled synonyms and homonyms do not exist.

As with any serious and valid database work, the data definition consists of a classification able to handle:

● a variety of contexts in which the data element will be used,
● the nature of the element,
● its technical characteristics,
● its description (nomenclature), and so on.

The description should be as precise as possible because it will be used repeatedly. During the modeling process each data element is examined, its description created or updated, and an abbreviation assigned. The abbreviation list itself must be updated whenever a new abbreviation is added. The dictionary listings must be available for all sessions.

After the taxonomical part and Further Definitions are established, the classification code is complete. It is then necessary to associate to it, in a one-to-one connection, a *basic code* whose object is identification.

The basic code should be short, and we have already spoken of the wisdom of using hexadecimal or radix 32 numbers. Since the basic code follows the classification and the latter rests on technical detail, it is advantageous to foresee two supplements:

- one is a *suffix*, typically two digits, to account for non-technical characteristics such as trademark;
- the other is *origin*, also two digits, to identify factory, branch office or whatever else of a topological nature needs to be described.

It is advisable that basic code, suffix, and origin be wholly numerical, constant-length codes ensuring that similar items are known by similar numbers.

Let me repeat the advice that not only drawings but also cost records, operation layouts, time studies and other documentation be classified/identified so that they can be quickly found through computer search. This facilitates the work of designers, estimators, planning engineers and administrators, making them more efficient and productive.

Implementing orderly solutions in an engineering firm

The orderly procedure of entification, classification and identification is fundamental for computer-aided design. It is just as vital for reasons of

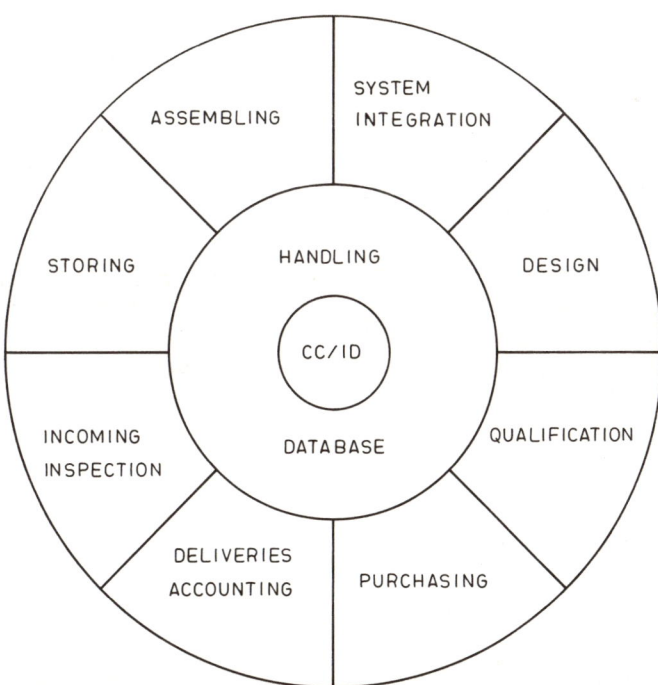

Figure 11.6 As mentioned, the parts identification should be the pivot point of the engineering database. The implementation environment must be designed around it

accurate, punctual and cost-effective management of engineering products – whether in stock or in process.

Let's consider an applications example. In Figure 11.6, the spares-handling database is the pivotal point. It belongs to an aerospace manufacturer, the process itself identifying an information flow with full access to the handling database from each activity within a system project.

In preparation for the proper implementation of CAD/CAM on a wide scale, management asked the engineering division to develop a classification/identification structure valid for the whole company. Part of this work has been the building of a library of standard symbols to be used in all applications as graphic standards. These are added to any drawing at any time during its development, ensuring accuracy and unified drafting results. There is no limit to the size of such a library.

Particular attention has been paid to the need for all drawing and symbol data to be interchangeable. There are no compatibility problems, even between metric and imperial users.

Drafting of construction and other detail drawings can be easily accomplished through the use of *part kits*. These kits contain all the basic components needed to assemble the detail drawing. The components can be easily and quickly moved, rotated, mirrored and replicated. This produces accurate drawings with uniform quality and appearance.

A detail drawing can be modified for other conditions simply by deleting the components and adding in, by drawing interactively, new ones. Thus, one drawing can be quickly used to produce a set of drawings for the various types needed.

Three-dimensional data can be viewed in *plan* or *elevations*, *isometric* as well as true *perspective*. As in the 2-D drawings, the data must be assembled from component parts and overlays. This gives the user the ability to pick and choose which aspects of the model are most relevant.

In perspective mode, the user can specify any viewing location and direction. He can *walk through* the object in a sequence of frames and locate himself inside the object. Slides and motion pictures can be taken from the screen for dynamic presentations to clients and end users.

Two-dimensional and three-dimensional presentations are composed of a number of overlays, each with its own information content. These can be defined in any way that the user chooses. In turn, overlays are composed of subparts also broken into components. This gives the user complete flexibility in the design and manipulation of his graphic data. He determines which components are to be included in a particular screen display or ink plot.

Thus, the data for one drawing can produce dozens of drawing plots, each with its own information and emphasis. There is no need to redraw structure or other underlay information for each experimentation or plot that may be necessary.

The positive effect of classification and standardization shows up in terms of usage. Once given the list of elements and the relationship values between each, the CAD equipment automatically produces an initial solution in form of a diagram made out of a construction kit. This can be easily manipulated into several alternative solution types.

At any time, the diagram can be checked against the original relationship values. Severe violations can be quickly seen and corrected. Then, the diagram can be instantly converted to a block plan. Each element can be moved and rotated to produce a solution. Because of the ease of manipulation, alternative approaches can be rapidly evaluated and the selected plan for this cluster added to the system drawing.

The effect of the preparatory work that preceded this application cannot be too often underlined. Classically with engineering work, difficulties with standards are of two kinds. First, there is the creative but also orderly effort that must go on classification proper, and second, there are the complexities of maintenance.

What is often overlooked is that departmental rather than corporate-wide standards are much more difficult and costly to maintain. Distributed icons, keys and standards spawn multiple update tasks, which may involve substantial upkeep and be a very severe overhead. Also, it should not be assumed that indexable operations cover the totality of useful functions and their utility should not always be taken for granted.

To the contrary, there are distinct advantages associated with the creation of subdatabases within a matrix of line departments-project management organizations for planning, designing, priority decisions, controlling, and so on. Closed user groups can be defined, based on the status of confidence of information – while definitions, classifications, symbols and keys can be corporate-wide.

For easy retrieval purposes, a classification scheme must include paging mechanisms and menu selection capabilities. The following functions are desirable:

(1) Record selection expressions that may involve nested boolean and other variables using the logical operators.
(2) Record selection expressions involving weighted threshold functions defined by the user.
(3) Counting occurrences of records satisfying a selection expression.
(4) Performing the summation of specified IE values in records satisfying a selection expression.
(5) The comparison of data item values of the same type to be available as a search term.
(6) Evaluating selection expressions across virtual records formed by joining two or more physical files.
(7) Projection of a set of records satisfying a selection expression.
(8) Subsetting of selected records specified by the task-generating processes.
(9) Masking of information elements as well as of individual terms.
(10) The use of maximum and minimum values of an IE as a search term; and a similar search through icons.

It should, for instance, be possible to access a string either by entering the proper icon, or through its basic code (if known), or by means of the classification code – for instance 825031, as indicated in Figure 11.7. This is a good demonstration of the fact that classification and identification are not end activities in building a CAD/CAM system: they are initial prerequisites to be followed by much more preparatory work.

154

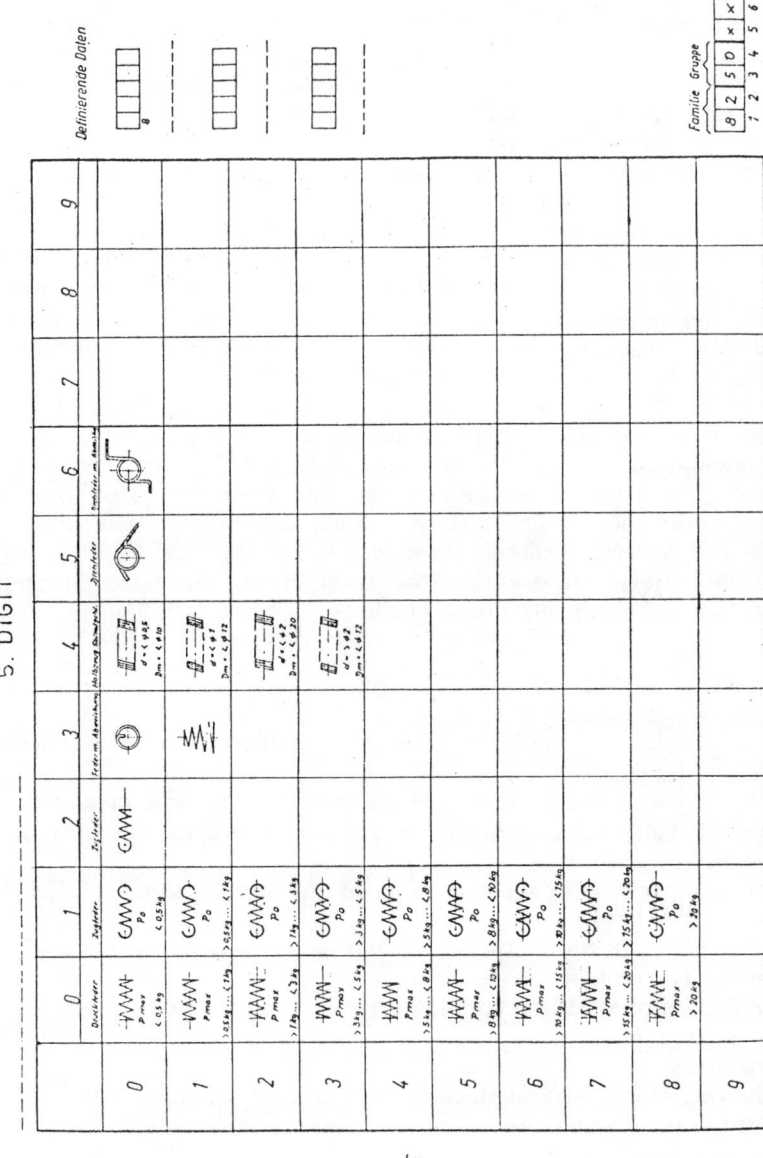

Figure 11.7 Example on classification for springs. Once implemented, it puts order in a classically poorly organized subject

Expanding into administrative procedures

Once the classification/identification work is properly done and includes all items in the organization – assets, personnel, accounts, products, materials, machinery, spares – it can be effectively used for other than pure design purposes; for instance, administration and cost control.

This was the path taken by a leading manufacturing firm. After the computer-aided design project was well-launched, its understructure was used to develop a Manufacturing Cost Performance System, with vital input data reflecting scrap and rework costs.

All product and manufacturing data are charged to specific accounts using the concept of *responsibility accounting*. Because of the emphasis on cutting down waste, quality control reports also feed into this system, which evolved within the framework of a manufacturing engineering program and led to new levels of technical competence and efficiency.

The story of the quality information system begins with the manufacturing engineering program. The ability to generate meaningful output from the corporate information system has been a direct result of the way the data are entered. The responsibility for the assignment of charge-backs has been established both by cost center and by item basic code. Each cost center is also identified by its basic code.

The numerical designation of responsibility for labor and material cost (including the deviations from standard) is entered into the system via a basic code followed by an *operational reason* (OR). This helps pinpoint responsibility. For example, all costs associated with quality deviations are assigned to one of five generic categories presented by the first digit of OR – failures due to planning, operator, job, machine tool or tooling.

The second digit of the OR assigns account responsibility by manager. Thus, not only are budgets established but also cost and quality variances by manager are periodically scrutinized. A third digit contributes further assignment of cause for cost deviation. For example, where a charge-back reflects quality deviation caused by improper material, the excess cost will be assigned to one of several different accounts: improper stock allowance, defective preproducts, distortion, etc.

Not only these references enter the database; the following information elements are also coded and easily associated to each step of the productive process by shop order: operator involved, shift, work center, tool designer, machine tool, vendor of material, set-up standard, production standard, item number (basic code).

Quality reports are generated as requested, but a dynamic follow-up is always done through a monitor and can be highlighted if a problem is suspected.

The information elements in the database are extensively used for simulation. Simulation helps in the investigation of different courses of action in a decision-making situation within a business or physical system. The use of computer-based models allows investigations which otherwise may be impossible, impractical, or prohibitively costly.

It is interesting that the administrative people in manufacturing operations now look at computer-based modeling as a realistic reflection of the behavior of the system under a given set of decisions. Because all items are classified, identified and managed in an orderly manner, the computer evaluates proposed decisions and provides information quickly and accurately to arrive at the effects of those decisions.

Within manufacturing operations, simulation is used to *determine production cycle time*. It assists scheduling to meet due dates; helps in parts and assembly manufacture; provides realistic due-date quotes to potential customers; and is also instrumental in purchasing raw materials.

Simulation also helps in *determining utilization of equipment and personnel* – from equipment selection to long-range facility and personnel planning. The same is valid for *determining the effects of operating decisions*, exploring the effects of various alternatives, evaluating subcontracting as well as scheduling of manufacturing procedures.

Through simulation, engineering administration is able to optimize *routing-cost frequencies*, get assistance in equipment layout, determine the effect of dispatching rules, evaluate in-process inventory versus risk, and select priority rules for various load mixes. This helps uncover salient factors and discrete manufacturing plant characteristics inherent in high-volume production.

Based on a steadily enriched database, simulation is used in connection with quality control procedures for fault determination. Resulting corrective action reflects background reasons underlining the need to learn more about the process, improve quality reporting, better preventive maintenance requirements, and reduce scrap.

This is achieved through a factory-wide computer-aided system which demonstrates a new but essentially simple systems concept. Namely, by providing functionally specialized and dedicated processing units operating under the overall direction of CAM software, performance gains stand at about one order of magnitude over past methods.

Such improvements could not have been achieved either by conventional techniques or by increasing the raw power of a central mainframe. A new balance was struck between hardware and software, having its major impact in interactive information retrieval.

Comprehensive language facilities may now be offered to users without incurring the high cost and slow response of conventional techniques. The system provides both timely and accurate responses to individual user enquiries, relieving the alienation frequency existing between data processing departments and their clients.

In its broadest sense, an information study must cover all of its functions associated with the manufacturing portions of business. CAD/CAM should perform long-term production scheduling, bill of materials processing, and inventory control. The simulator should monitor men, machines, materials and quality control.

Data must be stored in computer memory eventually to allow equipment modifications; additions; operational changes; information management modifications; redefinition of staffing needs; and retraining/reassignment of personnel. Alternative approaches must be evaluated against criteria considering cost, both initial and operating, timetables, deadlines, and effectiveness in meeting objectives.

In an operating system which permits simulation for planning and feedback for corrective purposes, reduction of the manufacturing cycle time results from control of parts and tool locations, control of actions upon completion of operations, closer monitoring of due dates, and assurance of material availability. A reduction of manufacturing cycle time, of course, reduces the work-in-progress inventory.

Computer-aided manufacturing systems have shifted away from the concept that dominated the past decade; that is, of equipment being primarily concerned with archives and static files. Not only are the information elements in the database properly classified, identified and indexed, but the whole system is designed for problem solving.

The user can search for answers to some particular questions. This is no longer a 'filing center' for archival materials, and it goes beyond the role of a 'switching center' providing services to acquire, select, and compress information. CAM is a service able actively to help solve problems.

Classification and identification provide a real convenience in indexing, storing, retrieving, and reading product, machine, and production-related information – including mail, memos, reports, and articles that usually occupy time. Engineers and managers with a heavy work load need a system able to cope with the clutter, confusion, and eye strain of everyday business life by:

- taking some of the paper out of the way;
- accessing the database interactively;
- having a system that separates the potentially useful information from the transient and trivial (so that the manager can ignore the bulk until he needs it);
- experimenting online to the computer resources;
- being linked in real enough time with the engineering design departments (which may be in any part of the world).

While hardware and software for computer-aided manufacturing are very important, such a system must be properly supplemented with a broad-band local area network (typically CATV), intelligent workstations, and large capacity computer storage. Such system components are here now, but they have to be integrated and combined into a system designed for the user. The user's skills must also be upgraded. Knowledge must be kept up to date, like any other system.

Chapter 12

Fourth generation languages and systems support

The CAD equipment at the disposal of engineers and designers must be programmed. Classically, this happens in either of two ways: first, by buying software packages suitable for the job to be done (whether turnkey or not); second, by writing the needed programs.

When it was possible to program only in FORTRAN or other nearly 30-year-old obsolete languages, re-inventing the wheel by reprogramming existing functions was considered almost as a criminal offense. Good engineering design programs were available and users were well advised to purchase them rather than rewrite.

The need for a package policy was further underlined by the fact that most engineering offices are undercapitalized. Many engineers have not been recycling their skills for years. As a result, there was a sizeable proportion of potential (not to say actual) CAD users who were poorly trained and who knew little of modern technology.

In the early 1980s, however, there took place three events which greatly changed much of this:

(1) As the user population increased – and, with it, the span of problems being handled – the available CAD packages were no longer able to answer the multiplying demands. This made it necessary to do some programming.
(2) A new generation of engineers reached the labor force with significant computer background gained during their university years. This injected programming skill into design professionals shying away from it.
(3) Most significantly, a new generation of programming languages was born, providing better than an order of magnitude in productivity improvements. This set new balances in the buy versus do-it-yourself equation.

The effect of Fourth Generation programming languages (4GL) can be dramatic if we focus on the fact that CAD/CAM depends on top-rate software. Yet the costs of software development are enormous – in time, manpower and money. Something must be done to increase productivity. While improving software quality, we have to minimize the time taken.

That means developing new technology and new techniques for the design and manufacture of software. This is precisely what we can do with 4GL.

We no longer need to tangle with 30-year-old problems of sequential coding. Instead, emphasis can be placed on how to manipulate patterns and combinations of patterns, including handling of error patterns.

The human mind seems to have a very high tolerance to pattern errors and can handle substantial amounts of erroneous data within a pattern before the pattern solutions are skewed toward unreality. Thus brain emulation calls for the linguistics of highly associative, pattern-based, so-called primitive languages integrating into an appropriate icon-based metalanguage.

Icons – that is, familiar objects – are a native characteristic of CAD/CAM. Hence, their use in this context is more than appropriate. At the same time, 4GL bring us other valuable tools, which fit perfectly within an engineering environment. *Prototyping* is a case in point.

Broadly, Fourth Generation programming languages fall into six categories:

(1) The simplest and most user-friendly form of 4GL is *spreadsheets*. They have been successfully used in simple engineering designs such as building logical circuits and in circuitry calculations (Figure 12.1).

(2) *Slightly* more complex, but also more complete, is *Integrated Software* (ISoft). Integrated software combines a spreadsheet with graphics, word

WE CAN BUILD UP LOGICAL CIRCUITRIES

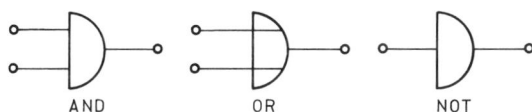

AND   OR   NOT

BY COMBINING SPREADSHEETS

ALSO CIRCUITRY CALCULATIONS

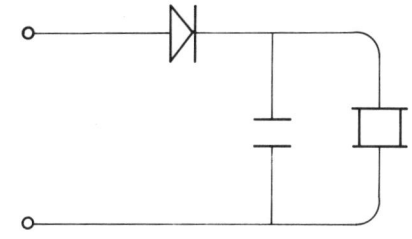

DIODE IS A NON-LINEAR ELEMENT:

    IF CURRENT NON-ZERO..........

    THEN..........

Figure 12.1 Spreadsheets can be used for simple engineering applications, making it feasible to do some elementary CAD on low-cost PC

processing, a database management system (DBMS), and data communications facilities. Newer generations of ISoft also incorporate calendaring services and other programs.

(3) *Query languages* generally, but also query facilities augmented by icon presentation, menu selection capabilities and DBMS support. The important issue with this, as with all other 4GL classes, is that while the original software package was intended to serve one objective it has now been turned into a programming language of very high level. In this sense, it enhances programmer productivity.

(4) *Graphics* systems, which to a very large extent have grown out of CAD packages. This is significant. By using the existing CAD software as a base, we can use the *system commands* to build a powerful language, which makes it feasible to tailor to our particular needs software written for general cases.

(5) *Prototyping* systems which, too, are based on system commands but not only of the CAD package. Prototyping often uses DBMS and operating systems (OS) level primitives. The great strength of prototyping lies in the fact that it permits a visual programming approach. The result consumes many machine cycles but it affords very high programmer productivity.

(6) The least sophisticated 4GL class is *precompilers*. Unlike the other five categories, which work on a run-time assembly principle (like translators), precompilers are one-shot assembly propositions. This leads to a more efficient object code, but the programmer's productivity is lower and the maintenance chores non-negligible.

In a certain sense, the generation of languages now gaining prominence may be short-lived. By the end of this decade, it will most likely be superseded by *expert systems* (ESystems). Contrary to current programming approaches, ESystems have a knowledge bank, a dynamic methodology and observe thousands of rules. Not only do they give an opinion (or solution) but they also justify it.

The possibility of attaining such objectives will become better apparent as ESystem tools roll out on a broad basis and the initial projects gain widespread acceptance. With successful implementation already under control, several engineering firms have gained valuable experience in promoting them.

A word of caution is necessary. New concepts and radically new tools call for a significant amount of education for the user. While the application itself is the best demonstrator, training in its use is fundamental – and this is just as true of ESystems as of 4GL.

One- and two-dimensional programming

Engineers, scientists and designers are primarily interested in a fully interactive programming system capable of fulfilling all their needs in the following applications: research projects; development projects; electronics; electrical engineering; mechanical engineering; architecture;

building construction; utility mapping; cartography; artwork; and general schematics.

Such work necessitates: a complete set of geometrical constructions; a powerful method of relating digitized points; relational tools to existing graphics on the screen; editing facilities; the ability to obtain rapid, accurate access to very large amounts of drawing data; extensible libraries of symbols and other reusable graphics. It also calls for a robust security system that fully protects the user's data from accidental or system errors.

Both input and query must be made using a highly developed interactive language, but graphics is not the only linguistic interface necessary for interactive purposes. As practically every chapter has documented, almost every modern CAD/CAM application involves a significant number of programming routines: bill of materials, inventory management, production planning, project administration, and query activities directed to the engineering database.

One-dimensional programming (1-DP) and two-dimensional programming (2-DP) (not to be confused with two-dimensional (2-D) and three-dimensional (3-D) graphics) come into play in connection with this last reference. There exist with Fourth Generation Languages different levels of sophistication in programming.

To understand the evolution in programming concepts and in the tools that go along with them we should first look at hardware and basic software. Over the last 10 years there has been a dual development (Figure 12.2).

(1) A layered structure involving one hardware level and four software levels.
(2) A trend towards added value, changing an initial offer in its content and also in its structure.

Evolution No. 2 is communications-intensive and moves from stand-alone and/or star-type solutions in engineering workstations towards interconnected engines and networks. Future developments should always be examined within this context.

It is just as important to appreciate evolution No. 1. Considering the workstation to be composed of hardware and software – essentially the operating system (OS) – the next essential layer is the database management system (DBMS). In this sense, the lower software layer is that of programmatic interfaces between the *back-end functions* of the relational DBMS and the *front-end tools*.

Both in the initial environment of the hardware/software offer and in the subsequently structured one, the DBMS layer is followed by programming languages, with FORTRAN conspicuously missing from the examples.

Pascal and BASIC are one-dimensional programming (1-DP) languages; they are not 4GL. But Fourth Generation programming languages can also be 1-DP. Typical examples are IBM's SQL and the RTI QUEL. Both are query-type data languages. From a programmer's viewpoint they are much more efficient than, say COBOL, FORTRAN, Pascal or BASIC. But, in a productivity-oriented sense, they are less efficient than programming By Forms/By Example.

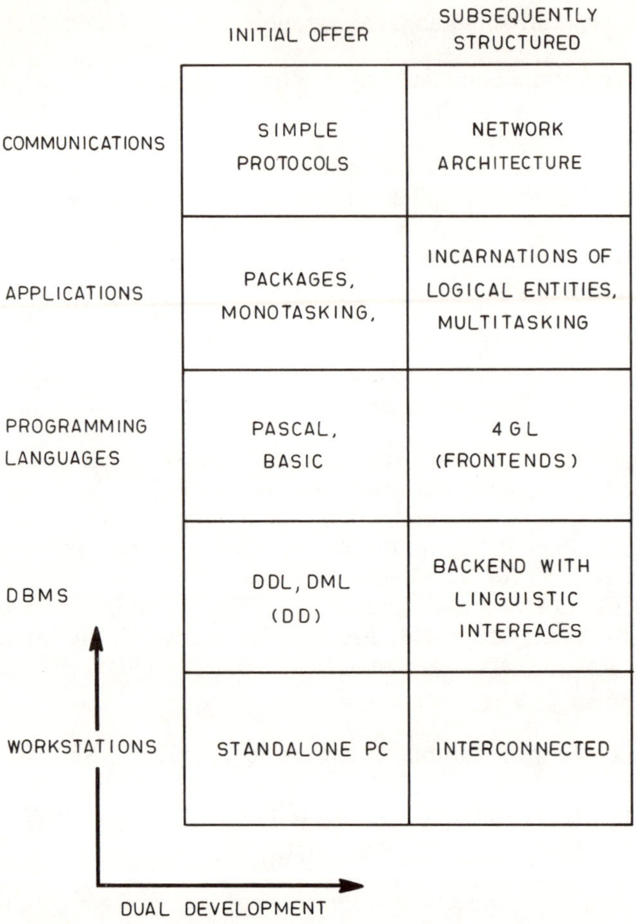

	INITIAL OFFER	SUBSEQUENTLY STRUCTURED
COMMUNICATIONS	SIMPLE PROTOCOLS	NETWORK ARCHITECTURE
APPLICATIONS	PACKAGES, MONOTASKING,	INCARNATIONS OF LOGICAL ENTITIES, MULTITASKING
PROGRAMMING LANGUAGES	PASCAL, BASIC	4GL (FRONTENDS)
DBMS	DDL, DML (DD)	BACKEND WITH LINGUISTIC INTERFACES
WORKSTATIONS	STANDALONE PC	INTERCONNECTED

DUAL DEVELOPMENT

Figure 12.2 A company finds significant advantage in organizing its software environment. A classification showing trends for applications, databases, languages, and communications can help

We said QUEL and SQL are examples of one-dimensional programming. Other query languages (and 4GL) follow this approach:

PRINT 1985-JUNE-DESIGN FILES, 1984-JUNE-DESIGN FILES
    (ALL ITEMS * AA – ZZ *)
WHERE (LAB = PHOENIX OR LAB = ZURICH)

A simpler (yet more powerful) example of one-dimensional programming is:

SELECT <drawing> FROM <file>
WHERE <product = incandescent lamp>

Some query systems present a dichotomy between form operations and the database operations. Database operations follow a relational query language – which, after all, is the job of the linguistic interface.

Query languages can be fairly sophisticated, supporting comprehensive prompting for users not accustomed to computer techniques, while experienced users can request reduced prompting. Also, depending on interfaces, input is switched easily between keyboard, digitizer, display cursor or file on disk.

For CAD purposes it is advantageous for all user input to be preserved in a file which can be re-input subsequently. Another important programming tool is the ability to use simultaneously menus placed anywhere on the digitizer. Menus should be created by the user and filed for later use. They may appear on the display screen and the user should be able to add to a menu any text (commands or data) that may be entered through input devices.

Menu management may improve the handling of virtual events by sorting them, so that commands may come from any input device. This includes the conversion of: a position event into a choice event; a character event into a choice event; and a choice event into a character event – if the content of a menu window which displays a keyboard layout is pointed to.

The menu management also highlights a menu item for system feedback. The same is true of special commands. A layered approach to natural language programming is shown in Figure 12.3.

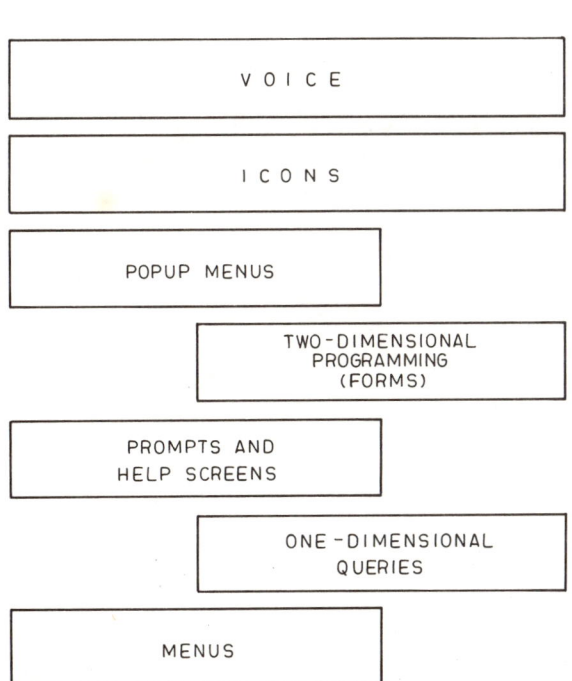

APPROACHES TO
NATURAL LANGUAGE PROGRAMMING

VOICE

ICONS

POPUP MENUS

TWO-DIMENSIONAL
PROGRAMMING
(FORMS)

PROMPTS AND
HELP SCREENS

ONE-DIMENSIONAL
QUERIES

MENUS

Figure 12.3 Natural language programming is one of the important fields of artificial intelligence. Some of the layers are already covered in an able manner

Commands can be grouped together by the user to form macro command files. Macro files can contain parameters which are input when the macros are executed. The user should be able to define his own prompting for a macro file.

A copy command is an example from the many generic commands used to exchange information between activities. Generic commands include communications primitives, supported by the network architecture or written *ad hoc*, as well as plotting, drawing and printing.

These references show that one-dimensional programming can be a powerful tool. Yet a better approach is to use the form's level to query the database. That is, formulating database queries by filling forms.

The filled forms are formats the system should try to find in the database. Such an approach can achieve a completely uniform interface. By contrast to the linear, one-dimensional programming structure of the simple query, languages working By Form/By Example are based on the technology of 2-DP.

Two-dimensional programming is more than a programming methodology. It is a method of database creation (and retrieval):

(1) allowing the end user to use very few entries;
(2) expressing the equivalent of a lengthy conventional language program; and
(3) obtaining the perception of directly manipulating the database.

Furthermore, users with no knowledge of formal programming language can, in the space of two days, formulate 2-DP programs to retrieve, modify, define, and control the database.

Retrieval is based on simple table selection. Suppose the task is to list article numbers and short descriptions of all items which belong to the design <basic code> including their status in inventory and expected deliveries. As a start, the user is presented with a blank table skeleton displayed on the screen:

Table name field →					

The user keys the appropriate name into the table name field: 52153 (the basic code of a defined engineering product). He may now either type in the column headings or let the system generate them automatically.

Having established the column headings, the user can program within the 2-D frame by making entries:

PRODUCT	Article number	Short description	Current status	Ordered amount	Delivery date

Entries will also be needed for cross-referencing between fields. 2-DP frames can be displayed on the screen and the name fields of both tables filled in. The formulation of this 2-DP query takes the shape:

PRODUCT	Article number	Short description	Current status
N			

SUPPLIER	Article number	Ordered amount	Delivery date
N			

The element N in both tables causes the listings in the 'article number' fields of the tables to match. Should there exist redundant columns they can be erased with a special function key. Cross-referencing can take place within a column.

Since the user can scroll the screen left, right, up and down, information elements (IE) do not need to be displayed simultaneously on the soft copy. This permits the handling of programs with many tables, each of which can have a number of columns.

One of the significant facilities of two-dimensional programming is data exchange between tables. To collect information in various tables and place it in a new, user-created table as an output report, we must map an example element from the base tables to a new format. The output table we are after is created by mapping data from the base table, but its headings do not need to correspond to the headings of the original tables.

Prototyping through 4GL

One of the major advantages with 4GL is prototyping. Rapid prototyping of computer applications is becoming a popular system development tool. The formal method of building software systems using structured analysis and pseudocode is abandoned by users who deplore its limited capabilities – and anyway it is ill-suited in a computer-aided environment.

Software prototyping is particularly important in CAD/CAM as end users have knowledge of system development from experience on their own workstations. Rapid prototyping techniques do not require much programming expertise – but they do accelerate time-scales.

A prototype is not a theoretical system; it is a working model which can be implemented on the machine and for the environment for which it has been conceived.

Engineers are also well acquainted with the idea of building and using a prototype. For over 50 years, prototyping experiments included the introduction of a physical (scale) model at the end of the design phase. Such a scale model was constructed to validate the system's specifications.

Simulation has been another approach: first, in the late 1940s/early 1950s, analog simulation through differential analyzers; then, in the 1960s, digital simulation with the development of specialized prototyping languages. They were used to create pilot systems for testing the feasibility of a new proposal. These approaches represented steps in the development process. Simulation languages produced software that was intended to be thrown away when the production version was implemented.

Rapid prototyping capitalizes on the experience gained through these methods. It does not require add-on development time or throw-away software.

- Prototyping is the first activity to occur in a development project.
- It continues through all phases of the system life cycle, even after a refined version of the prototype software has been implemented.

Natural languages, expert systems, and knowledge banks will provide users with still more powerful development powers. But not all tools apply to all situations.

Let us return to the fundamentals of analysis. A very important technical requirement is to provide tools for:

(1) understanding,
(2) evaluating,
(3) modeling,
(4) experimenting, and
(5) designing new systems.

Human intuition is not always present to catch abnormal behavior and handle special cases. If there is a design oversight, the system will malfunction. This is as true of product design as it is of software.

Abnormal situations cannot be detected by informal or manual techniques. There is a need to prototype:

- the flow of documents,
- coordination requirements, and
- the structure of an office information system.

An engineering design department, an architectural study, a manufacturing operation, are all typical office information system structures. They face basic needs for specification tools, database access mechanisms, efficient presentation, and control procedures for corrective action.

The prototype may address traditional data processing, word processing, document handling, electronic mail, etc. As stated in the introduction, it can be done through a spreadsheet or database-type language; but it should be specific to the job to be accomplished – not a generality.

Engineering work will be modeled in terms of text and data in databases containing records created and manipulated by computer-aided design tools. Models involve procedural steps and operands (units of information). They emphasize the task-orientated nature of office work. Each procedure is designed to perform a particular task. They also identify important and often unpredictable roles played by component functioning.

Thanks to computer-run prototyping procedures, we can forget about the requirement to have design specifications complete, approved and frozen before development begins. We can also eliminate a good deal of hard-copy output and report formats. A working prototype is more useful than paper records during analysis and design.

Technical specifications can be derived from a user-approved prototype. This can completely alter our perspective on the traditional life-cycle methodology. This refers to software development, but precisely the same principles apply in engineering design work.

Working interactively on the computer, a complete but not necessarily efficient model – in terms of machine cycles used – should be drawn up. This will aid the designer in determining database structure, access/ presentation forms and functional modules for the prototype. Important elements of such a model are:

(1) system context,
(2) information elements, and
(3) essential functions.

The system context shows where the system will obtain and deliver information. The definition of the information elements can be used to create a database structure online. The designer need not be concerned with the possibility of the schema requiring changes as new needs and/or possibilities are discovered during prototyping.

Data elements and data tables can be added or deleted online with little effort and no loss of stored data. The essential functions refer to what the system must perform to deliver required information.

Using the power of abstraction, models provide insight into important characteristics of complex systems. They can be used to assure:

- rigorous, tractable characterizations of, or approximations to, engineering systems;
- insights into complex products, their assemblies, sub-assemblies, and elementary components;
- a sufficiently high level of abstraction to make feasible the discovery of individual differences and inconsistencies which would not otherwise be apparent.

Insights obtained by modeling lead to better understanding, the testing of theories, and a consistent, well-structured design. Models have a potentially strong impact on implementation, and practical direction.

Models also pose requirements. They demand that collected data or observations from existing implementations (or simulations) are used to drive the model. Valid data represent 80 per cent of a model's success. At the same time, if the algorithmic part is done hastily, haphazardly, and imprecisely, it will produce misleading and grossly incorrect results.

To establish which prototyping solution best fits an engineering design need, it is necessary to:

(1) analyze the candidate applications;
(2) determine the potential size of the engineering database;
(3) evaluate the number of the probable concurrent users – as well as communicating databases;
(4) estimate performance requirements;
(5) establish user preference for interface characteristics;
(6) provide efficient communications tools; and
(7) assure the necessary training.

Beyond doubt, it is necessary to provide the proper training for rapid prototyping. Users should not become uneasy with the transition to prototyping concepts. They should be put into a position to use the tools they have available in an effective manner.

Facilities must also be provided to assure that prototypes can be expanded into production systems. The prototype's structure must be reviewed to determine the functional modules to be developed. There is usually a one-to-one relationship between essential function and a module in the prototype.

4GL structures see to it that modules can be invoked at run-time from the appropriate menu and aggregated by type to function. An important feature is the ability to:

- rapidly modify data storage structures online,
- create and run the prototype using menus,
- employ screen forms that minimize programming effort, and
- make available testing procedures, so that a resulting prototype can be used as a first-phase production system.

A relational database management system (DBMS) makes it feasible for storage structures to be modified quickly without regard to record management. At the same time, there should be no danger of losing stored data. It is not enough to learn the new facilities. We must also learn to put them to work effectively.

Placing emphasis on communications

The need for communicating engineering workstations has been duly emphasized. No project should be undertaken today in computer-aided design without communications being an integral part of it. Most particularly, an open systems architecture should be observed.

An example of open systems architecture is the ISO Reference Model of Open Systems Interconnection (ISO/OSI). It establishes a data communication path which is logically composed of an ordered set of layers. Through these layers, application programs communicate.

Each of the seven layers of the ISO/OSI model is composed of *protocol* entities. Those that exist at the same layer are peer entities, communicating with each other using peer-to-peer rules of *format* and behavior.

A communication uses formats and protocols in order to operate. These are the two pillars on which any information system rests. The network must define *formats* of the information transferred between its nodes over links connecting them. It must specify the *protocols* – the rules – associated with the transfers.

Formats and protocols are fundamental in a functionally layered system. They are necessary to represent a form of *meta-implementation*, which means decomposable into components that are essentially protocol engines

(1) generating a valid output sequence
(2) in response to input sequences
(3) subject to the rules for information transfers.

Computer programming and communication systems have in common the notion of a *finite state machine*. Its *states* are the time sequence in which commands and headers may be sent. Typically, these are memory states.

A basic requirement for a computer program – whether for communications, processing, or databasing – is the *set of rules* whereby the machine's responses to all input sequences are properly defined.

A protocol engine can have routing and *checking logic* that performs a mapping of *inputs* (basically message units and finite machine states) into *outputs*. Another view of a protocol engine is that of a block diagram. It represents the decomposition of the finite state machine into component sub-machines, signaling paths between them.

Within the concept of the total engine defined by the systems architecture, peer entities receive data from the next higher layer, attach the appropriate protocol control information to those data, and then pass the result to the next lower layer.

To communicate with a peer, a transport entity (layer 4) passes its control information and data to a networking entity (layer 3). The network entity adds its own control information to the transport data and passes this new construct as data to a data link entity (layer 2). Layers 4, 3 and 2 are logical, hence software supported.

The lowest level (layer 1) is physical. The ISO/OSI model also features three higher logical layers: Presentation Control (layer 5); Session Control (layer 6) and Applications (layer 7).

Each one of these entities can communicate with another peer level supported by the appropriate software. At the destination system, a network entity will receive data from its immediate lower entity, remove its own control information, and forward the remaining data to the receiving layer. (In the example we have considered this has been the transport entity.)

We said that the best system architecture for CAD/CAM is that of an open system. Open systems differ crucially from traditional data processing systems. Their users are able to select and integrate new services; facilities can reach new users; and flexibility in implementation takes place in a way not possible with closed systems.

Open systems reach beyond the confines of an operating organization. The user can see directly the improved service, which is seldom true of the old 'EDP' kept closed within the organization. This gives a great opportunity both to the end users and the open system operator because they can add to the service's becoming more competitive.

This is absolutely necessary with CAD/CAM, as continuing advances in computer and robot technology give impetus to efforts in design automation. The availability of efficient programming mechanisms and communications features are key factors to success.

One example is the need to incorporate robotic languages at future stages of development. Conventionally, such languages have been developed *ad hoc* and are, therefore, geared toward specific robots and/or computers and their applications.

Any serious effort in flexible computer-aided design and industrial automation will explore current and future directions of robotic languages, including in-depth analysis of what exists; global issues in relation to an integrated design and manufacturing; requirements/specifications for future implementations; and ways and means to put it into effect.

These development needs are part and parcel of a CAD and CAM coordination – which in its fundamental characteristics calls for much more than the ability to integrate linguistic structures. The pivotal point is communications, and here the chosen protocols must provide reasonable assurance of error control and guaranteed engineering file delivery.

- the supported *communications band* must be wide enough to cover the projected application(s), accounting for emphasis on design.
- The featured *services* must answer the applications requirements in a cost-effective manner.
- The *strategy* should be to develop an architecture which can promote lots of parallelism – and be open to future developments.

We must make sure that we build an engineering design system that is flexible and expandable. It is almost certain that within a CAD environment, as applications experience accumulates, we will need to increase the number of attached nodes; accommodate diverse types such as storage nodes and multifunction workstations; blur the distinction between one processor and the other; and pay particular attention to end use considerations.

Since emphasis is increasingly placed on communicating structures the system must feature software properly supporting user ports such as *in-out baskets*. In-baskets and out-baskets provide a mechanism for receiving and sending information from and to other people or engineering workstations.

- When we have mail waiting, an envelope appears in our in-basket.
- When we open our in-basket, we can display and read the received documents.

Document, folders, information elements, can be mailed. Documents need not be limited to plain text. They can contain illustrations, mathematical equations, and other non-text material. Folders can contain any number of items.

Activities may update a large virtual window on the engineering workstation, of which only a small section is visible on the screen. This visible part is the *viewport*. Input may be directly reflected on screen through this viewport. It limits the viewing space of an activity that may perform actions outside it.

The management of communications sessions requires procedures for updating the viewport size and for scrolling the viewport contents. We will return to these notions in the next chapter when we talk of interfaces for interactive man–machine communication.

Finally, it is proper to stress that with open systems there are no benefits to be obtained without exposure to risk. Three major risks can be identified. They relate to possible loss of control over: features being supported; users having access to the system; and the security mechanism which should be in operation at all times.

Interactive videodiscs

Global communications are one of the pillars on which efficient implementation of CAD/CAM rests. Another fundamental aspect of systems support is the implementation of interactive videodiscs (IVD).

In a CAD environment, interactive videodiscs can be used for generic file systems providing cross-vendor data compatibility, as well as image and document storage (archival). Another interesting area of application is as a backup subsystem to CAD/CAM.

Other fields are appealing both for CAD and in a broader industrial applications perspective – for instance, computer-supported two-way video and audio systems; large information databases including the integration of text, data, graphics, image and voice; electronic publishing as well as authoring and editing tools. The same is true of IVD use for training purposes in engineering, manufacturing, sales and service.

What these have in common is the IVD ability to respond to the growing need for low cost/large capacity. Augmented by computer power, interactive videodiscs may become the first effective integration of text, data, graphics, image and voice at the end-user level.

The IVD is therefore becoming a likely adjunct to the engineering workstation. Depending on its manufacturer, it can store between 0.6 and 5 gigabytes of data, text, graphics, on both sides. Access time to any track within a sector is less than 100 ms (less than 1 second for some models). Figure 12.4 shows two alternative lens-based mechanisms: laser diode and laser tube.

The optical pickup system developed by Olympus (called 'Taohs') uses two-dimensional lens-moving, making possible a reduction in the number

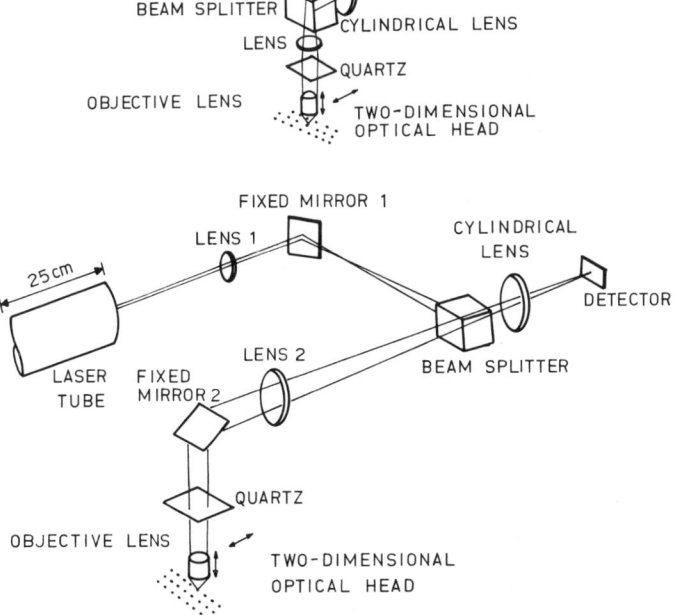

Figure 12.4 Two alternative lens-based mechanisms for laser beam positioning: laser diode and laser tube

of lenses and mirrors otherwise necessary. Also, lenses used for the Taohs do not need to be of extraordinarily high quality like those for the conventional system, so mass-production of lenses is possible.

The Taohs system shows its efficiency if combined with a semiconductor laser as a laser emitter, bringing the production cost of a whole optical videodisc player unit well below $500. The videodisc, 30 cm in diameter, can store 54,000 frames of images or 50 times as much information as a reel of computer film (2400 feet in length). Allowing for space needed for the correction of errors, a disc will store an equivalent of 25 computer reels. (An alternative solution, Philips/Sony standard, is 12 cm, with less storage capacity.)

With present videodisc technology information once recorded cannot be erased from the disc. When this is seen as a shortcoming, the remedy is to use a combination of videodisc recording and magnetic disc recording – the latter being used for rapidly changing information. (There are cases, for instance legal records, where non-erasable storage media are an asset rather than a liability.)

Recording on IVD can be analog or digital. Digital audio and video recording techniques that have been explored in the R&D community for over a decade have now come to fruition.

The underlying principle with videodiscs is that any signal can be recorded and then fetched as binary information. A greater precision is afforded because of:

- the exactness of binary information, and
- the immunity to background noise inherent in the recording medium.

Because the signal is subject to distortion, modern audio recording has had to bring the most minute sonic details under electronic control with computerized mixing boards and devices like digital delay lines, which are used for special effects, ambient reproduction and so on. Digital recording avoids such complexity, and silicon has the lifespan necessary for archival storage.

Computer facilities can be used to enhance three technical classes of dynamic image management:

(1) the acquisition of image and sound, and its storage for retrieval purposes (generally known as production);
(2) the processing of the stored information to create inference, extrapolation, derivative designs or animation (post-production);
(3) the distribution of information to its target address, and its display or presentation in a chosen format.

One of the earliest implementation examples with IVD was an MIT project jointly done with the US Department of Architecture. Analysts walked through the streets of Aspen, Colorado, videotaping the view. At an intersection, all four directions were traversed and taped. In some cases, the person entered a store and taped the view of the inside.

This video material was cataloged and transferred to videodisc. When the videodisc machine was connected to a microcomputer, a person could walk through Aspen, turn in any direction at an intersection, enter some stores, and visit places as if he was there.

The computer can make picture and sound sequences immediately available on request, connecting them with information stored in the hard disc or received through communications lines. Five areas are outstanding in terms of implementation:

(1) the whole area of office automation (OA);
(2) CAD/CAM applications for the archiving of all drawings;
(3) integrating graphics and images into DP/WP/CAD for patents, court action, transfer of DB from supplier to consumer or vice versa – hence for *full product documentation*;
(4) marketing activities of all types, in a wide variety of industries ranging from banking to retailing;
(5) PC augmented by laserdisc capability can be effectively used in computer-aided instruction (CAI), giving a new perspective to 25-year old efforts.

One of the earliest uses of IVD (in 1980) was for boosting productivity through training and education. Hughes Aircraft completed a project for the US Army replacing a tank maintenance manual through interactive videodiscs. A microcomputer program allowed the learner to continue along the branches of a procedure as the material was absorbed. Hughes also worked on another step-by-step instructional program for a maintenance application. This time, IVD was used with full sound and motion.

Among the functions the IVD unit can be programmed to perform are: play forward/reverse at normal speed; scan forward/reverse at 75 times normal speed, with sound muted; fast forward/reverse at three times normal speed, with sound muted; slow-motion forward/reverse at an adjustable speed, with sound muted; slow-motion speed control adjustable in 16 steps from 25 frames/second down to 1 frame per 4 seconds; still (forward/reverse) freezing playback on a picture, and on command (for further operation of appropriate remote control/keyboard button) advancing or reversing one frame at a time.

The system can pause temporarily, stopping playback with sound and picture muted; go-to-picture (number, search mode); go-to-chapter, also with sound and picture muted; go-to-time; autostop, defining the point at which playback must stop automatically; segment (referring to that part of a disc program bounded by two specified picture numbers); freeze segment, restricting functions to within a specified segment; repeat (allowing a predefined segment or chapter to be repeated once); loop, for automatic, continued repetition of predefined segments or chapters.

To understand how a computer-based IVD system works, we must distinguish between the user (man or program) and the logical blocks constituting the IVD.

(1) *The user level*. The user level must be provided with the appropriate interface for inquiring, retrieving, storing data – and for issuing the appropriate commands to the MCA manager.

(2) *IVD manager*. This has three missions: handling the user's requests; communicating with the monitor of the information resource (eventually a DBMS); and running the foreman or foremen directly dependent on it.

(3) *The information monitor*. The role of the information monitor closely resembles a knowledge bank in an expert system. It contains problems and relations providing the linkages between text, data, graphics, moving image, and voice contained in the database.

(4) *The foreman*. The foreman controls the workers: receives internal system commands, queues these commands for execution, schedules worker functions, issues commands to workers, combines worker responses into a single answer (text, data, graphics, image, voice), and sends data bottom up to the requesting authority.

(5) *The worker*. The worker has a polyvalent mission: updating the user information elements; combining updates with original information; executing tasks such as window processing and grid conversion; encoding and decoding image data; interfacing with the controllers of the laserdiscs. Workers are accessed in parallel and specialized by function: text, data, graphics, image. Voice capabilities can be added.

Interactive videodisc technology is especially interesting to business using mountains of information that does not require constant updating. Companies like GM, IBM and McDonnell Douglas employ it: McDonnell Douglas, for example, estimated that it could put its 20,000-page DC10 maintenance manual on a single disc.

Chapter 13

Expert systems for computer-aided design

As Chapter 12 underlined, industry leaders are fast adopting *information engineering* solutions and 4GL methodologies. In so doing, they keep their options open to the inclusion of *knowledge-based tools*.

Before the end of the 1980s, expert systems (ESystems) will provide fifth-generation languages – and their impact will be more far-reaching than that of 4GL. Artificial-intelligence tools will support a wide range of users through:

(1) Interactive dialog with the engineering database.
(2) Easy access to and manipulation of text, data, graphics, image.
(3) Balanced answers to queries posed to the computers and communications aggregate.
(4) Computer-enriched presentation with full screen-editing capabilities.
(5) Logical pathways to the solution sought by the engineering designer.

Expert systems are here to stay. After we strip off the scientific glitter, it becomes apparent that expert systems are simply a new and advanced programming paradigm. The human windows, logical inference, and algorithms used are fairly straightforward and can be easily understood by every designer.

However, one important thing to remember about the current state of ESystems technology is its intrinsic capabilities and limitations. These systems are rule-based, using sets of IF . . . THEN . . . ELSE guidelines to process the required information or knowledge.

This is why expert systems can be applied to problems defined and solved using sets of logical inference. The expertise can be easily extracted from various sources, including human experts, texts and manuals. Rules are built based on such expertise.

Advantages of an expert consultant system for computer-aided design are that the interactive explanation facilities provided with the ESystem can be a significant aid to simulation and debugging of an engineering design. The human window (man-machine interface program) provides a means of presenting an acceptable picture of exactly what the CAD tools in use are doing.

The use of expert systems in the engineering sciences can assure automatic knowledge elicitation so that informal design approaches evolved in R&D can be made explicit, evaluated and possibly incorporated into a larger system. Efficient use of expert systems should also assist in closing the present gap in understanding between the company's design engineers and its purchasing staff.

Since purchasing executives rarely have an engineering background, they find it difficult to follow the diversity which now exists in CAD gear – and appreciate its implications for the suppliers. In the UK, for example:

- Austin Rover uses Computervision equipment for both body design and transmission.
- Ford has it for transmission, but uses Prime Computers for body development.
- Vauxhall is standardizing on IBM, while adopting the target date of a unified supply base by 1990.

Small-to-medium-size firms who depend on the big three auto manufacturers for their survival, cannot afford to invest in three or four incompatible systems. But they can make ingenious use of the tools provided by modern technology. This means front-ending through expert systems to create a homogeneous presentation environment, and back-end (again through ESystems) to implement intelligent databases. See also: D. N. Chorafas, *The Engineering Database*, Butterworths (in preparation).

Why artificial intelligence?

An efficient investment in computers and communications should definitely be end-user oriented. Eventually, all services of an information society should be addressed to the person with the problem, and the design should lead to an integrated system.

Software should be made to optimize not the way machines work – but the way people think. This is in the process of being achieved through Artificial Intelligence (AI).

Artificial intelligence is the scientific field concerned with creating computer systems which can achieve levels of reasoning. The broader objective of AI is to build both

- *cooperative systems*, which will closely assist humans, and
- *autonomous systems*, which can function without human intervention.

Such goals are pursued through a dual track: first, hard-wired AI machines, with intelligence embedded on a chip; second, expert systems written for equipment ranging from PCs to very large computers. Expert systems are the first practical application of artificial intelligence, just as in about 1835 the telegraph was the first practical implementation of the electromagnetic laws elaborated by Michael Faraday (1791–1867).

AI focuses on developing computer programs able to perform tasks normally associated with intelligent human behavior:

(1) engaging in dialog,
(2) understanding natural language,
(3) speech recognition and synthesis,

(4) computer vision,
(5) problem solving,
(6) knowledge representation,
(7) inference capabilities.

Its objective is to endow machines with reasoning and perception. That is why AI is so important in robotics.

Characteristic of AI is that it manipulates symbols rather than numbers; makes inferences and deductions from information; applies knowledge in solving a problem; uses such knowledge, and its associated rules, to prune the exponential growth occurring in complex real-world situations.

One of the more distant engineering applications of AI will be in the areas of voice recognition and voice synthesis, developing a system able to help the designer. But there are also immediate possibilities for implementation closely linked to our developing knowhow.

The knowledge revolution impacts on this approach to engineering design, for four reasons:

(1) The rate of growth in manufacturing industries has created a need for more and better-qualified engineers.
(2) Fast-moving automation (including robotics) requires that skills are better analyzed and made explicit.
(3) Product development cycles have been greatly shortened, thus calling for appropriate tools to handle compressed timetables.
(4) Product diversification (rather than homogeneity) is the new characteristic of product development.

Diversification requires a greater degree of intelligence to see it through while preserving the benefits of low-cost production.

The Japanese auto industry shows the way. Between 1975 and 1985 the Japanese focused on cost competitiveness through the use of technology (from CAD/CAM to robotics), but they are now adopting a new strategy: car personalization. This can be helped through expert system usage at a higher level than CAD/CAM. The key is to preserve the low cost while individualizing the product. This tells us much about the use of artificial intelligence as the science of making machines do things that would require greater perception, inference, and individualization if done by people. While the theoretical goal of AI is to make computers more useful by understanding the principles that make intelligence possible, there are also practical goals which are both more concrete and attainable.

For the first time, there is a consensus that AI is a technology which can be applied to solve real problems today in isolated instances, and very soon in a broad range of applications. This is reflected by the tool vendors, who are publishing extensive lists of customers and applications; by the application vendors, who are reporting non-trivial sales activity; and, most importantly, by the customers, who are talking about a large number of expert system applications now or soon to be in practical use.

In terms of implementation, it is relatively unimportant to AI who is doing the thinking or perceiving – human or computer. Important, in an implementation sense, is how we put to practical use our developing understanding of symbolic, non-algorithmic reasoning processes, as well as the representation of symbolic knowledge for use in machine intelligence.

The other side of the coin is the use of AI systems to help discover previously unknown algorithms for problems that can then be solved by conventional computing methods. Hence, both analytic and synthetic approaches should be used.

For instance, on the analytical side, a certain user organization saw to it that for the purpose of mass production the range of skills possessed by a single craftsman were broken down into their component parts. These were simple actions that could be performed by a less skilled person or by a machine. As an example of the synthetical approach, an ESystem was built to coordinate body shapes, engine performance (and structure of an engine, the configuration of wheels, chassis, and so on. This is an approach with evident impact on design methodology. It is more far-reaching than a limited use of technology which, say, allows the implementation to be physically smaller.

A similar statement can be made about the use of AI for better communication. Years ago it became obvious to users of CAD tools that unless computer output was easy to understand and human input to computers was carefully phrased, the system did not work. Now AI helps provide a much more efficient man-machine interface by shaping a comprehensive computer-led dialog (the human window).

Among AI implementations in engineering are SRI's *Prospector*, which helps a geologist search for mineral ore deposits (Hart et al., 1978), and Schlumberger's *Dipmeter Advisor* to aid in borehole analysis in the search for oil deposits (Smith, 1984).

At Schlumberger, the expert system helps in the interpretation of scant clues, projects from information on the incline of a subsurface sedimentary deposit, and manipulates logs showing the degree and direction of the tilt (dip) of sedimentary beds. Petroleum geologists studying the log will be looking for evidence of ancient reefs or channels in which hydrocarbon deposits could be trapped by impervious rock. The Dipmeter Advisor transforms the measurements in these logs and adds local geological knowledge from its knowledge bank.

The aim is to produce *answer products*, the Schlumberger phrase describing the information it sells to petroleum company geophysicists, geologists and engineers. The Dipmeter Advisor incorporates the knowledge of the user in an interactive session divided into eleven phases. Only four of these phases in the interpretation session use rules.

The ESystem codifies the expert's view of interpreting dipmeter data, and

- confronts the operator with a choice of conclusions in order of probability, or
- displays all the possible conclusions to the expert user.

The user can add his own conclusions or modify the conclusions reached by the expert system. It is a combined effort, with the expert system interactively incorporating the knowledge of the user.

Cadcons is an ESystem for computer-aided design. Design operations are modeled by system functions: specify, generate, simulate, refine. Cadcons executes hypothesis testing:

(1) An engineering design is projected, modeled, tested.
(2) The design hypothesis is modified according to the results of testing.

Specification and refinement is done automatically at all but the topmost level of representation – that is, specifications.

One of the better-known ESystems in engineering is *Sacon*, and for computer-aided instruction is *Sophie*. *Gummex* (by Battelle) makes it possible to generate production plans for rubber diaphragms automatically.

Alcoa is using an ESystem (the Carnegie Group helped develop it) which enables the user to model and derive new alloy mixes more rapidly. Sohio developed a seismic workstation for data preparation to help with the analysis of seismic data. Kodak is doing business planning and process control.

Search problems in chemistry are handled by expert systems like *Dendral, Sechs* and *Synchem*. Problem solving approaches include *EL* for circuit analysis, *Molgen* for genetics, and *Mecho* for mechanics.

Stanford's *Dart* project and Nixdorf's *Faultfinder* system help localize and repair faults in computer systems (Savory, 1984). Nixdorf's *Conad* provides configuration advice when building up computer orders (Savory, 1984); and DEC's *XCON* assures similar functions. (XCON is a development of the R1 ESystem by Carnegie Mellon (McDermott).)

As an expert configurer, XCON configures VAX systems in less than two seconds of CPU time. In its five years of operation it has processed nearly 100,000 customer orders for both VAX and PDP-11. Each computer system is tailored to specific customer requirements and constraints, enabling DEC to provide computer systems that are virtually custom-built.

As an AI tool, XCON has brought easily quantifiable financial savings, but also has a strategic benefit. It has provided spin-offs such as *XSEL* (expert salesman). It also generated a level of competence in AI within Digital Equipment that is vital to its future progress.

Critics say that XCON has become a maintenance nightmare, that it is poorly understood, badly structured and, hence, hard to change (David Lorge Parnas: 'Software Aspects of Strategic Defense Systems', *Communications of the ACM*, Volume 28, No. 12, December 1985). Such critics must be unfamiliar with software! We have not reached even a reasonable level of software dependability and, for the time being at least, AI has not addressed this subject – though it should.

Software is the soft underbelly of computer science, and this is just as true of sophisticated programs as of simple subroutines.

Expert systems components

As the products and processes we handle through computer-aided design become increasingly complex, they require intelligent planning and control strategies. Expert systems can contribute to both product design and systems management, provided we have a model of the aggregate to be managed; a situation assessment function for interpreting input data; and rule-based functions to select desired activities.

A valid way of looking at artificial intelligence in CAD is to compare twenty years of contribution by CAD with what was known in the early and mid 1960s as *scientific calculation*. This was basically a manual design process, but, as we discovered, manual design of large-scale integration (LSI) chips is almost impossible. Only through the implementation of CAD technology were we able to produce chips having 5, 10 and 25 thousand gates. As design sophistication increases, it is understandable that there is a great interest in improving existing CAD systems. At the same time, the more automated a process or product becomes, the better understood it has to be. Hence, the management perspectives ESystems should be addressing.

System management is an ideal area for artificial intelligence, as management functions require knowledge-based methods, including planning, designing, evaluating, and controlling activities. The ESystem represents the elements of the domain to which it is addressed and their interrelationships. It provides a basis for linking observable data to apparent system states through diagnostic reasoning.

Such reasoning is not unlike a human experience. When we observe certain data, we attempt to find the possible states of the system which the model suggests would produce those data. In a similar way, ESystems can support future projection, examining one or more alternative simulations to identify an objective outcome among options.

The expert system, for example, can project technical data more accurately and quickly than the designer. On the other hand, the designer can often prescribe plan revisions that achieve desired results simply and efficiently. Thus, efforts should be aiming to articulate the elements of the problem-solving task, developing functions to accomplish subtasks, and integrating humans and machines in cooperative, problem-solving teams.

Like creating design, management is a fertile field for ESystems implementation, given that artificial intelligence has started as a sector of computer science oriented toward simulating human cognitive behavior on computers. At the same time, AI is only a small component of an expert system. The major parts are:

(1) Designing the interactive dialog interface.
(2) Engineering the system to fit the organization through approaches leading to logical manipulation.
(3) Addressing the crucial issue of data management.
(4) Training and adapting the organization to use the ESystem successfully.

The expert system itself is made up of software, computer programs that perform tasks usually associated with human intelligent behavior:

- understanding language,
- learning,
- reasoning,
- problem-solving.

Successful applications help demonstrate that machines can exhibit artificial intelligence. They can think and reason somewhat like man, and understand information conveyed by sight, motion and speech.

This is a process which well suits our knowledge-intensive society, as increasingly our output consists of information, services, experiences. The domain where expert systems can be successfully implemented increases with time, as does their structure, which basically consists of three distinct components:

(1) a knowledge bank of facts and methods;
(2) rules about a particular problem or application;
(3) a global database which can be accessed online.

Knowledge-based systems provide facilities well beyond the decision support capabilities we have known during the last 15 years. They make feasible the creation of *knowledge banks*, whose facilities can be employed to assure new system capabilities. When such knowhow-dependent processes are useful for solving problems related to a class of objects, we talk of expert advice.

In the general case, knowledge-based systems make a wide use of methodology and specifications integrated into the components forming the aggregate. Such methodology implies a rigorous discipline. In terms of computers and communications, a knowledge-based system acquires a fourth dimension, beyond the three already provided by databasing, datacomm, and data processing.

Knowledge banks are typically constructed to address only a narrow domain of expertise. Often they are unreliable at the boundaries of such domain, including a limited explanation capability, while they are at their best within the implementation domain for which they have been designed.

The aggregate of rules is the *inference engine* – a program that interprets the information; makes a judgment; draws a conclusion; and justifies the advice which it gives.

Rules attach certain factors to conclusions. But the calculations and extrapolations that the expert system performs may employ probabilistic reasoning. Efforts to build a better inference engine have in common a basic methodology. Their strength lies in lessons learned.

Current work is concentrating on improved methods for representing knowledge, building knowledge banks, and encoding heuristic rules. These reflect, in a larger sense, a new approach to modeling, contributing new capabilities, employing new languages, and developing new architectures – including non-procedural descriptions, and intelligent methods for manipulating modeled entities.

A knowledge bank should not be confused with a database. A knowledge bank handles the rules it stores through multiple cycling. The database contains information elements which must be easily accessible to the inference mechanism.

A communications discipline is necessary to provide global access to the information resources of the firm. The better these resources and the more complete the database, the more rewarding the result of expert system implementation in computer-aided design. The use of expert systems in design increases the need for a complete, consistent, and accurate engineering database.

A theme central to all AI applications areas is *knowledge acquisition and representation*. Major methods of knowledge representation are inference nets, logic programming, frames, semantic nets, production rule systems, and so on. Logic programming includes predicate, modal, temporal and fuzzy logic.

Intepretation requires rules to govern the flow of control, and in this sense expert systems use the kind of knowledge that a human does. They can justify their judgments in terms intelligible to users.

Because of their inherent behavior and computer support, ESystems bring all the benefits of computer-based processes to the tasks being executed. That is why cognitive psychology, complex information processing and machine intelligence are different perspectives on the same aggregate.

Useful development rests on the premise that to manage a system we need to understand what it is doing and how it will respond to potential interventions. We also need a method for generating and selecting actions that will produce desirable outcomes. This leads to *situation assessment*, the task of understanding the system's behavior.

Rules must be explained to the machine through linguistic interfaces. There are a number of knowledge representation languages now available. The most popular first-generation AI language was Lisp. Prolog (from the University of Marseille) and OPS (from Carnegie Mellon) are logic-oriented languages. Other second-generation AI languages included Planner and Conniver from MIT, Rosie from the Rand Corporation, Fuzzy from Rutgers and Smalltalk from Xerox.

Amord from MIT is a language designed for antecedent systems; KPL from Xerox, FRL from MIT, KL-ONE from BBN, OBJTALK from the University of Bonn, and M-Actors from the University of Kyoto are actor languages. there is also a golden horde of system shells which are excellent for prototyping. Emycin, Hearsay III, M1, S1, and Expert Ease are a few examples. The use of shells invites end-user involvement in the modeling process.

Expert Software International (of Edinburgh, Scotland) has developed a software package that allows the development of an expert system in prototype. Dubbed *Expert-Ease*, this language can run on a microcomputer. One of its uses has been in the upkeep and repair of machinery, such as estimating the service life of a helicopter gearbox.

Once Expert-Ease has enough examples, it determines the rules that led to the expert's conclusions and develops questions that could guide someone who is not an expert. The program produces a series of multiple-choice questions that a non-expert user seeking help with a particular gearbox will answer. After the ESystem has enough answers, it tells what action to take.

Knowledge environments

An *expert* is a person who possesses extensive knowledge in a finite domain. The logical process this person follows in his thinking is too complex to be described through an algorithm. We need to map it as a logical structure.

A key feature of expert systems is therefore the representation and processing of knowledge. As stated in the preceding sections, the fundamental difference between traditional data-processing systems and expert systems lies in the nature and the treatment of knowledge: in DP, it is numeric, factual, procedural; with ESystems, it is symbolic, heuristic and declarative.

Knowledge acquisition is very important because the expert system's expertise rests on technical knowledge received from human specialists. To apply it to varied situations in order to reach conclusions, they must first acquire it. (Indeed, this is a comprehensive and concise definition of the current state of the art in machine intelligence.)

Several successful artificial intelligence efforts have aimed to improve the technology for modeling and simulation. The same is true for systematizing situation assessment methods and expanding the repertoire of planning strategies and tools.

Designers of expert systems have found that dredging general rules from the subconscious of human experts is a huge challenge. Yet it is a necessity. Expert systems must have a model of the domain of expertise. In this way, deeper reasoning is possible whenever the rules are deficient.

Knowledge and advice available from expert-system consultation comes at the end of a question-and-answer session. During this session, users describe their problem. Similar sessions have taken place for knowledge acquisition purposes, during which the experts described their thinking process. In this connection it is important to underline the concept of metaknowledge – knowledge about knowledge.

Knowledge sources usually transform entries at one level of abstraction into entries at another level. Some knowledge sources operate bottom-up. They aggregate several lower-level entries into a smaller number of higher-level entries. Other knowledge sources operate top-down, exploding a compound knowledge source into its components.

Metaknowledge handles knowledge about:

(1) representation of objects (through schemata);
(2) representation functions (function templates);
(3) reasoning strategies (by means of meta-rules);
(4) inference rules (rule description).

Metaknowledge avoids the rigidity of always having to apply hierarchical structure for abstraction. It provides for flexible structures and can therefore make a significant contribution to expert systems development.

Just as important is the role of *symbolic computing*. It allows the processing of thoughts and concepts in addition to numbers, and makes possible the handling of *knowledge intensive* and *reasoning-intensive* activities.

Concepts embedded in metaknowledge can be instrumental in knowledge acquisition, as this is achieved by extracting and formalizing the knowledge of an expert for use by an expert system. Examples of knowledge to be framed in rules are descriptions of objects, identifications of relationships, and explanations of procedures.

Software engineers called knowledge engineers specialize in the techniques of knowledge acquisition. We said that knowledge representation forms include production rules, frames, and semantic nets. Different representations are suited to different types and different uses of knowledge.

'IF . . . THEN . . . ELSE' rules lend themselves to the representation of deductive knowledge – situation/action, premise/conclusion, antecedent/consequent, and cause/effect knowledge: for instance, 'If the temperature exceeds 80° Fahrenheit, then turn on the airconditioning'.

- The rules with Emycin are of the form:
  IF <evidence> THEN <conclusion>.
- In automatic control, rules are of the form:
  IF <measurement> THEN <action>.

The chosen representation approach should simplify the problem of encoding knowledge. It should also provide an intelligible encoding of the knowledge that is the property of domain experts, making it available to a larger user population.

In this sense, frames are well-suited to representing descriptive and relational knowledge that clusters or conforms somewhat to stereotypes. An example is the description of an accounting or a statistical process.

Semantic nets are useful for modeling classifications, physical structures, or causal linkages, such as how various elements of a given model influence each other. With these knowledge representation forms constructed, the production rules are the most widely used for current applications.

Eventually all intelligent CAD workstations will use expert systems to make product-development decisions, optimize designs, repair machinery. While until recently only major corporations could afford expert systems, as they were designed for mainframes starting at $200,000, now ESystems run on PCs.

The development of PC-based ESystems is a direct out-growth of nearly thirty years of mainframe-based study into artificial intelligence. When confronted by a problem, such as insufficient data, the flow does not stop. The system

- asks more questions,
- draws more tenuous inferences from the knowledge bank,
- reaches conclusions which emulate the way a professional would hedge his bets.

The knowledge representation scheme in the ESystem works with information flows and linkages which are transparent to the human user, though the latter is provided with a meaningful dialog capability.

Microcomputer expert systems have burst onto the marketplace after decades of fermentation. As with all new products, the first ones available were not 'ready for use'. But if you needed expert assistance you could live with the small knowledge bank, rather lengthy inputting procedures, and other problems found in this first generation of micro-ESystems.

The new development machines are available for about $50,000. These are generally high-power workstations running CommonLisp. Examples include offers by Apollo, Hewlett-Packard, Digital Equipment, Symbolics, LMI, and Xerox. At the low end of the business, there are the IBM PC/AT-type machines at the $5000 level.

If we wish to appreciate the future trend in terms of expert systems, we should ask ourselves:

- What are the key developments in software and hardware stimulating ESystem usage?
- What are the implications for the user interface?
- How can information be represented in an expert form?
- What are the costs and benefits of using ESystems?
- The pitfalls?
- How do the commercially available, state-of-the-art expert systems compare?
- Should mainframes, minis or micros be used for their implementation?

The answer to this last question is that to be effective a knowledge environment must be distributed. We should not operate centralized expert systems. The AI component must be integrated into every engineering workstation.

This poses lots of challenges not only in knowledge acquisition but also in supporting facilities – such as (several) inference mechanisms, database access(es), natural-language dialog interfaces, attached procedural interfaces, explanation facilities, and so on. One of the most vital elements in an enlarged ESystems implementation will be the upkeep of domain knowledge till this process can be supported by the expert system itself.

A valid natural-language interface, visual recognition and voice recognition are among the next steps in ESystems technology. More precisely, they are the stepping stones toward the development of truly artificial intelligence.

Advantages of an intelligent CAD system

We said that expert systems are the first business and industrial implementation of artificial intelligence. We are still a long way from expert advisers, able to see, hear, talk and think, communicating via worldwide electronic nets. But we are presently able to implement AI in computer-aided design.

Starting with the fundamentals, four sorts of operation are performed by an intelligent CAD system:

(1) specification,
(2) abstraction,
(3) optimization,
(4) testing.

Specification involves a negotiation between the designer and the computer about what constitutes a valid product. The designer has a concept which might be more or less clear, but the CAD machine has to present specifications which are formal, verifiable and enable the larger system to work properly.

The use of AI tools is further promoted by the fact that expert system techniques are more rapidly accepted among the end users – especially those who have viewed computers as 'useful, but they can't solve my real problems', the reason given typically being that real problems involve a lot of judgment.

At the specifications level of engineering design, expert systems provide the ability to arrive at an interactive solution while trying a greater number of alternatives in the time available. They also make easier the duplication of expertise.

Working within this context, an expert system would allow the designer to intervene in a controlled way with the design, interfacing between the end user and the process of automatic generation. Depending on:

- the representation appropriate to the application and
- the relative compatibility of this representation within the larger system,

the user might be able to contribute his imaginative approaches to the design in successive stages. The ESystem facilitates this intervention and also sees to it that as much use as possible is made of past designs in the generation of new models.

End users and computer-based processes are no longer distinct. AI tools provided by modern technology help bring them into one aggregate. ESystems can assure the connecting link.

A farsighted approach to fundamental design requirements is vital in terms of competitive advantages, with investments in new products and processes running into billions of dollars. At the same time, *competitive pressures see to it that value-added features are part of further refinements in implementation. The expert system is a value-added tool in CAD.*

With time and experience, off-the-shelf knowledge banks will appear with thousands of rules – while current AI applications typically use a few hundred rules, easily stored on a single chip. Chip manufacturers are working now to develop these larger building blocks on an expert system.

Such systems will become transportable and marketable, comparable to books and software. They will:

- represent knowledge in an organized but adaptable manner;
- support knowledge in terms familiar to end users;
- employ user-friendly interface functions;
- exploit the kinds of reasoning which are available.

No wonder the US Department of Defense has identified AI as one of the critical technologies for national defense and for continued economic leadership in the 1990s.

For any product and for any process, the initial specification and the resulting criteria for a successful design are essentially responses to market needs and reflect ever-changing values. Given an adequate specification and the means to modify it according to requirements, there is no reason why intelligent CAD tools should not be made for all areas of engineering design.

Abstraction is a fundamental activity in engineering design. We have known this for centuries, and for over 50 years have appreciated the asistance to the human mind offered through scale models, wind tunnels, and differential analyzers.

Simulation can be of significant help to abstraction, so successively we have moved from analog simulation to digital simulation. At the same time we have enlarged the population of products and processes subjected to similation, as well as the size of the systems we simulate. But while in the past simulation basically concerned physical characteristics, AI tools now make it feasible to simulate logical processes. This is a new dimension in abstraction of which the design engineer must be aware in order to appreciate it, and use it.

This is an exciting field of research in a discipline which has come to be known as *cognitive engineering*. It lies at an overlap point between psychology and mathematics, where the theoretical and the arcane come to have practical applications.

In an era of increasingly complex engineering projects, there is every reason why AI tools are necessary to technological progress. At the same time, their creation gives a rare opportunity for real-life experiments with models of the complex cognitive processes involved in design.

Often it is not sufficiently appreciated how important non-technological considerations are in engineering design. Even if we pay close attention to algorithmic processes, knowledge representation and control structures, out project could fail in application if we do not assure the quality of human interfaces. Careful consideration must also be given to how the system is introduced to its users and how it will affect their work patterns.

Optimization is a more complex process than the preceding two. If done automatically, there is an advantage in that simulated data are generated in one step of the design process. Then experimentation takes place to optimize a product, process, or system which has already been found to be feasible.

ESystems can play a key role in optimization, for two reasons:

(1) They can bring into play the way the real expert works in optimizing product characteristics – making this knowledge widely available to other engineers.
(2) In implementing this process they structure and formalize the methodology to be used, thus making feasible a homogeneous approach.

Logical methods supported through AI enable us both to employ and to control upward-propagating constraints. This gives the designer the opportunity of doing with the ESystem what is done in classical design: feeding back information. But it also provides the added facility of studying difficulties in implementation details to higher levels of representation, which can then be modified.

Looking carefully at such problems, the designer is naturally led to the identification of areas about which not enough is known. Many questions, however, still need to be answered:

• How can algorithmic and heuristic knowledge be combined?
• How do we elicit the knowledge needed for building AI aids for specification and for optimization?
• What kind of formal language should be used as an internal representation?

Representation has an important influence on logical problem-solving. The wrong representation can make even the most competent problem-solver inefficient. (If you don't believe this, try doing multiplication with ancient Greek numerals.) A good representation can lead to problem solution – it can also extend the power of a problem-solving strategy into new domains.

Through a good representation, an expert system may be able to learn to do more than the original expert could achieve. The bottom line is that there is more than one way of acquiring knowledge from the expert than by asking direct questions. Methods of deriving rules from examples are being developed, and rules established by this method have been found to be quite efficient in performance.

Particularly in the fields of optimization and testing, *representation by example* can make previously obscure domain knowledge explicit, coherent and logical. This deepens and extends our grasp of the domain.

Testing is the final phase for every product. The evaluation of the final, optimized design can be subjected to tests produced by expert systems where, once again, homogeneity and consistency can dominate the picture.

In developing intelligent testing systems one of the main aims should be to isolate criteria for a good design. The topmost issue, for instance reliability, must first be determined – with the ESystem paying due attention to it. Other requirements at the top of the list may be an effective man-machine interface and/or a supportive, crash-proof environment.

Through expert systems CAD can be placed in a context in which the values used to produce judgments about what makes a good system are more evident. This enables the designer to identify salient problems and address them effectively.

As experience in the implementation of expert systems in engineering steadily grows, we will be able to address issues which the manipulation of the electronic or mechanical parts of the system cannot ameliorate. Typically, such problems are logical in nature and require new techniques for their solution – such as the incorporation of knowledge expressed in rules.

The *provision of advice through a consultant program* assists in the analysis of the design task and reveals the influence of logical processes. It can also be of assistance in the social organization of the design team, on the way the design task is partitioned.

Another class of results can be obtained by matching technical solutions to practical problems. One of the key questions in a recent implementation was: *What can be automated and what cannot?* This led to the consideration of some fundamental issues of formalism and representation.

Design has long been considered an ill-structured problem which is difficult to handle through software. Research into AI has revealed *the importance of using the correct logical representation of the problem as the key to making its solution a distinct possibility*. This has its counterpart in the way that good notation in mathematics makes thinking about mathematical concepts easier.

Through CAD algorithms we now have at our disposal formal mathematical methods for automating design. With ESystems we should aim to capture informal knowledge. This is the concept of an *expert consultant* approach to CAD through a knowledge-based system.

Let us conclude with the following thought. In the next few years, advanced CAD equipment will incorporate expert systems as a matter of course. Once computer-based methodology moves into the domain of the designer, it will be employed in a growing range of tasks, including user-assistance.

Expert systems facilities will become major sales features in an increasingly competitive market. They will:

- allow us to describe many types of entities and behavior that do not readily submit to algorithmic or state-change representation;
- support deductive inference and analysis;
- promote logical problem-solving methods;
- incorporate mathematical as well as non-mathematical relationships.

They will provide the base for integrating models of physical processes and human behavior, subject to various constraints with goal-seeking capabilities.

Within the next ten years, both the Americans and the Japanese plan to develop knowledge machines able to handle tens of thousands of inference rules and one hundred million objects. While not yet realized in hardware, such machine architectures are generally viewed as comprising an essential feature both of the fifth-generation computer and of artificial intelligence at large.

Let us hope that the European Strategic Project for Research in Information Technology (Esprit) and the Alvey Directorate in the UK will see to it that Europe is an active participant in the development of intelligent systems. Competition is always healthy. Our future depends on our ability to face challenges and overcome obstacles. This is what divides man from other animals.

Chapter 14

Graphics languages

We have established that the engineering designer on his workstation will be carrying out much broader functions than simple design. It is therefore proper to look into the most effective ways and means to shape the *dialog* between man and the information contained in the machine.

Purposely, the last chapter avoided making reference to graphics languages as these fit both within and outside the area of programming concepts. *Graphics is a system of signs and rules*, and we should properly appreciate that this is much more a means of dialog than of machine instruction.

Dialog is a generic word for a preplanned man–machine communication. It encompasses:

(1) formatting capabilities regarding the information to be presented,
(2) formal programming languages to release the functionality of software and hardware,
(3) interface languages for interrogating a database and, eventually,
(4) non-formal conversational interchanges.

Many of these last will be projected for one specific application or type of interchange. This requires more analysis – not less.

Even within a predominantly engineering environment, we should be interested in determining whether some office forms get into infinite loops. We must also characterize the forms that end up at a specific engineering workstation, as this information can be critical in our specifications regarding initiation, usage and termination of technical forms.

When we study form processing, we should be interested in determining the logical and physical paths that are followed: defining the action(s) of each workstation on the forms it originates, transits, stores and retrieves during a project's life cycle; and evaluating the loads which form traffic poses on engineering workstations and channels of communication. Such references help show that dialog procedures (and languages) must go well beyond what was thought of them even five years ago.

Query, electronic mail, data and graphics manipulation languages permit engineering users to communicate effectively with one another, accessing the other party's database(s) – doing so in a way transparent to the non-computer professional.

As stressed in the chapter on 4GL, the user should say *what* is required. *How to do it* is the business of the Fourth Generation Programming Language. We have also spoken of the wisdom of standards for communications purposes – such as the Open System Interconnection (OSI) of the International Standards Organization (ISO).

In that discussion reference was made to the seventh (highest) layer of the ISO/OSI standard. The User (Applications) Layer is of basic importance to an engineering firm as it affects the structure of an interactive system. Such a structure is most vital to the *man with the problem* for whom the workstation, database and network are provided. A similar statement has been made about the Database Management System (DBMS); file access for handling text and data; the applications programs to run on the system; and the end user functions as a whole.

The reason why in the introduction to the present chapter I am highlighting key issues already discussed is to help to show that the source of design concepts and tools is shifting from people to software. The days of the programmer's influence on man–information dialog to be used in engineering applications may not be entirely over, but there is a great change. Machine intelligence and polyvalent software are more than ever focusing attention on the end user.

The need for graphics languages

Pictures and signs have always been used to convey information that transcends language barriers. From ancient hieroglyphics to the icons of modern computer systems, symbols are the most effective way of providing information without in-depth knowledge of a particular linguistic structure.

Icons are familiar objects which help bring together means, of representing abstract concepts. They are important to engineering design because they enhance our ability to process information by applying proven techniques for needed representations and their subsequent translation.

Icons, and the graphic concepts behind them, provide the user with a powerful tool to present and analyze information. This is just as true of charts – which highlight trends and relationships within the data – as it is of engineering graphic displays.

One of the earliest uses of computer graphics was during the 1950s in SAGE (semi-automatic ground environment). The system presented the operator with symbols and identifiers he pointed to with a light pen. The computer also generated map outlines to provide context.

In the same period, drum and flatbed plotters were developed, allowing computer users to obtain a graphical output in place of alphanumeric printout. A few years later (late 1950s, early 1960s) researchers at industrial and university laboratories were connecting CRTs (cathode ray tubes) to computers to view output.

As video displays converted radar data into computer-generated pictures, the need for graphics-oriented input means became felt. SAGE is considered to be the first installation to use the light pen, which allowed the operator to select information by simply pointing at the appropriate target on the CRT screen.

These were formative years. The logical understructure developed around the mid-1960s. Ivan Sutherland's MIT doctoral thesis (1963) described the Sketchpad; it contained theoretical work on data structures and laid the software basis for computer graphics. At about the same time, also at MIT, Steve Coons began developing surface patch techniques for computer-graphics modeling.

The GM-promoted DAC (Design Augmented by Computer) has been another significant step. From the early to mid-1960s, DAC/1 evolved into a major computer-aided design effort, and became a key element in the design of cars and trucks. (As a matter of fact, the Alpine Display of DAC/1 gave the basis for the IBM 2250 graphics console, introduced with System/360 in 1964.)

Almost in parallel with this effort, Lockheed-Georgia worked on the use of computer graphics for programming. Itek's Digigraphics dates back to about the same period. (This project evolved into the line of CDC's interactive computer graphics.)

By the mid-1960s several other major aerospace corporations (like Rolls-Royce, McDonnell-Douglas and Boeing) began to explore the use of computer graphics for aircraft and missile design. IBM worked with Lockheed, McDonnell-Douglas, North American Rockwell, Rolls-Royce, and TRW in an effort to evolve CAD and CAM techniques. IBM's 'Demand', McDonnell's CADD and Lockheed's CADAM computer-aided design and manufacturing programs are examples of this effort.

With experience, interaction between man and the information stored on the computer system became a major driving force behind computer graphics terminals. MIT's TX1 featured an interactive graphics console. DEC's interactive computer displays (type 30) were modeled after the TX1 system; while DEC's 338, introduced in 1968, was probably the first intelligent graphics terminal offered to the business market.

Management applications were not among the early goals of graphics systems, but the interest was there from the early days. A 1966 American Management Association (AMA) publication listed 'appropriate industry characteristics' of users that could expect a reasonable pay-off from computer graphics. Among them were:

- better experience in R and D,
- improved computer performance,
- a closer relationship with the computer manufacturer, and
- numerical control possibilities.

A basic prerequisite, AMA said, was a management receptive to innovation. But at that time, graphics were not recommended for companies without technically complex, multiple system products, reasonably large engineering staffs, product performance standards, a high rate of change in technology or design, and the need to maintain a posture of competence.

The same year, 1966, the *Wall Street Journal* published an article on computer graphics and the assistance they could offer to design problems. Professional societies were also being formed: the Society for Information Display, in 1963; and the ACM Special Interest Committee for Computer Graphics, in late 1966.

Other contributions are also worth noting. For instance, from 1974, SIGGRAPH (ACM's Special Interest Group for Graphics) took an active role in the standardization of a hardware-independent graphics system.

We have come a long way since those first steps in the re-introduction of *graphics languages* in human civilization. Today, graphics languages are commercially available, featuring:

(1) easy man–machine interfaces;
(2) powerful systems commands;
(3) built-in editor(s);
(4) calculation routines for diagram details;
(5) enriching diagrams with headlines, dates and explanatory text;
(6) scaling capabilities and division of axes of reference;
(7) ability to output between different graphic machines (screen, plotter, printer).

The desired diagram is defined in the dialog, the input being done through functional commands. The result is available on the screen and can be changed in an interactive manner.

The state of the art in graphics languages goes well beyond the production of drawings. It starts with origination and follows with the routines necessary for communicating with the engineering database, minimizing input operations, using precision hit codes and line styles, proceeding with dimensioning and with constructions, selecting text and character styles – as well as editing and viewing.

Three ways of providing the designer with an opportunity to compare what he thinks he has with what he really has – and which is reflected in the EDB – are as follows:

(1) Dynamic rotation, zooming, dimensioning, view selection through the image control unit. This will not only allow the structure to rotate but also enable the designer to view different sides of a construct at a chosen scale, with characteristics updated to the last change he or any of his co-workers made to the product.

(2) The use of color, at the workstation level. Color makes a big difference and helps comprehension. But color standards must be established organization-wide and observed by everybody working on the system.

(3) Hidden line removal and other editing capabilities. This facility permits the engineer to give one command and the system will remove any line and/or subsystem. Automatic editing obviates much manual work. It can be of major help in a dynamic situation where the designer can stop at any stage of his work and experiment. Through hidden line removal he can take any selected piece of information out of the complex design in the EDB. He can treat it as a separate plan, and provide it with full documentation.

Stored in files, graphics are callable at any time. The design validation process, full debugging aids and other tools are included within a package. We will be talking of windows in a following section but, as a preview, we can think of a given character as being a small window which will be transferred to the specific screen.

Furthermore, there are similarities between this new generation of languages and database programming systems: both have as their primary goal the ability to operate on data, with calculation becoming a subsidiary activity. Also they both tend to show relational characteristics.

A new class of graphics languages is characterized by the *merger of programming and display features with the operating system*, as well as databasing, datacomm and flow control characteristics. This will have implications both for engineering and for managerial implementation of graphics systems.

A valid philosophy in this connection is that CAD is just another tool, albeit a very sophisticated one. Therefore, whether in engineering or in management, the best people would be more likely to learn faster and use the equipment most effectively in the design mode. To be effective, we must:

 (1) idealize the project (conceptual design);
 (2) analyze the entification of the fundamental parameters;
 (3) proceed with the definition of the general architecture;
 (4) assure the detailed examination of all components;
 (5) effect the integration design;
 (6) do the proper testing through computer-based routines;
 (7) relate product design to manufacturing engineering;
 (8) provide full, comprehensive documentation;
 (9) produce the drafting chores; and
(10) guarantee the updated bill of materials.

An engineering project must properly relate the process under discussion to the three fundamental design procedures: abstraction, experimentation, concretization, to be supported through CAD/CAM.

Using computers to assist in conceptualizing, analyzing, and documenting designs, and in converting design information into the actual product, can help in increased productivity and profitability, eliminating the need for paperwork in the design process. But to obtain such results, the concept of graphics communications must become second nature.

Query through graphical symbols

A construction line facility available in both two-dimensional and three-dimensional CAD programs allows geometric data to be computed through graphical operations. These can be looked at as analogous to slide rule and calculator but with geometric curve and surface forms – and therefore ready for the construction of bodies. When this results in bodies separating into two or more pieces, CAD retains each piece as a separate body, as well as the original body.

The same sections can be used for visual inspection at the display as design proceeds - for cutting portions away or drilling holes, for interference checking and the like. Such usage suggests the existence in the designer's mind of definite images, which can be employed in communicating with the machine.

The existence of images suggests that graphic displays of data can communicate ideas quickly and effectively. In fact, the value of graphics stems from the ease with which trends and relationships within the data are made apparent – and/or information elements in the database can be called through graphical query capabilities.

Two basic ideas help justify this process. First, graphic displays emphasize and call attention to visually defined data characteristics, hence promoting more effective communication. Visual characteristics under-score a point that could have been overlooked in a one-dimensional textual query or in a tabular report.

Figure 14.1 demonstrates the use of seven graphic signs as system commands in the bottom line of a soft-copy presentation. Through cursor positioning, the user selects the process behind the icon which he sees – for instance, a phone set, calculator, or routines for charting.

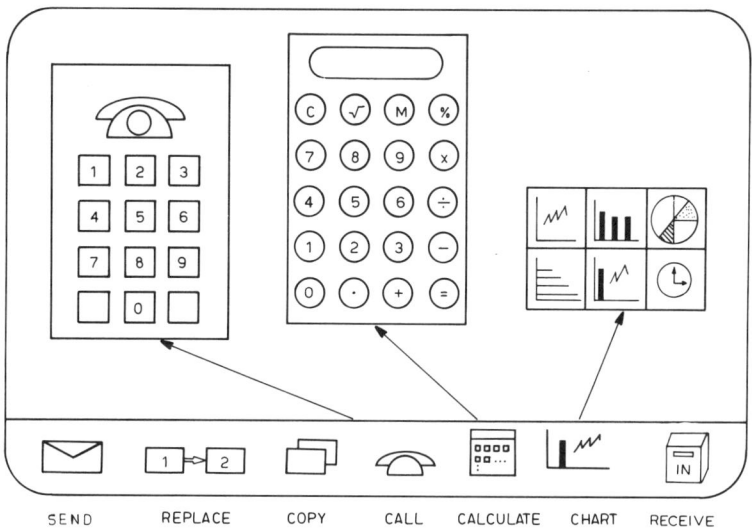

Figure 14.1 Icons are familiar objects. Their interactive use on video simplifies the programming job

Second, current projections tend to indicate that graphic displays will be still around long after the textual languages we know and use today have disappeared. A good example of this is a US Department of Energy study which recommended that the government establish a non-verbal system of warning the next 300 generations of the presence of radioactive dumps.

The report, *Communication Measures to Bridge Ten Millenia*, assumes that present-day languages will be incomprehensible to inhabitants of Earth in 10,000 years. Yet the need is there to leave warnings that will survive and be understood as long as existing nuclear waste dumps remain toxic. Among the recommendations were creating a modern Stonehenge, ringing the dumps, and erecting huge cartoon narratives depicting the danger of the nuclear material.

Regarding the monoliths, the suggestion was for a waste repository with a series of raised earth barriers built around it in triangular pattern. Within this wedge would be monument-like markers, as durable and detectable as England's Stonehenge. For the warning symbols was advised something as simple in design as the 17,000-year-old cave drawings by Cro-Magnon man in France.

One proposed sequence of drawings is: three human figures stand by a dump site: one of them drinks from a bubbling well; and falls dead. The task force – involving physicists, anthropologists, linguists, and psychologists – cautioned that there is controversy among historians over the efficacy of different types of transmission for accurately conveying information over long periods.

In this, as in other studies which have taken place, the underlying concern is that of a lasting relationship with the system. Design features should serve the needs of the user but also provide for continuity. The system has to work within well-established parameters – and this is just as valid of query as of design proper.

Returning to the fundamentals, query can be done through graphical symbols as well as through verbal expressions. In either case, since the engineering designer will very often interact with the database, the effective incorporation of a DBMS and the support of the right linguistic interfaces are vital.

When in the early to mid-1970s database interactivity became crucial, man–machine communications were enhanced through the development of structured query languages. The earlier ones, such as SQL, were characterized by one-dimensional programming, its functionality expressed by the statement: 'select from where'.

Newer programming languages are rather table-oriented, providing two-dimensional programming. Examples are IBM's QBE (query by example) and RTI's QBF (query by form). As stated in Chapter 12, two-dimensional programming goes beyond information element selection because it involves a presentation structure.

These points are quite important because, while the earlier engineering design work was primarily demanding an efficient graphics support, newer approaches are much more global. The designer needs linguistic supports able to help in:

(1) reaching the database in a dependable manner;
(2) composing messages;
(3) mapping data from tables into the body of the messages;
(4) sending messages to other users;
(5) importing/exporting files;
(6) branching to other activities;
(7) specifying key conditions triggering actions and events.

Graphical presentation essentially focuses on the interfacing routines – hence, the foreground. There is, however, in the background a layered functionality the system must support. Figure 14.2 presents the key components of the supporting services necessary for man–machine interaction.

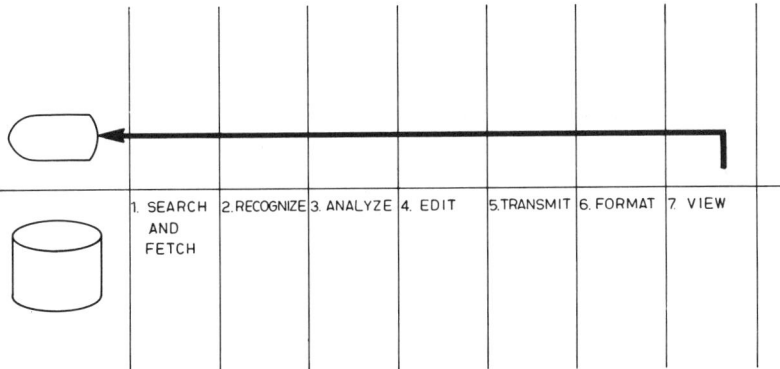

Figure 14.2 Man-machine interfaces require the appropriate infrastructure. This figure shows a 7-layered solution

Furthermore, in a computer-based system, the handling of graphics, text and data structures runs concurrently with processes embedded in applications programs. This further underlines the interest we should focus on information management (retrieval, transmission, storage). The processing activities (including those of a number-crunching type) should be concurrent and properly dimensioned.

Some of the elements helping design proper can be ingeniously used in strengthening dialog features. Users, for instance, can shift the coverage of areas to be displayed on a screen through a *graphic* facility.

There is also *semantic usage*. By properly selecting a function for going up, going down, or traversing a tree (which defines logical hierarchy of categories on a displayed menu), users can shift their interest to another class of elements. These are related to each other in their semantics but are of different categories, resulting in a single map image.

Supporting software must be characterized by *shell functions* corresponding to the work to be done – which involves both managerial and engineering design functions. A shell is in a privileged position to implement generic commands because it detects the activities the user communicates with.

Closely relating to the operating system to be used, a shell understands events and sends them to the various activities, follows up on menus and their routing, interfacing between the user and the computer resources and also between computing and databasing. This is quite important in assuring flexibility and logical portability between different jobs.

As the design environment evolves, we need flexible means for the structuring of our systems. We already know from 30 years of computer experience that adding facilities and equipment is a permanent job. The more we can do through shell interfacing without upsetting established systems, the better for all concerned.

Another advantage of the shell is that it eases *end user access*, permitting processes to communicate with one another, transfer messages, and access a common engineering database and support the symbols we choose to implement – for instance, graphical. This is, after all, the main objective in establishing efficient and comprehensive query facilities.

The important message to convey is that it is not only the system designer who needs to change his attitude toward supporting greater user friendliness in interactive applications, but companies too, must alter their policies and the way they perceive things. It is sometimes difficult to understand how CAD/CAM manufacturers (to take an example) with all their human resources and research facilities can stick to products which have outdated design concepts in regards to their use of symbols and their semantics. A system made for graphics applications should first of all employ graphics in communicating with its users.

Viewports, windows, menus

Because the features of interactive systems will continue to be in the hands of the individual designers it is important to underline efficient principles. If the design team observes them, the resultant system stands a chance of being good.

At the user's workstation level, input commands are generated through:

(1) a cursor pointing into a menu window;
(2) a keyboard with function or control keys; or, eventually,
(3) a voice recognition device.

Input commands require the proper interfaces. We have spoken of menus, prompts, help screens, icons and natural language approaches as examples.

Any input (and output) man–machine communication is characterized by physical and logical elements, as Figure 14.3 demonstrates. Presentation of the reply to the user can take the whole screen or part of it, defining a viewing window.

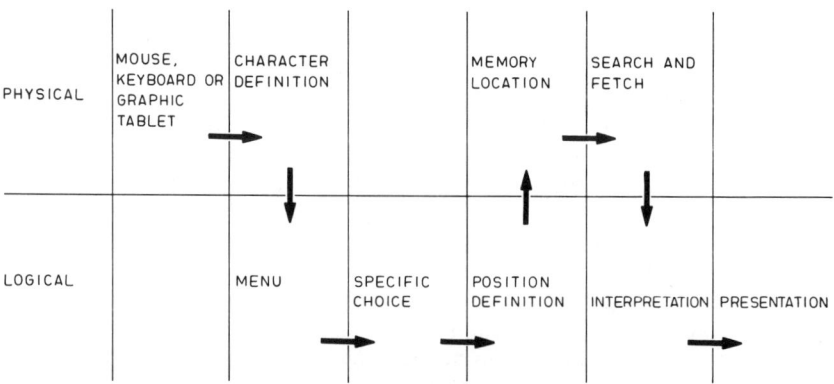

Figure 14.3 Man-machine interfaces involve both logical and physical elements. There is also a grey area where logical and physical components can be exchanged for one another

A window is an independent format-handling device which responds to standard input/output calls. Every window has an independent multi-font map. It answers commands to manipulate attributes such as:

- location,
- size,
- font-usage,
- exposure,
- keyboard status.

Typically, a window is associated with the raster-scan video unit upon which it is displayed. A window can be opened, manipulated, and closed – and while active it may or may not have a one-to-one relationship with a given process.

Generally, a window attaches itself to a process-group to which a signal is sent whenever:

(1) the window changes size or location,
(2) becomes exposed or covered,
(3) gains or loses current keyboard window status, and so on.

Only the user has control over the windows in the system; but a window can be manipulated by a process in its process group, or by a process with write permission on the window.

Stated in different terms, a screen can be divided into fixed or user-defined sections to be manipulated at the user's command (keyboard, function keys, mouse, joystick, graphic tablet) or process device. They may be opened or closed on the screen, each presenting a mapping of the contents in computer memory.

Thus, windows enable the user to bring to the foreground information elements in the engineering database. A window may contain one block of data or several. In the latter case we talk of *paving stones* (tiling).

Each paving stone corresponds to a rectangular surface in the window. It is a logical structure of an image and offers the following advantages;

- The possibility of partially modifying the image at a level of a paving stone through its creation, suppression, or modification.
- The feasibility of composing an image through windows, and paving stones within windows.
- The flexibility to use, if need be, the same paving stone(s) within different windows.
- The possibility of designing a video presentation through forms which may become synonymous to paving stones at the building block level.
- The ability to use alphamosaic, alphageometric and alphaphotographic representations, assigning a different paving stone at each level of definition.

Such a logical structure remains very simple in itself and easy to manipulate. One of the forms of manipulation is by default: if there is no indication to the contrary, the whole image on the video is by default created by one and only one paving stone, which corresponds to the whole surface available for presentation.

Upon creation, all windows are entered in the file system as character-special devices. In the directory they have a filename specified by their user-supplied label.

Windows are dynamic in that their location, size, exposure and font-map can be modified at any time under user/program control. When a window is created, it can be used in a variety of ways by the process that created it.

When a window is covered, output to it can be saved in a buffer and displayed when the window becomes exposed again. This way a process will not be halted because it wants to output to a covered window.

Windows lead to the implementation of a simulated virtual memory environment, allowing combinations of applications to run concurrently which would never fit into ordinary personal computers. User creation and control of windows is accomplished through a set of calls. These allow a user-process to:

- make and initialize a new window,
- draw or erase a window,
- insert a selected window,
- obtain the current state of a window,
- modify the current state of a selected window,
- select and manipulate the fonts utilized by a selected window,
- read the state of the input device in a selected window, and
- obtain the current state of the display to which a given window belongs.

Typically, a window has a *border* which encloses the user's *viewport* so as to separate it from others. Such a border may include:

- a title,
- commands, and
- scrollbars,

which may be enriched by the computer or represent user inputs. Thus, in addition to managing the windows, the window manager has to handle the input devices.

Window management must therefore offer: creation and updating title and commands; setting scrollbars and commands on and off; and highlighting a border component for user feedback. Window handling involves:

(1) moving a window to a new position;
(2) changing its size;
(3) shrinking it to (or expanding it from) a title header.

Windows may occupy independent and changeable rectangles of video screen surface and may overlap each other. They help users move easily between graphical presentations, spreadsheet pages, word processing functions and other packages.

Window management will also be in charge of screen designations to match them with appropriate windows. If the window manager is used by more than one process it must provide mutual exclusion for the sharing screen and its windows.

Window management facilities permit sharing of the screen between several windows which may overlap. They also make feasible the implementation of procedures for creating, destroying and updating the location of a window.

The other basic component in man–machine interaction is the support of menus. They make possible multiple choices for the end user and also help in replacing methods which have been largely manual:

- paging through listings;
- scrolling through blueprints;
- hunting through references which are rarely updated, usually non-coordinated and often unclear.

This is important because it is necessary to understand that the key to the automation of engineering design lies in recognizing what a designer does, hour after hour. He is mostly reading, writing, and modifying bits of text and of drawings.

The challenge of design is to perceive, monitor and control this extended system in a series of specialized symbolic views. It cannot be repeated too often that engineering design is a symbol processing task. We will return to this notion.

In substituting for manual operations, computer-aided selection begins with the choices of data input and reporting. Each level of the menu hierarchy (routing, structuring) should include an online help facility, prompting, browsing, forward, and return to the preceding level.

Routing features are indispensable in a system able to help the designer conceptualize elements like icons and other graphic forms, tables, attributes, and screens that need to be included in the prototype. Typically, such capabilities are software-based and operate on the engineering database.

From the operating system to the DBMS, software supports create a common base upon which is built a range of common access facilities (Figure 14.4). Then come the towers of functionality – such as windowing,

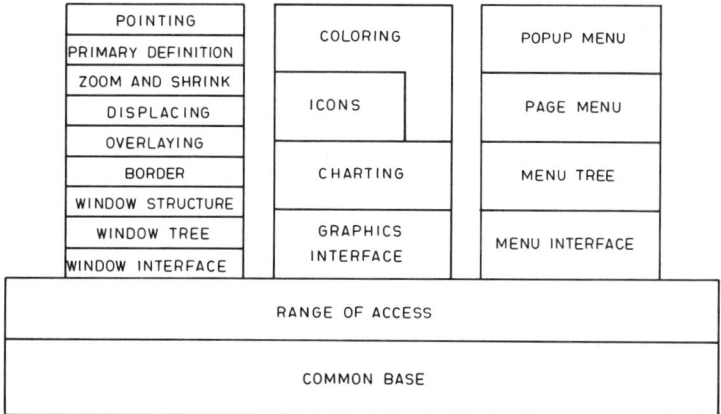

Figure 14.4 Three towers of access facilities are built on common layers. They are: pointing/windowing, presentation and menu structure

icon representation, color usage, and menu services available to the end user.

Menus are a visual interfacing facility providing connection with stored information. Here again, design perspectives can find successful implementation – for instance, *semantic zooming*.

By properly selecting a function for zooming-up or zooming-in on a displayed menu, elements to be displayed are selectively controlled according to the degree of interest previously assigned to them by designers. This can have important functional implications in managing a displayed image.

Icons and menus should invoke the various functions to be manipulated. Routing procedures should permit users to branch to menus such as data entry, analysis, fetching of graphs and bills of materials from the EDB, various reports and other presentations.

Help screens should list choices of graphical and tabular reports the user can produce. The appropriate level of menu nesting depends on the size and complexity of the application – but the facility should anyway be present.

A software service is necessary to manage the content of the viewport. Such contents may be composed of text, data and simple graphical objects. For each, procedures must be offered for:

* painting;
* updating subsequent to a user action;
* pointing;
* highlighting for system feedback.

Current activity switching can have side-effects: for instance, the menu windows of a disabled activity vanish. Or those of an enabled one appear and its main window comes forward.

A screen-sharing policy must be established. For instance, overlapping of windows may be prevented. Alternatively, the software can define that the topmost window is the active one.

Alphageometrics, alphamosaics, and unit screens

Geometric operations ensure the capability of drawing circles (and segments), lines, rectangles, polygons. Each is specified as a series of coordinates, within the framework of the supported protocol to be presented on screen. Presentation poses three challenges:

(1) *The resolution of the screen on which the presentation will be made.* This is expressed in a physical sense through the *pixel* (picture element), which is a unit of measurement of video resolution. There is also a logic unit, the *pel* (logical presentation element), which can be mapped on video, through one or more pixels. The pel allows conversion of text in coded form.

Under current technology, *low resolution* relates to 256/320 × 256/280 elements, hence 0.06–0.09 Mpixel. *Medium resolution* works with 512/640 × 512/480 elements, or 0.26–0.35 Mpixel. *High resolution* demands

1024/640 × 1024 elements, or 1.07–1.31 Mpixel. Engineering applications require 1 Mpixel or better.

Future screens will be of greatly improved resolution – at least 80 pixels per inch and eventually more than 100 per inch. New developments will eventually do away with CRT technology.

The same reasoning is valid for monochromatic and color raster systems, with the difference that in the color case we have three electronic guns rather than one. This is necessary since the phosphors deposited on the screen are three (red, green and blue).

(2) *The bandwidth necessary to feed the video presentation.* Image-showing video devices work at 30 screens per second, thus requiring at least 30 MBPS (millions of bits per second) for steady transmission if the graphics terminal is of 1 megapixel. This capacity, which characterizes today's engineering applications, may tomorrow be commonplace because of compound electronic document implementation.

A compound electronic document includes voice annotation, text, data, charts, images. The system architecture must handle every aspect in a reliable, efficient manner without creating a bottleneck. This is a different way of saying that modern applications require efficient means to understand and interchange requests for different types of information. An architecture should assure the needed means, at the same time being open to future enhancements.

(3) *The type of character handling of the graphic sets being supported.* The finest picture is given by *alphaphotographics*, implemented through raster scanning, with the pixel codes transmitted sequentially. *Alphageometrics* correspond to vector generation displays. Images are composed of points, lines, arcs, polygons, and text.

Alphamosaics were the first graphic characters (more precisely, semigraphics) to be supported by videotex. They are based on a grid-like division of the screen: typically 40 columns by 24 rows. Each cell contains any one of a fixed number of predefined graphics characters.

Mosaic characters can be displayed in two modes: contiguous and separate. In the former, the mosaic elements in a character should completely span the given character field, at any size. In the latter, each of the mosaic elements is reduced in the horizontal dimension by the width of the pel size – and in the retrieval by the height of the pel size.

Alphamosaics and alphageometrics fit the objectives of management graphics – at different levels of precision and of cost. Alphageometrics and alphaphotographics answer the CAD/CAM requirement and bring computer-assisted engineering within everybody's reach.

Furthermore, macro features offer the capability of encoding sequences of presentation level codes to be executed upon command. A macro can be used by designating the macro set as one of the graphic sets (G-sets), followed by invoking the macro set into the in-use table and transmitting the macro code. A nesting capability is feasible.

A service reference model outlines a set of specific implementation parameters for a particular service. Thus it defines the functionality available to an information provider, and service operation for text, data, image generation and display. New features can be grouped into logically consistent classes to be employed for the definition of additional G-sets and control sets (C-sets).

Though this discussion basically focuses on videotex, it is of great interest as all future systems will include a much higher graphical content; graphic communications will be dominant, and the present deficiencies in integrated data, text and graphics in office systems will disappear.

Dynamically redefinable character sets (DRCS) allow each page to use a tailored character set by:

- first, transmitting the cell display corresponding to each code, and
- subsequently, one or more grids of codes that define complete display images.

The coding techniques for dynamically redefinable character sets should be resolution-independent so as to accommodate developments in technology.

A DRCS is a set of characters whose shapes are sent from the service and downloaded via the line. It may be used to represent alphabetic characters, special symbols, picture element symbols, or construction of fine graphics. Once loaded, the DRCS are regarded as members of a library that can be designated by appropriate graphic set sequences.

Bit combinations from any control or graphic set may be used, including picture definition code (PDI), primary, supplemental, mosaic, macro, and the DRCS set itself. With the North American Presentation Level Protocol Standard (NA PLPS) graphic sets provide the option of selecting 7- or 8-bit ASCII codes.

Graphic sets are managed by the presentation level protocol (sixth layer of ISO/OSI). Each type of the presentation process within the terminal can be in one of three states: active, suspended; or terminated (inactive). One and only one presentation process may be active at any given point in time. This is the process that will be participating in the presentation level data exchange.

The NA PLPS standard supports two kinds of display screen. One is the *physical screen*. The other is the *unit screen*, the one-by-one portion of the coordinate plane, providing coordinate axes for use in reference to the physical display screen.

The notion of the unit screen is important. It represents the virtual display address space, within which graphic set characters are deposited and all picture definition codes executed. Horizontal (X), vertical (Y) and depth (Z) dimensions are defined – the last only in 3-D mode.

Another basic notion is the Presentation Protocol Data Unit (PPDU). It is made up of two parts: Presentation Protocol Control Information, and Presentation Service Data Unit. The syntax used inside the latter is designed to be compatible both with ISO 2022 Code Extension standard and ISO Open Systems Interconnection. It is intended to be usable in both:

- character-oriented systems, where each character is examined by the receiving presentation process, and
- bit-oriented systems, where the use of a length field in the header is common practice.

The presentation data syntax is prohibited from containing certain code combinations lest they be misinterpreted as presentation level commands. To accommodate future data syntaxes, which require full use of the address space provided by the presentation level code, a transparent mode can be selected.

Chapter 15

The interactive workstation

For over two decades we have become used to talking about the way in which the computer alienated the user, divorcing him from information he needed to carry out his job in the manner which was most convenient to him. Times have, however, changed and there is no longer any excuse for such behavior.

On a system-wide basis, integrating operations in computers and communications enables companies to shrink the layers of people reporting to the corporate staff. The future office will have fewer, more productive people interacting electronically.

The desks of managers and professionals will be equipped with intelligent, interactive, multifunction workstations. A *workstation* (WS) is the centerpiece of a distributed information systems strategy. It will:

- make feasible personal computing and personal communications,
- with the beneficiary being the actual user of the system – as an individual.

Personal computer (PC) based workstations mean functionality at an affordable cost. The workstation provides its services through software which has now become commercially available. At the same time, Fourth Generation Languages (4GL) ease tremendously the problem of instructing the machine.

Workstations are becoming increasingly potent, benefiting from steadily improving cost-effectiveness. The eight-chip micro VAX II has the power and functionality of a full VAX 11/750. It reduces the footprint from 4000 square inches of board space to 18 square inches; and power from 1000 watts of consumption to 20 watts.

In terms of computer-aided design, this type of intelligent workstation is leading toward two developments, both of significant importance.

- The first is the distribution of significant computer power at each and every engineering desk – with the integration of data, text and graphics.
- The other is the fading-out of the long favored solution to CAD/CAM – the turnkey concept.

Typically, turnkey systems have involved the applications software, the means to structure databases, data management procedures and component libraries. The better developed ones featured efficient command languages, able graphic tools, communications capabilities, and online connection to a host or similar resource.

Fourth generation languages and graphics tools available on a commodity basis have greatly reduced dependence on turnkey-supplied software. Local databases and processing power at the workstation level have made obsolete the notion of time-sharing central resources and of host-centered systems for access to information elements.

Sure enough, microdatabases will not replace mainframe-supported solutions for large warehouses of text, data and graphics. Should this happen it would be like going back to single-user systems that provide redundant information and low information systems performance. But the role of the mainframes is radically changing.

The role of the mainframes has evolved over time from being a data processor to assuring a link between personal computers, the local databases running on them, and the corporate database which is centrally and regionally distributed. A user's directory facilities enable him to find needed information no matter where it is located.

At the same time mainframes have become big communications switches, making it feasible to interconnect thousands of WS in a manner transparent to their users. This is bound to have dramatic effect on the way we handle design, manufacturing and field maintenance information.

The new demands for expertise

The use of local intelligence, standard software, database facilities, online links and presentation protocols allows the workstation to offer – at point of access – graphics, text, data and commands. Standards are particularly important for repetitive types of operation, for file exchange, as well as for formats. They must be universal within a given organization.

The requirements of an engineer who handles graphics, performs intricate computations, and displays complex products on his video station are different from those of a manager who needs occasional access to financial information and charts. In this sense, the notion of a universal workstation may look like wishful thinking. But it is not so.

The applications software will be different. Something that is equally good for everyone may not be worth a damn to anyone. Something that serves very different user populations equally brings limited support to each one.

The basic software, however, will be very similar if not the same – Unix being an example. Still more pronounced is the similarity of the hardware. Technology sees to it that, at about equal cost level, what is an engineering workstation today will become a managerial workstation tomorrow.

Five thousand dollars today buy a 16-bit machine with less than 0.5 million instructions per second (MIPS), quarter-to-half a megabyte (MB) central memory, a 10 MB hard disk, and a 0.3 megapixel video. In a few years, the same money will buy a 32-bit microprocessor, 1 MIPS or more power, more than 1 MB central memory, 60 MB disk and – most important – 1 megapixel video.

The last description is that of an engineering workstation today, and it cost $25,000. In a few years, the $25,000 engine will be a symbolic machine with 6 MB central memory, 200 MB hard disk, voice input/output, and user-generated computing rich in algorithms and heuristics.

The new generation of engineering workstations will concentrate on expert systems – rather than image processing – and on speech input/output, which will reside in the human interface area. They will aim to assist the engineer in design beyond CAD.

This last point means larger design problems than so far encountered; problems which cannot be handled with one set of rules but need thousands of them – as well as the methodology to develop the fundamental tools. Tell the machine the results you want and the relational database will ask the questions and do the job. This means embedded expert system facilities. It also calls for a tremendous amount of preparation and of training.

This great amount of preparation and training is the most important issue engineering and managerial workstations have in common. That is why, before discussing workstations, it has been necessary to detail what that preparation means.

The tools are there, but are we ready? Have we done our homework prior to acquiring and introducing these powerful tools? Have we analyzed the job to be done, structured the environment, established the standards? Are we in a position to protect applications investments as technology moves forward, our needs increase and our tools expand?

It is not enough to have the best product. It is also necessary to provide for continuity through time. The same is true of an online handling capability, which can be automatic and transparent if devices are architectured.

Only when we have reached a level of preparation that makes us confident can we talk of workstations as being the:

(1) merger of data processing, word processing and graphics;
(2) tools that make possible *personal* computing, presentation and communication;
(3) centerpieces of a distributed information systems environment.

Preparatory steps must not only study local needs but also exchanges. networked CAD workstations have an inherent need to exchange files. Are file standards valid and observable throughout the organization?

Distributed systems span long distances, connecting installations in different factories with the work in the engineering office. Designers and managers need to process messages, obtain up-to-the-minute monitoring of product status, check inventory levels, handle financial information. The system must assure quality and timeliness.

With distributed systems, equipped with software able to answer workstation requirements at the touch of a few function keys, any department manager can look up his current expenditure versus budget, ask for incoming emergencies and flash reports, or select any document he chooses for display on his screen.

To check on key commitments and due days that may be approaching, the project engineer will typically invoke the follow-up file, which will list all items in the chosen order, and which will be updated as new transactions come in. He will send and receive electronic mail, call the telephone log to see what telephone messages are waiting, or display his calendar – first the highlights and then the details of the appointments.

As workstations are linked among themselves and with the central resources, the user has to channel through and access the files containing the required technical designs, even if these files are distributed in other workstations or stored on mainframes. The prerequisite is that the person doing so has had the necessary authorization.

Far-reaching solutions, such as those briefly described, do however require a golden host of supporting studies. Because man–machine interface and workspace design are so critical, there is then the need not only for hardware and software, but also for behavioral and human engineering expertise, to help develop and coordinate the discrete elements that will ultimately form tomorrow's communications world.

This balancing problem confronts us in many areas, impacting on *the amount of preparatory work to be done.* We slowly come to appreciate that as the demand for individual, polyvalent WS increases, the systems expertise is no longer hidden in the classical DP department. Design engineers and technical managers must themselves be computer experts – otherwise they will not remain top-level professionals for long.

One terminal per desk

Technology will continue to change. Hardware will become less expensive and more powerful. Software and programming languages will develop – and in any case software has generally been in advance of our capability to exploit it effectively.

With the increasing levels of automation in an enterprise, it has become quite common to see two or more display terminals on the same desk. This is done in order to satisfy the need to access different systems at the same time.

Companies often fail to realize that this redundancy is costly not only in terms of the terminals themselves and in the inherent communications capabilities that support them but also, and most particularly, in the human usability of such a solution. A key ingredient of the preparatory work is to ensure *generality in the capabilities of workstations,* and to streamline the system fully.

As an increasing number of terminals require access to more and more database/datacomm facilities, the importance of system solutions increases. The number and type of users operating online should definitely influence the design of entire information systems rather than just the communications end of them.

An efficient computer-aided design system depends on more than hardware and software. If a system is to work, we have to consider the most important variable: *people.* How do we manage our engineers and designers for highest productivity? How do we establish workable, cost-effective solutions? How do we select the software and hardware suited to our requirements?

It is now widely believed that microcomputer-based personal computing has made obsolete time-sharing on supermicro and mainframe systems. The sharing of centralized computer resources and its heavy overhead have been displaced by the low-cost supermicro. At the same time, the workstation is substituting for 12 things that were on or near the desk:

(1) paper of all sorts, including drawings;
(2) pencils and other writing material;
(3) inter-office memos;
(4) official and unofficial reports;
(5) storage and presentation media; from microforms to foils;
(6) calculators;
(7) typewriters;
(8) copiers;
(9) filing cabinets;
(10) dumb terminals;
(11) telex units;
(12) voice stations.

Workstations able to merge data, text, graphics and voice coordinate these 12 elements, which, taken together, make up all the office chores.

This point is just as valid whether we talk of managerial or engineering workstations – though emphasis on certain facilities may better characterize the one or the other. The *managerial WS* will use personal computers with spreadsheets, calendaring, business graphics, word processing, electronic mail.

The *engineering WS* will use a supermicro, have a design orientation, software for modeling and experimentation, support data reduction and data analysis, make feasible integration studies, and be oriented to complex graphics. However, as already stated, with powerful microprocessors and very high resolution video, the two tend to converge.

Let us never forget that not only the manager but also the engineer needs business functions such as spreadsheet and list processing. The new software technology can offer these functions in a much more improved form, given machine potential: multiple font text; pagination, repagination; diagramming; tiling and integration; 3-D graphics; fast changes in graphical presentation; structured document editors; and pop-up menus.

Fundamentally, there are four key components interactive intelligent workstations must have:

(1) personal computing (DP, WP, icons)
(2) microfiles (distributed databases, information elements);
(3) gateways (distributed communications, networking);
(4) the organizational framework (functions, nodes).

It should be no surprise to anybody that the *hardware components* are and will remain: microprocessor(s); central memory (CM); basic input/output system (BIOS); monochromatic and color video; line discipline; hard disk; optical disk; keyboard; graphic tablet; mouse or tracking ball; printer or plotter; and other devices the user needs. The power of these devices will, however, develop, an example being the 32-bit microprocessor.

The main advantage of the 32-bit machine is that of superior memory addressing. A 32-bit word can be used to access up to 4096 megabytes of main memory. A 16-bit word allows only 64 kilobytes without the use of memory bank switching.

Additional addressing power comes in handy as supermicros are asked to handle larger databases, teleprocessing, time-sharing and transaction processing. Another advantage of the 32-bit machines is their ability to do more work in a single cycle. For all these reasons, additional power at the central processing unit is not only welcome but also necessary.

The *software components* are and will remain applications generator and DBMS facility (4GL); integrated software with spreadsheet; protocols/communications programming; and vertical software offerings of all sorts. Today a key ingredient is *bit-mapping*, that is memory association with screen display, enabling the processor to address any point on the screen.

Software is necessary to handle typical end user operations such as formatting, visualization and copy. Typically, the software supports generic commands or primitives. These are a small set of native commands that can be used throughout the system. Examples are the commands *rename, format, move, copy* and *delete*. Each performs in the same way regardless of the type of object selected.

In a CAD/CAM system native routines go well beyond the command level, supporting a well-rounded functionality. The latter must be tuned to the work on hand, reflecting specified organizational and user needs; analytical tasks; design jobs. It is around these missions that we select suitable interface equipment; project a user/system dialog; support windows and menus; generally sharing the functionality of the workstation.

As stressed from the opening chapters of this book, when talking of CAD/CAM most people think only of graphics, but this is a distortion of reality. An engineer uses data tables and graphics.

- Text is supported by word processing and text formatting, and by newer editorial functions like spelling checking.
- Data is classically handled through computers.
- Tables are supported by report generators, screen painters, spreadsheets.
- Interactive graphics support icons, shape generators, simulators, color overlays, etc.

Systems offer high-resolution graphics hardware and specialized use of those graphics for design and documentation. At the same time, design environments are an area of rising competition.

Competition is further fueled by computer-based solutions and the fact that CAD has developed tools for improving development and testing. These include editors, optimizers and generators. The generators are greatly appreciated because they can also solve the portability problem by producing code that is transferable among a number of different machines – provided file transfer standards are observed.

Hardware features

The micro revolution is fueled largely by its potential to bring an organization into a new era built around users. It may sound ironic but *cost* is the first and foremost hardware feature we should consider.

Reputable low-cost producers are those destined to survive – and with CAD/CAM we cannot afford to invest in equipment of manufacturers who are fading away. The most critical question to be asked when we contemplate the establishment of a source of supply for engineering workstations is: will the manufacturer be here 10 years hence?

Cost per bit of information storage and/or per million of instructions per second is closely associated with higher densities per chip, greatly automated production methods, the availability of CAD/CAM/robotics and of highly trained engineers. The evolution of microprocessor architecture since 1971 has progressed from the primitive 4-bit level Intel 4004 to the present spectrum of sophisticated 32-bit microprocessors. They incorporate: astonishing computational capabilities; high level languages; silicon casting of DBMS and datacomm protocols; and technical innovations only recently introduced on larger mainframes.

This has become feasible at affordable cost levels as solid state circuitry integration has progressed exponentially (Figure 15.1). In one and a half decades since the first primitive microprocessor was introduced, these devices have proliferated to such an extent that it is hard to find an application of computers and communications where they are not used or are not being considered.

Chips are now manufactured to respond to software control; to handle specific user problems; to process and store speech; to cast on silicon a

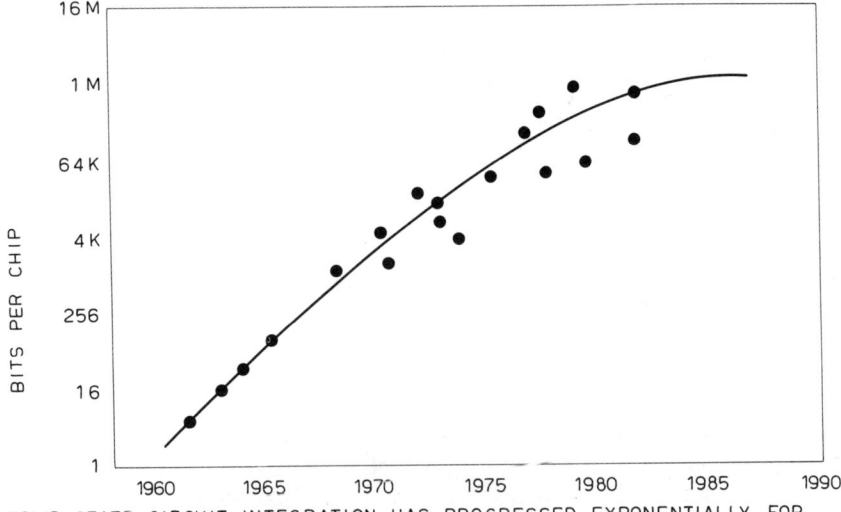

SOLID-STATE CIRCUIT INTEGRATION HAS PROGRESSED EXPONENTIALLY FOR THE PAST TWENTY-THREE YEARS. THE POINTS INDICATE MILESTONES IN INTEGRATION FOR SILICON MEMORY, SILICON LOGIC, AND BUBBLE MEMORY.

Figure 15.1 In terms of cost/effectiveness, CAD benefits from VLSI breakthroughs

DBMS; to perform signal switching; and to respond to datacomm needs of all sorts. They incorporate interface requirements and conform to one or more standards.

New channel concepts for direct memory access go together with the upcoming generation of processors. Direct memory access controllers feature four independent channels, each with a separate register for:

- auto-initialization of all intelligent channels;
- mode control, current address, current word count, and base word count;
- block, demand, single word, or cascade transfer modes;
- memory-to-memory transfer, as well as memory to I/O;
- address increment or decrement;
- enable/disable control of individual intelligent channel request.

Communication facilities support full duplex asynchronous channels, buffered sender/receiver registers, programmable transfer rates from 50 baud to 9.6 kilobits per second (KBPS), and false start bit detection. They also operate in a programmable channel mode.

All this consumes cycles, and microcomputers increasingly feature both multiple, dedicated microprocessors and a greater power processor unit. This is made feasible through steady developments in physics and in engineering design, each successive breakthrough having a great impact on cost (Figure 15.2).

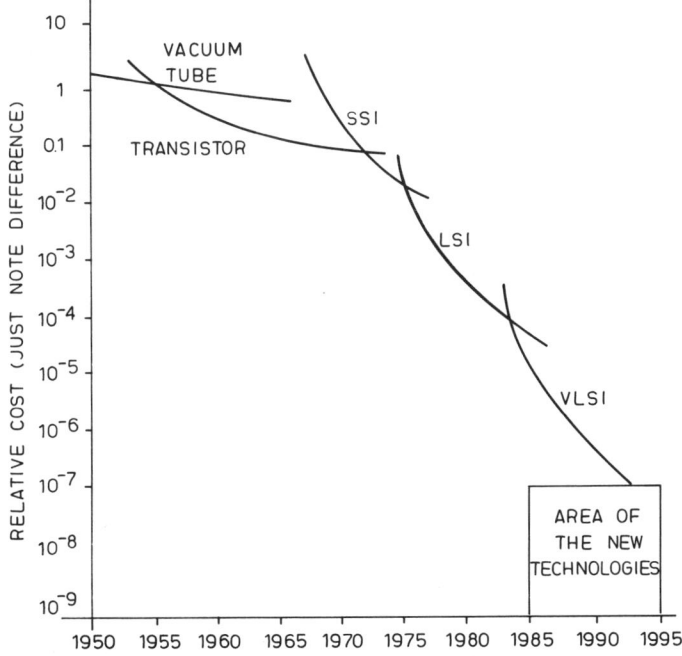

Figure 15.2 Three different integration levels have followed vacuum tubes and transistors. An era of new technologies is beginning

The now obsolete Apple IIe personal computer could execute about 100,000 operations per second (0.1 MIPS). Microprocessor power is now an order of magnitude greater, and we can foresee 32-bit workstations operating at 10 MIPS with up to 16 megabytes of central memory and 400 megabytes of disk storage.

The opportunity for the winners in this race is that whoever first builds the next generation of computers will have a huge technological and commercial advantage. Among other areas of application, the new computers will be used for microelectronics design to build even smarter and more powerful machines.

This is power at the individual WS level. The centralized computer resources will continue to grow with multiple machines per center, roughly at 35 to 50 per cent of the MIPS installed at the periphery as workstations.

Broad-band communications networks will tie together various levels of computer power. The centralized systems, or glasshouses, will typically address themselves to the tasks of big communications switches and very large text and databases. Data processing will not be their function.

The big computers will feature:

- 100 MIPS uniprocessors;
- transaction rates of 10,000 per second;
- hierarchy of storage speeds and sizes;
- digital PBX front-ending;
- integration of text, data, image, voice;
- compound document handling within and between enterprises;
- file sharing among non-similar WS and networks;
- software that integrates systems across the network.

The key to this kind of implementation will be the new generation of software. Service quality, fast online access to distributed resources, data privacy and security, response time requirements, error detection and correction, and better than 99.99 per cent availability will be design goals – and this requires vastly increased computer power.

Fifth generation projects aim to design and produce computer hardware and software for *knowledge engineering* in a wide range of applications: expert systems; man–machine interfaces that permit significant use of natural speech and images; natural language understanding by machines; robotics. Workstations are the desk-level extensions of such supercomputers and, as stated, their capabilities improve dramatically.

Memory capacity is the other subject of steady, major innovations in technology. Very large databases (upwards of 1 trillion bytes) will enable the new generation of computers to:

(1) support knowledge-banks,
(2) allow very fast associative retrievals,
(3) perform logical inference operations as fast as current computers do arithmetic instructions, and
(4) utilize parallelism in program speed and file transfer.

The physical disk has been steadily improving through the development of the overall disk system. This is an across-the-board reference including the location mechanism, the channels, the cache interface. As Figure 15.3

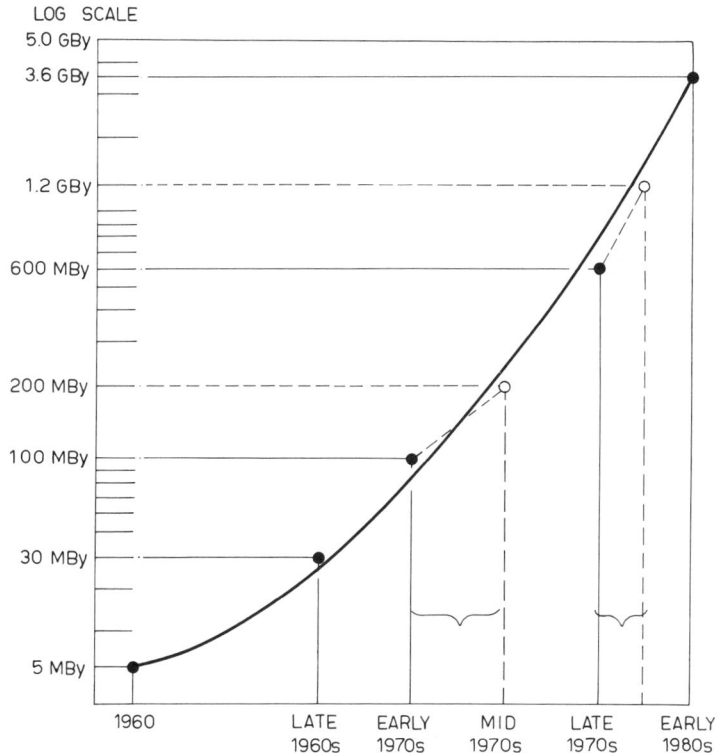

LOG SCALE

5.0 GBy

3.6 GBy

1.2 GBy

600 MBy

200 MBy

100 MBy

30 MBy

5 MBy

1960   LATE   EARLY   MID   LATE   EARLY
       1960s   1970s   1970s   1970s   1980s

Figure 15.3 Recording densities have drastically increased. New methodologies are now needed to push beyond current frontiers

demonstrates, recording densities have dramatically increased. Further improvements in disk technology are in process, both in terms of a bigger memory capacity and better access time.

At the current state of the art, hard disk controllers feature programmable track format, multi-sector and multi-track transfer capability, data scan and data verify features. An integral part of these features is error-checking with detection and correction facilities.

Disk units have become intelligent by using dedicated microprocessors and programmable storage. Self-contained control units have emerged for running the disk storage system. Rear-end solutions are not new, but they are now subject to decentralization at the drive, channel and interface levels.

New technologies evidently open new horizons and bring about cost-effective solutions. Optical disks are by now a current technology, holding upwards of 10^{11} bits per disk. 'Juke boxes' (still in development) can reach 50 gigabytes (see also Chapter 12).

Optical recording media are of great importance to engineering designers as they make obsolete the use of microforms. Optical disks make feasible the storage and easy retrieval of engineering designs of all sizes (replacing microforms and aperture cards). They also present an ideal carrier for the transfer and easy retrieval of old drawings.

It is quite safe to foresee that there will be a drive toward electronic libraries able to hold billions of bytes online. This will be characterized – and propelled – by a steady decrease in cost, which in turn will feed a tremendous growth in storage capacity resembling three-dimensional memory cells with the power to replicate.

As we are discussing hardware features for engineering workstations it is time briefly to review means of input. This adds up to the selection of the proper cursor controller and largely depends upon both technology and the application being served.

For many applications, the *light pen* is the quickest and easiest to use. Display system response can be elicited simply by pointing to an object on the screen with the light pen. This is most useful for obtaining information about an object on the screen and for choosing items from a 'menu-type' instruction list displayed on the screen.

While it is fast and easy to use, major drawbacks to the light pen are its low accuracy and its color sensitivity. A better approach is the *graphic tablet* used to digitize drawings and enter graphic information into the display system. It is frequently used for schematic diagrams, process control applications, and to enter maps for a command and control user.

Graphics can be input simply by placing the drawing or map on the tablet and touching the stylus to the end-points of the lines. The graphic tablet can also be used to steer a cursor for identification or menu selection purposes.

The *trackball* is useful in high-resolution graphics and imaging systems. Trackballs are suitable for drawing objects on the display and are particularly useful for outlining regions of interest on the screen.

The *joystick* is less expensive than the trackball. A cursor is steered by moving the stick, controlling both the direction and rate of cursor movement. Joysticks are easy to use and can target objects with single-pixel accuracy.

The physical units we have been discussing are supported by the appropriate software, which identifies higher level objects and produces viewing transformations to be applied to a picture by the display system. For example, the operator might enlarge a portion of a plant diagram, then point out a particular control device and menu element.

Assuming the menu element instructs the computer to open the control device, the computer could be given this information along with the identity of the selected control. Thus, the task of issuing the appropriate command is simplified. It is important that the operator be able to communicate with the computer by pointing to the picture it has presented.

Finally, in computer graphics the display is the most critical factor. An engineering workstation should use the most advanced computer display available. It should present the user with a clear image that responds to his changes. Alternative solutions are covered in the following section.

Video display technologies

To generate screens from data stored in the machine, manufacturers have turned their attention toward soft-copy presentation, using one of four possibilities:

- raster scan,
- storage tube,
- refresher,
- plasma screen.

Raster scan technology is that of common television, though computer-oriented offerings are more sophisticated for the requirements of the applications they handle. The electronic beam scans continuously the screen (525/625/1000 lines per 30/60 times in a second). When one or more vectors have to be visualized, the video generator lights up the points for each single line of scanning.

The support memory of the screen must be dimensioned in a way that earmarks a particular number of memory cells for visible and addressable points on the screen. We have spoken of the *pixel* (picture element) as the unit of measurement.

The grade of screen definition is expressed visibly in the uniformity with which we see curves and icons. Picture definition will be higher the nearer together the pixels are on the screen.

Currently, there are mainly two limitations that hinder the universal use of raster technology in all applications of computer graphics. First, the maximum resolution, though high, does not yet allow really continuous curves as with storage tubes and refresher (stroke) memories. While with the last two solutions the vectors are designed through a continuous trace, with raster they are constructed through pixels. It is however true that this is visible, with low to medium resolution. With high resolution, the image closely approximates a steady line.

Second, raster scanning is not yet fast enough to permit the rapid animation of solid objects in real time. This limitation, too, is being overcome as raster scan technology steadily develops.

Let us now look at alternatives. *Storage tube* was the first technology to be used for graphics presentation. The surface of the screen, on which is deposited a high-persistance phosphor, has also been employed to memorize the vectorial image (hence the tube's name).

In principle, this storage capability requires no refresher memory. In practice, this is not quite so. Spill-over effects develop when some points are regenerated quickly while their neighbors are not.

Furthermore, while this technology permits the use of a high resolution screen (1024 × 1024 addressable points), it is not adapted to many applications. With even the smallest modification of the design, the rewriting of the complete image is necessary. We will be looking into advantages and disadvantages.

Instead of memorizing the information of the vectorial picture directly on the screen, it is also possible to first store the data in a random access memory. This is the sense of *stroke writing* technology. Subsequently, the picture generator picks up the coordinates of this memory and presents them on the screen.

The electronic beam travels through all the vectors in the picture at least 25 times per second, a frequency that represents the threshold for the human eye, so that it sees a stable luminous source and not a pulsating one. Hence, if the object becomes very complex, the coverage time of all the vectors augments. The operator can notice an annoying flickering of the picture.

Plasma panel display is the only technology that does not use a vacuum tube. The screen consists of two or more plates sealed together. They have a high number of cavities in which a gas is present. Between the internal surfaces, either in the vertical or horizontal sense, small conductive courses are created. This is the mechanism through which a potential is applied to the gas in the cavities to maintain it in a wanted condition, given that the gas is bistable. One state of the gas can emit light (usually orange/red in color), the other cannot.

Through simultaneous impulses between the horizontal and vertical courses, it is possible to change the state of the gas at the intersection point. Once this point has been excited it is not necessary to refresh the information. Plasma display is supported through flat panels – and this is a major advantage.

There are also disadvantages. One is the relatively high cost. The other is that, with initial offerings, resolution was limited and, as in the storage tube, the low intensity orange color constitutes the limit of the image memorized on the screen. This is, however rapidly changing. Recent research demonstrates that flat panel displays have become impressive in their resolution.

Let us now summarize the positive and negative aspects of each technology, starting with the *advantages*.

Raster
(1) Handles easily both gray scale (black/white) and color.
(2) Makes possible many tones of gray or color.
(3) We can modify or change one part of the design selectively.
(4) We can create graphics and alphanumeric images, with high contrast icons.
(5) We can split the picture, and we can also obtain multiple resolution.
(6) It is a compatible technology with standard TV (RS 170, RS 374).
(7) It permits a programmable background and supports local intelligence.

Storage tube
(1) Helps design vectors and curves in a continuous mode.
(2) It is of relatively low cost.
(3) Offers good resolution, high graphic density, no flicker.
(4) Assures photographic reproduction of the picture.

Stroke writing
(1) Projects curve design in a uniform mode.
(2) Supports good interactivity.
(3) Helps manipulate objects dynamically.
(4) Exhibits high resolution.

Plasma screen
(1) Assures flat screen capability.
(2) Does not need memory refresh.
(3) Presents uniform visualization.
(4) Exhibits increasingly high resolution.

The *disadvantages* with each technology are as follows.

Raster
(1) With low to medium resolution the curves are not as continuous as with storage and stroke writing.

Storage tube
(1) It is not possible to upload the information from the screen to the host.
(2) There is relatively low contrast.
(3) The operation is not fully interactive.
(4) No partial modifications of the picture can be effected; it must be completely redesigned.

Stroke writing
(1) Relatively high cost.
(2) Further cost increase for color picture – while only the basic colors can be obtained.
(3) Cannot support scales of gray.
(4) Limits to the vectorial density.
(5) No possibility of reconstructing the picture.

Plasma screen
(1) High cost
(2) Relatively slow in update.
(3) Low contrast.
(4) No possibility of reconstructing the image.

Chapter 16

Strategic planning for CAD/CAM

Strategy is a master plan against an opponent. Planning is the key ingredient in ordering our thoughts, goals, ideas, resources and proposed acts. Since CAD represents not only a good size investment but also a change in the ways, images and means for design engineering it is only right that it be subjected to vigorous strategic planning procedures.

Strategic planning for CAD/CAM goes beyond what is usually happening in most companies, where cost jusitification is the beginning and the end of management's interest. Once the CAD equipment is implemented, there should be monitoring of engineering productivity, steady follow-up of product quality, and ways to channel our recources into making the best use of the facilities offered by CAD.

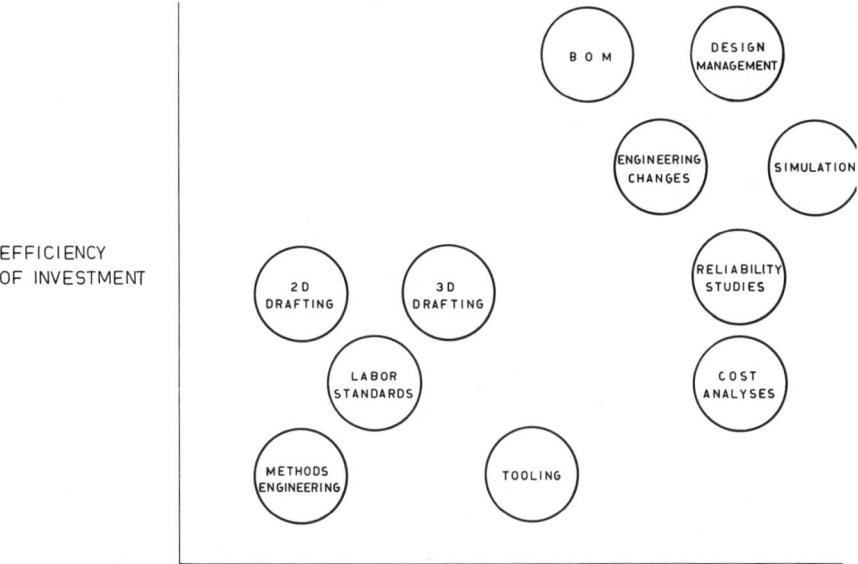

DEPTH OF CAD PENETRATION

Figure 16.1 The efficiency of the CAD investment increases dramatically with in-depth preparation of the engineering process, and also through the integration of many, until now, diverse disciplines

Even the comparative evaluation of CAD investments should be seen as a tool for strategic planning (Figure 16.1), providing management with the reference needed for productivity decisions. At the same time, assurances should be given to guarantee that the organization can handle the swift changes induced by technology.

This is exemplified when we consider that in the 1964–83 period productivity increased a meager 20 per cent in the United States, nearly 60 per cent in Britain and in Germany – but an impressive 270 per cent in Japan. Such lags in productivity improvements price a country's labor and products out of the world markets.

Changes in management thinking on how companies should be run are part of the shift taking place in all industrial countries. Such a shift has in the background the movement away from blue-collar production of goods to white-collar, knowledge-intensive work.

First, management must reach decisions in unpredictable markets. More than ever, this requires *fast response* from product design to production, an aggressive commitment to sell, and the readiness to listen to a competitor's pitch and react to it.

Second, *greater productivity* – from the design board to the production process and the sales effort – has become a key ingredient of success. Fast response and productivity are fundamental in remaining a low-cost producer and, therefore, apt to survive and prosper. Investment in high technology – from brainware to software and hardware – should be examined from this point of view.

Five top issues have been identified by a study conducted by the Brookings Institute. Together they determine the degree to which each of several factors helps in increasing productivity:

(1) technological innovation – 44 per cent;
(2) capital investments – 16 per cent;
(3) economies of scale – 16 per cent;
(4) education – 12 per cent;
(5) better response allocation – 12 per cent.

The Brookings study brings into perspective the known but not always appreciated fact that technology can make a major contribution: information technology offers a very attractive solution, especially while computers are comparatively inexpensive and when a scarcity of good engineers dictates automation.

There are emerging computer technologies important to design engineering and manufacturing organizations: office automation; factory automation; computer-aided design; decision support systems; expert systems. All five converge upon the fact that *the principal role of an engineer in an industrial environment is to bring the appropriate applications of scientific principles to practical use.*

Why a strategic plan?

In an industrial organization, the designer is the engine of the creative process, and computer aids can be employed in virtually every engineering area. Among the expected benefits are: the enhancement of design capability; shorter design cycle times; cost reductions; product quality improvements; a better utilization of engineering manpower; and the possibility for comprehensive management controls.

While these points may be seen as valid for most organizations, and users can expect to benefit from them, the degree of profit will be highly variable. Profit is a direct function of preparation. This also accounts for the fact that, in many instances, the real engineering weaknesses of a company are hidden. In such cases, it is difficult to enhance a department's overall strengths.

The right planning should weigh all engineering functions in order to determine their eligibility with respect to expected benefits. This, too, is a strategic planning action from an advanced system technology viewpoint – and it contrasts with the often followed approach: first come, first served.

While first come, first served solutions are often instrumental in breaking the ice toward CAD/CAM in an organization, successful implementation experiences demonstrate that maximum productivity benefits require a company-wide effort which should be accompanied by overall planning. To do so, management must have a conceptual framework.

Engineering management can be guided in developing a sound CAD plan if it comes to appreciate the effects experienced in the overall data processing sector in the firm. Time and again we have evidence that DP expenditures take the pattern of a growth curve, which fully represents the process of organizational learning coupled with:

● the building of a portfolio of applications to support business functions;
● developing personnel resources to face the burden of maintenance; while
● raising and managing the users' awareness of DP potential.

Yet the large majority of classical DP solutions are neither brilliant nor rewarding. To avoid a repetition in CAD/CAM of the poor practices often experienced with DP organizations, it is important to determine the stage of growth of the company's CAD function and to assess how to go from there.

A careful comparison with appropriate benchmarks provides the foundation for developing a valid strategy. Furthermore, the planner needs tangible information to support him in the next step: to define the engineering activity areas with the highest potential for overall productivity improvements.

In this particular sense, a comprehensive functional assessment of applications can lead to an understanding of what CAD may be doing for the company's business. such an evaluation of the engineering applications portfolio should be conducted from two viewpoints:

(1) the possible rate of effectiveness of CAD systems, and
(2) the contribution of each engineering function to the company's overall performance.

Strategic planning should integrate both assessments and provide a map of opportunities for computer assistance to each engineering activity. User collaboration can be a great contributor to better performance.

Westinghouse experience suggests that the company was able to design and install a computer-aided design system far more quickly after spending a few months facilitating a Quality Circle in the engineering department.

(Quality circles are a Japanese innovation which have spread in American industry. Watching them deal with huge quantities of data about facilities or products has persuaded the management of several firms to provide subordinates routinely with more information than usual to fill their immediate needs. In one specific case, an engineer needed a system to process printed data in equation form, for instance. Though it had no immediate applicability, the company provided the possibility for graphical output from the computer, and this got the ball rolling for computer-generated graphics to do a job which normally would have been done manually at a much higher cost.)

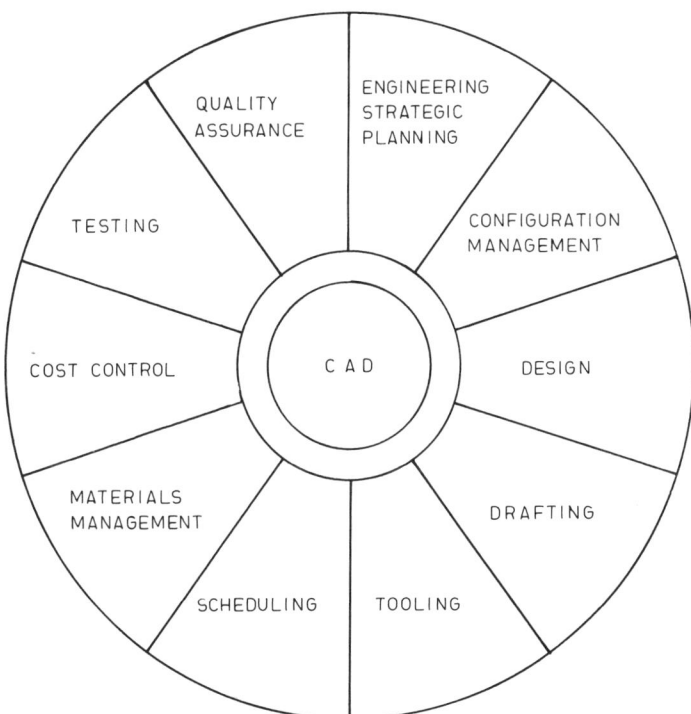

Figure 16.2 An integrated approach for technical operations should use CAD as an enabling technology. However, it should not forget the organizational perspectives which are most important

Using CAD as a pivotal point, a company can support an integrated computer-based approach toward ten vital segments of an engineering organization (Figure 16.2). This:

- helps resolve a classical difference which exists between the engineering management and the company's business management, and
- clarifies the references which should be made when approaching problems related to software and hardware choices.

An issue on which both business management and technical management should find no difficulty in agreeing is that the competition between the leading contenders amont the vendors should be largely based on factual findings regarding criteria to be detailed in the following sections.

The solution sought after should serve, in the best terms possible, pre-processing, processing, and post-processing requirements, as discussed in the next section. It should do so in an interactive way, covering the whole range of user interests; for instance, structural/civil engineering, metallic structures, topography, piping, electrical engineering, flow sheet, bill of materials.

Having identified his application areas the user should examine the response he gets from the system. For instance, flow sheet may be feasible, but in the larger sense of general layout the size and resolution of the available video units obliges either a summary view, or a detailed view by section. Is this satisfactory?

Questions and answers of this type should be kept in mind in decisions regarding the use of CAD equipment. Not only is it proper to ask what the CAD vendor has to offer but also: Is *our* organization ready? Have all machines, links, spares, materials been properly classified and identified?

Remember always that wishful thinking is of no avail. The hard facts of life will show up. Results come from preparation – not by throwing money at the problem. That is why the *user* departments should be the first to detail the applications for CAD:

(1) immediate, and
(2) desired expansion.

This report must both qualify and quantify their needs and involve a number of examples which will subsequently become a basis for benchmarking. But what do qualify and quantify mean?

Qualify: describe the work in terms of
• pre-processing (manual to interactive),
• processing (manual to TS or automatic),
• post-processing (manual to interactive),
• archiving (paper to EDB),
and also to assure the right interdepartmental exchange.

Quantify: establish for the above phases the
• computing,
• databasing, and
• reporting requirements.

For *examples* it is advisable to take typical application areas. This is the best way for evaluating the *benefit* the user will derive from the investment. And there should always be an associated timetable for action.

Pre-processing, processing, post-processing

Although this is a management-oriented chapter and should not include technical details, it is proper to underline the wisdom of organizing CAD work around pre-processing, processing, and post-processing phases.

Several turnkey manufacturers offer this approach as a matter of course, but if the company develops its own systems some highlights should be kept in perspective.

The following steps identify the pre-processing, processing, post-processing procedure to be followed and the possible outcome. Starting with pre-processing:

(1) Interactively, we describe on video the structure under study and define all elements.
(2) We link to the engineering database and proceed with the selection of the elements.
(3) We may, on request, obtain an initial bill of materials.

Once it is clear engineering-wise *which* elements to include, we can study and decide on dimensions. Automatically, the element is visualized; then divided into its components. This being done, say that:

(4) We wish to experiment; for instance, with the goal of changing certain parts.
(5) Such a study may involve the evaluation of boundary conditions, loads, and kinds of loads.

Throughout the experimentation and evaluation the possibility is open to have more than one load. The computer program (pre-processing) produces a file with the elements' descriptions for processing. Modeling is part of pre-processing. The same is true for geometric evaluations.

The processing software starts with the transit file and calculates the loads for each element. This can be directly contrasted to pre-processing, which is load evaluation at system level.

Let me add one more thought on this subject – albeit one that might mature by the end of this decade. Two MIT researchers, the late Dr David Marr and Dr Tomaso Poggio, have advanced the concept of a *regularization theory*. It considers vision as an example of, in a mathematical sense, an ill-posed problem.

An *ill-posed problem* is one whose correct solution can be found only by injecting knowledge about the world. By treating vision as an ill-posed problem, mathematicians try to devise algorithms that can behave like our brain – which means discovering the principles behind vision.

Dr Marr began with the assumption that opaque surfaces were the only raw material of the visual world, and set about finding a way to capture in three dimensions the 'reality' of an object from its photograph. He concluded that a three-stage process was needed:

(1) converting the image on the photograph into a primal sketch, showing all the boundaries and discontinuities;
(2) reconstructing the likely three-dimensional shapes of those surfaces (he called this the 2½-D sketch because it contains only those surfaces visible to the viewer, similar to a fresco);
(3) arriving at a full 3-D representation of the objects.

I see pre-processing as evolving toward this role, integrating into it different disciplines and, by so doing, becoming the true interface between the man and the information system. When this materializes, pre-processing will become the really indispensable prerequisite to processing, which is not necessarily true today.

The results of processing are visualized through post-processing. This phase leads to drafting, bill of materials, and so on.

Thus, it can be appreciated that the three activities are interrelated – and though they can be treated on separate equipment, continuity is at a premium. But well above the mechanics are the issues of:

- strategic decisions,
- goals,
- preparation to reach the goals, and
- training.

Part of the challenge is for management to decide which kinds of organization and methodology it wishes to have: A machine-centered approach? Or a user-centered approach?

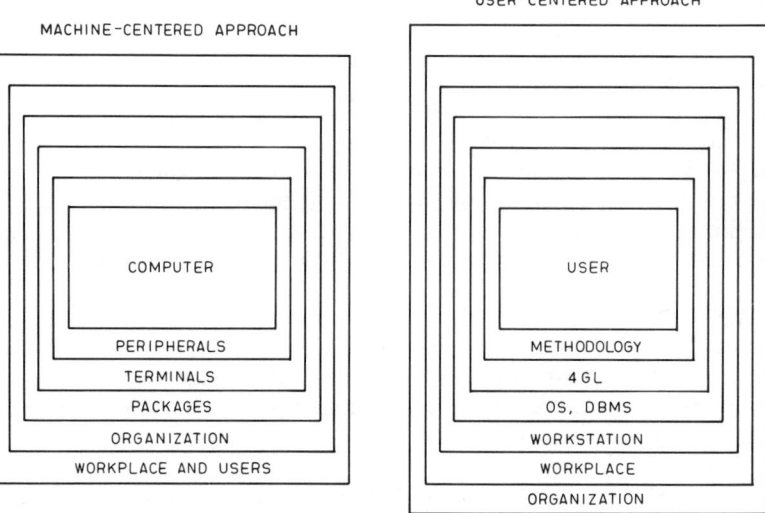

Figure 16.3 The old systems approach has been computer centered. This is both obsolete and inefficient. A valid solution should be user-centered

Figure 16.3 identifies priorities and points to the differences in the two solutions. Without any doubt the user-based approach should be selected. This has prerequisites implying indispensable preparatory steps.

A user-centered methodology is, first of all, responsive to user needs. Then, in concentric circles, it

- establishes and observes the rules to be followed,
- chooses the programming languages to be used and *therefore* the OS and DBMS,
- reflects on the workstation chosen to optimize the workplace, and finally
- is responsive to organizational needs.

A user-centered methodology is adaptive and supportive. It sees to it that equipment comes in second place, with the key criterion being that it is unobtrusively integrated into the user's workplace.

A user-centered methodology is flexible in its implementation. It provides management with the ability to manage the system, make changes, add/delete functionality, dimension the tool to the needs of the user.

By dividing the procedure into phases – pre-processing, processing, post-processing – we make it feasible for the end user to open the black box and change for himself the software configuration. He can personalize the engine at his disposal – starting with a base machine and increasing the configuration as his skills improve and as his job demands.

Just because of the significant implications in engineering design, the choice of a productivity aid is not as important as *the decision to choose*. Provided the decision to use CAD/CAM in a strategic manner is made, among the important tools to consider are development compilers, enabling the user to prototype, and complete pre-processing environ-ments. Other critical issues include testing facilities and communiations links.

One concept that has been used for some time is the establishment of a library of standard functions. The problem has been the high overhead cost of maintaining the library until the concept is established and repetitive use of the code occurs.

It is for this reason and no other that I would advise considering *applications packages*. But beware of traps. Shy away from the opinion that the basic software only comes from the CAD/CAM manufacturer. This is strictly a turnkey orientation and if you go that way you will be tied to his applications programs.

Packages can be procured from other sources: sofware houses, and other CAD houses. Most importantly, the user organization can become a significant source of applied programs. CAD manufacturers themselves are quick to capitalize on this source. For instance, the Applicon Library is combined with the DECUS Community (of Digital Equipment). (Applicon uses for computer support the PDP 11 and the VAX series.) Some 80 per cent of the programs are engineering and can be obtained at the cost of only tape and documentation (about $100).

As a CAD manufacturer, Applicon also supplies a software system called Image, which includes among other programs a 3-D environment and a 2-D environment, claiming that the whole applications environment and its mechanics are transparent to the end user. Other design tools offered by the manufacturer are AIM (Applicon Interactive Model) suitable for structure and SUPERTAB (also supported through GEIS).

Both AIM and SUPERTAB are modeling packages allowing the user to create geometry, analyses, drafting, and documentation. The 3-D application package is a set of geometric instructions that assists in diagramming, dimensioning, the creation of models, automatic updates of model changes, projection of components parts of a structure, and the analysis programs to study the model under development.

On this same equipment, the analysis area is supported by packages like SUPERB, SABBA and FRAME – which have been acquired from SDRC.

Other packages are ASSYS and NASTRAN, offered by software companies but interfacing with the Applicon CAD system.

For the study of structures, there is a program called BASE A/E, which supports a variety of applications, including structural analysis, pipelining and isometrics. Each has a set of routines available in the library. But I think support is lacking for topography, though some existing programs do help in site preparation.

Some of the aforementioned programs are complete in their range of facilities, others are still in evolution. Manufacturing capabilities are provided for numerical control machine tools (in both two and three axes).

Other CAD/CAM manufacturers have their packages, and it is not the object of this chapter to review them. Rather it is to say that no matter how complete the library offering is there will always be a need to complement it. Such complements can be made by the user organization or brought as commodities.

There are testing aids, such as static and dynamic analyzers, that give designers a picture of exactly what is happening with respect to their code. A valid aid is a test-bed model used in a quality control environment for defect identification. Such a model can be created along with the application. It trades design time against computer support to provide online assistance.

In the area of documentation aids, the most widely known and used are graphic products such as logic and flowcharters. Other aids include program organizers and analyzers. These aids address the problem of keeping the documentation from getting out of synchronization with what is being run in production. Combining a design maintenance effort with a documentation effort accomplishes two valuable tasks.

Let's always recall that providing adequate documentation has always been an engineering goal. Yet elegant documentation has often been considered a waste of resources. Automating this function helps change such ideas and approaches.

It is quite proper to underline that computer-aided design simplifies the documentation and permits the use of graphics and icons within systems. User documentation can be improved through computer-based facilities, online help capabilities and program tutorials.

Maintenance of engineering design is an area of tremendous concern. Any successful attempts at improving engineering productivity must of necessity address the design maintenance problem.

Because maintenance includes the functions of design, development, testing and documentation, computer-oriented tools used in these areas are most appropriate. Many can be found integrated in Fourth Generation programming Languages. The same is true of testing procedures and associated tools.

Criteria for CAD/CAM choice

Although software is a key consideration in selecting the sort of equipment best fitting the user's needs, it is not the only one. It is therefore proper to outline some basic criteria for a CAD/CAM choice. Different organizations may have different priorities, but there is near-universal agreement that, next to software, the top five are:

(1) *Job specifications*. This is closely related to software (operating system, DBMS, 4GL, packages) but starts with a more fundamental consideration – the job which needs to be done.

The design of any user system calls for specifying objectives, doing task analyses, proceeding with job evaluation, then doing dialog and workstation specification. This work should be done by the user (not the manufacturer) and, once done, it will provide a valid basis on which to call for offers.

From task analysis and job design it should be possible to differentiate those tasks that might still be best performed by people from those best performed by computer. The relationship and interface between the two should be established and this is most important.

Without such preparatory work it makes no sense to talk of applications packages, even if it is irrational to choose CAD equipment without first examining the applications software available with the system. Let me once again underline that the reference to applications packages should include not only processing routines, but also:

- pre- and post-processing;
- tools to structure and manage the engineering database;
- datacomm facilities and the supported interfaces to other equipment, in use or projected; and
- friendly end-user interfaces and functions.

Only after the technical criteria have been established in a fundamental manner, does it become sensible to talk of:

(2) *Throughput*. This involves several references, from OS to MIPS, central memory size, disk storage, and the all-important response time.

Typically, response time is a function of the applications environment (including its evolution) and of the throughput capabilities of the equipment. A realistic response time must be ascertained through benchmarking – and benchmarking makes sense only when the applications definition has been done.

Carefully prepared benchmarking will focus on software and hardware. On the software side, it will distinguish between OS, DBMS, 4GL and applications programs. Latin squares and greco-latin squares are a good approach for making a multifactored distinction.

The user organization is well advised to write its own programs and not to take manufacturer-supplied standard routines for that purpose. The reason for this is that users have to live for many years with the equipment they are about to select.

(3) *Best fit within the existing environment*, that is the other computer and communications equipment already in operation within the firm.

With the exception of companies just starting with computers and communications, which today are unusual, an organization has a significant investment in data processing gear. Such investments have to be protected in the sense that any new equipment must demonstrate availability of interconnect routines.

While an *open vendor* approach is a valid policy to follow, a prerequisite to it is the ability to maintain networking functions at all times. This means both file transfer and online connection.

The reason for underlining these subjects is that they are often overlooked. Organizations find after the fact that incompatibilities exist. By then, it is too late.

(4) *Reliability*, involving system availability and measured on the basis of effective uptime, which is a function of product quality and proper maintenance.

Reliability is built into the system at the design level. As such it either exists or it does not. To be protected, the user must imply specific, quantitative uptime and mean-time-to-repair clauses in the contract with the CAD vendor.

Let us not underestimate the importance of reliability on CAD/CAM. To appreciate it, we should recall that a great deal of design graphics and the associated bill of materials will be locked in the engineering database. The company will not be able to operate without nearly 100 per cent availability.

Design automation, office automation and the increasing use of computers and communications generally are excellent goals to pursue in order to improve human productivity. But we should not fail to appreciate that new systems bring with them technical prerequisites which unless observed can lead to catastrophies.

In this sense, the CAD manufacturer's maintenance service, as well as the dependability of his equipment are prime issues in choice. CAD/CAM is a strategic product. Let's treat it as such.

(5) *Cost*. When it comes to cost, like must be compared with like. It is not possible to contrast and compare the cost of package deals without defining what is in them. Hence, the need to stress first the technical detail.

Cost will be affected by many technical criteria. Invariably there will be differences between CAD proposals which cannot be weeded out to create a fully homogeneous basis. The reasons for these differences may lie in:

- intelligent versus non-intelligent workstations;
- color versus monochrome terminals;
- raster versus alternative video approaches (refresh, storage tube);
- different levels of DBMS and 4GL support;
- different types of datacomm protocols;
- applications libraries included in the price of the total proposal, and so on.

Such differences should be first analyzed, the proposals then clustered and an effort made to evaluate their impact on cost-effectiveness without entering into weighting factors, which are often misleading.

For price evaluation purposes it is advisable to establish a *standard configuration*, supplemented by modular pricing indicators. To participate in the competition, the CAD manufacturers must:

- comply with all technical requirements of the user organization;
- guarantee both reliability and throughput capacity;
- provide all information required by the user, with particular emphasis on the criteria which have been outlined.

At the same time, it is wise to recall (as mentioned on several occasions) that equipment costs are steadily dropping. Twenty years ago (in 1965), the CAD cost per contact hour was in the range of $75–250. Taking the lower range as a reference point, personnel costs then stood at about $15/h, and $15 + $75 = $90/h.

This $90/h price tag meant that unless we increased productivity by a factor of six we would not break even. By 1980, CAD cost dropped to about $15–30/h. And with personnel costs at $25/h (always lower range) the equation became $25 + $15 = $40/h. The multiplication factor is less than two, which gives a low break-even figure.

In the 1981 to 1986 time period, this low break-even point became even lower. At the same time productivity claims by well-prepared users have multiplied, which help further to justify the proper implementation of CAD/CAM. These are points which should be kept in perspective in a return on investment evaluation.

It is also interesting to note that computer-aided instruction presents similar figures per contact hour: military special training, $15/h; university level training, $5–10/h; high school training, $1–5/h; and elementary school training, $0.20–0.50/h. The last figure is the cost level associated with personal computers.

A last word of caution about costs is appropriate. As with all computer operations, hardware costs are only part of the picture (and quite often a small part). For instance, one CAD/CAM application found that:

- hardware costs amounted to 5 per cent;
- the initial software cost another 5 per cent.

The 90 per cent was the personnel cost to keep the system running.

As cannot be too often repeated, the system must be designed, from the drafting board onward, to operate in an automatic way – without any human intervention – and to address itself to the end user, not to different translators and intermediaries. Otherwise, a CAD/CAM system risks being too costly and give less than commendable results.

Taking charge

Engineering management would be well advised to attend personally to the preparatory studies, the choice and the implementation of CAD equipment. Since software sells hardware, engineering management must become familiar with both issues and form a personal opinion on software and hardware tools that permit execution of all phases of the work which needs to be done.

To define the work to be done in a factual and documented manner, management must be careful to establish proper job definitions: for managers, professionals, secretaries, clerks. It must also have clear ideas about productivity goals.

It is not enough to say: 'The goal is design automation and/or the integration capabilities of graphics with text/data resources.' Describing is not defining. It is therefore necessary to define in both qualitative and quantitative terms.

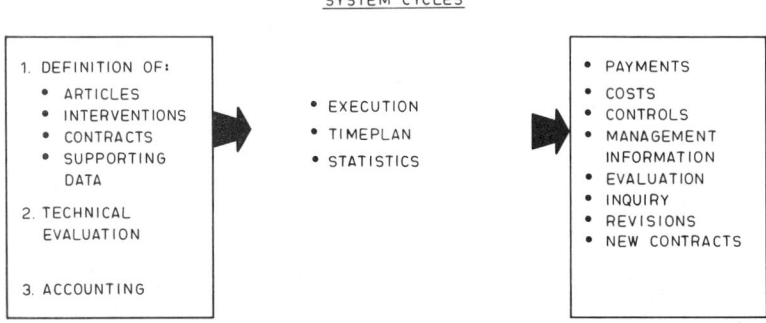

Figure 16.4 Don't confuse system cycles with machine cycles. The finer is the definition of system cycles, the less machine cycles you need

To better exemplify what this means, let's follow a case study concerning the functions of technical operations in a construction business. The system cycles are shown in Figure 15.4. In this particular firm, installation management involves:

(1) technical studies (construction),
(2) permissions and authorizations,
(3) bidding and decision on contractors,
(4) work supervision,
(5) accounting,
(6) direction and assistance,
(7) technical tests,
(8) plans versus actual: budget,
(9) plans versus actual: timetables.

Management decided to proceed with computer-assisted functions from planning to control, and while architectural design and civil engineering work is done through CAD/CAM, a significant part of the process is office automation. This is, for instance, the case with the decision on contractors, including the selection of the enterprise:

● call for offers,
● evaluation,
● definition of the contract.

Computer-assisted processes characterize the definition of the contract (previously a long typewritten document) and the execution of the contract:

- realization of the work,
- on-the-job measurements,
- credits to the contractor,
- accounts payable,
- cost control,
- management statistics.

What this outline may not make apparent is the amount of organizational work which went into the preparatory phases. Among other things, it has been necessary to classify and then identify all interventions, from the global proposition to the work element.

This meant establishing a classification code; assigning basic code and clear text; identifying origin and type of operation; and working out a machine-processed debit code. To keep timetables and budgets by computer, it was necessary to work on milestones, budget per milestone, elapsed-time calculations and end of work criteria.

With CAD providing the design support, it was decided to put on computer all contract management procedures. This work started with *identification of the contract* (basic code, classification code, clear text, registration number, date of registration, origin, date of completion, revision of prices) and proceeded with *list of prices*:

- suffix,
- clear text,
- date of validity,
- revision of prices.

The prices themselves were composed of basic code of the article, starting price, and basic code of price increases. The computer-run list of prices included work at completion (turnkey); measurement of percentage of work completed; price revision.

Price revision considered both articles and price changes. The following issues were defined: basic code, classification code, clear text, unit of measurement, full description.

While the preparatory work seems significant, and it was so, a different task group worked in parallel to prepare for CAD/software/hardware selection and installation. The timetable can be nicely generalized as a suggested procedure:

(1) *Top management decision* regarding the use of CAD and the range of its implementation. This demanded practically three calendar months during which engineering management visited similar installations to obtain first-hand experience on requirements and results obtained.

(2) *Preparatory work on the first priority of implementation* and the overall perspective of future usage. The first priority issue is important because it provides concrete applications on which benchmarks can be made. At the same time the overall implementation picture should not be forgotten as, with accumulating experience in terms of applications, it will eventually be necessary to dimension the equipment to meet the system perspective.

Though timetables can vary from one organization to another, six months often prove sufficient if, for two projects, groups are progressing in parallel: one on the first priority, the other on the system concept. The outcome of these two projects should be integrated prior to calling for bids.

(3) *Call for offers and lead time to the installation.* First of all, the call for offers should be made on a properly documented basis. To demonstrate the rational approach followed by at least one user, we will consider as a specific case the experience of an organization which undertook a very thorough study on equipment selection.

Properly to define the work to be done, qualitatively and quantitatively, a comprehensive list was compiled, to be answered item by item as the research went on. This list involved areas of possible CAD usage: design goals; interfaces to existing computational facilities; supported subjects; hardware-oriented criteria; software-based choices; and other factors. The following highlights some specific questions by chapter:

10. Areas for CAD Usage:
11. Projecting (flow control, layout)
12. Layout Planning (site plans, isometrics)
13. Electrical Engineering (wiring etc.)
14. Machine Construction (new equipment, variations)
15. Civil Engineering Construction (cement and steel construction)
16. Topology (mapping)

20. Specific Goals
21. Engineering Design
22. Simulation, Experimentation
23. Model Testing
24. Drafting
25. Project Documentation

30. Interfaces to Existing Facilities
31. Interface to other Computational Systems already in Operation
32. Communication to the Infosystems of Subsidiary Companies

40. Key Subjects
41. 3-D Capabilities
42. System Analysis
43. Interactive Graphics
44. Easy Object Description
45. User Friendly Approaches
46. Usage Possibilities for all Kinds of Construction
47. Software Assistance by Vendor
48. Facilities Supported at the Graphical Workstation

Immediately thereafter came *software-based choices*: applications software libraries; experience in the development of an engineering database; communications capabilities; dialog functions; object description (interactive, graphical, alphanumerical); manipulation of points, lines, areas, variable positions, geometry, etc.; ease in handling user elements, user-defined symbols, parametric object description, and so on.

Precise questions were posed regarding group formation – views, cuts, perspective, shadowing, measuring; helpful facilities – geometric construction and the like; basic graphical functions – input of elements and their handling; video work – zooming, windowing, scaling, storing (with names), cataloging, calling-up, modifying; and calculation – geometry, volume, weight, simulation of movement, definition of centers of gravity.

The technical people outlined questions on tolerance analysis, while management was more interested in data security by user data. Both technical people and management paid attention to reliability/availability.

This was followed by *hardware-oriented criteria* such as expandable CPU characteristics; multi-user support; flexible system periphery (graphic video screens, graphic tablets, plotter(s), printer(s) and so on); memory facilities; access times; system response time for typical configuration; hardware maintenance by vendor.

The main object of these lists was to clarify what should be asked of the system vendor. They were followed by a chart which outlined the projected action in six layers:

(1) Information collection.
(2) Quantitative definition of work spectrum; evaluation of product range; comparison of this range with organizational facts.
(3) Precise definition of CAD facilities and comparison of the flow of graphics, text and data as seen by the users.
(4) Run of pilot projects and benchmarking on selected projects.
(5) Comparison of CAD systems in terms of cost-effectiveness.
(6) Final choice, followed by contractual negotiations. ,

Quite often among the issues which play a significant role in the overall evaluation is the vendor's ability to provide a valid approach to the customer's requirements, including 2-D and 3-D systems. Also, its ability to handle one of the three main WS types: refresh, storage tube, raster scan.

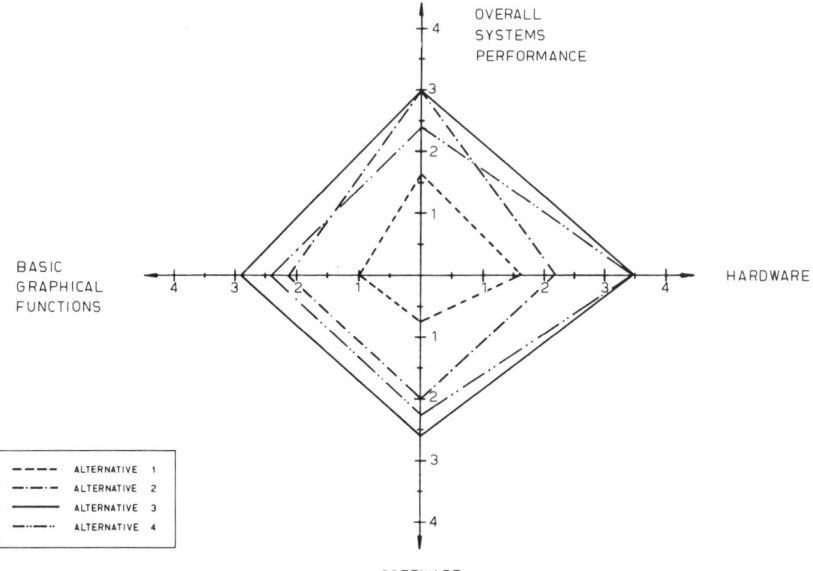

Figure 16.5 Four alternative solutions have been compared with an equal term of salient factors. The outcome proved to be quite reliable

In a similar sense, other criteria are the maximum number of WS per graphics processor; plotter perspectives, including interactive plotter; digitizer(s); menu tablet(s); hard-copy devices (A4); and automatic scanner. The support of magnetic tapes and disks per processor was also examined.

I would dissent from this last point. My top choice would be for fully distributed CAD/CAM resources with intelligent workstations, as discussed in the last chapter. These should be linked together through a local area network (LAN) and communicate with central computing through the appropriate protocols and broad-band channels.

Hence, to the critical question list should be added the support for LAN, the communications protocols, and the intelligent multifunction workstations – typically based on a dedicated supermicro. It is around this engine that the software endowment should be built and the evaluations made.

After the company management and its engineers have clarified their views on CAD/CAM and fixed their sights on desired performance comes the time for the selection chores. The following paragraphs and figures outline the path followed by a leading user organization.

Starting with a fairly impressive list of components which involved 70 firms, vendors, universities and service bureaus, the competition centered on nine alternatives: Applicon, Aristo-Werke, Calcomp, Calma, Computervision, CDC, IBM, M+S, and Terminal Display Systems. Prior to the final test that led to the choice of the supplier, this group was reduced to four CAD/CAM suppliers.

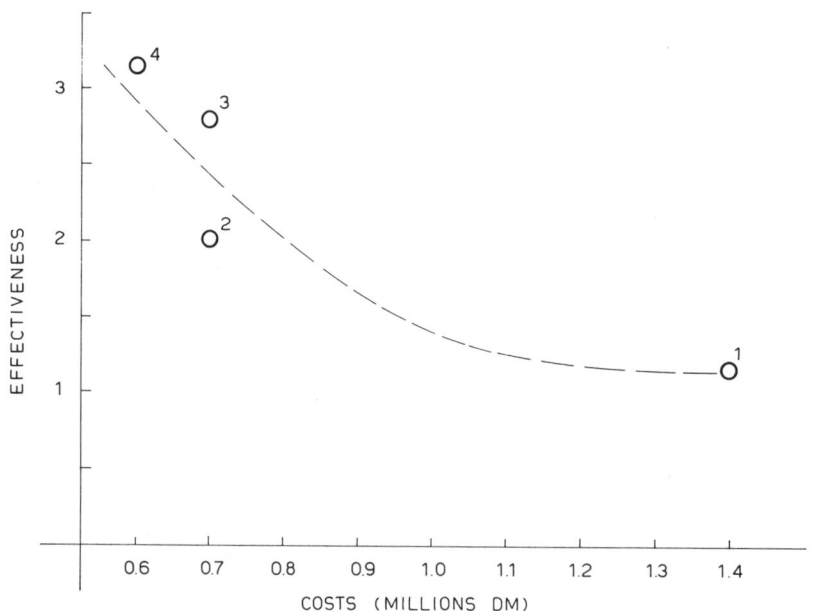

Figure 16.6 The best alternative is not necessarily the one of higher cost. In this case, the lowest cost solution was by far the most effective

Figure 16.5 demonstrates a graphical approach to the relative capabilities of the equipment presented by each of these four firms, along the following dimensions:

- overall system performance,
- basic graphic functions,
- software,
- hardware.

Subsequently, the results were plotted in a cost-effectiveness chart (Figure 16.6), which identified one of the prospective suppliers as way out in terms of high costs and rather low effectiveness. The other three tended to cluster together, with Alternative 4 presenting the best results in terms of the criteria under consideration.

While a thorough and documented study, like the one we are describing, does not necessarily ensure that the CAD effort will be successful, the lack of it will guarantee near failure. *It is the emphasis on the quality of the work and on preparedness that makes the difference between success and failure – and that is what the reader should store in block letters in his mind.*

Index